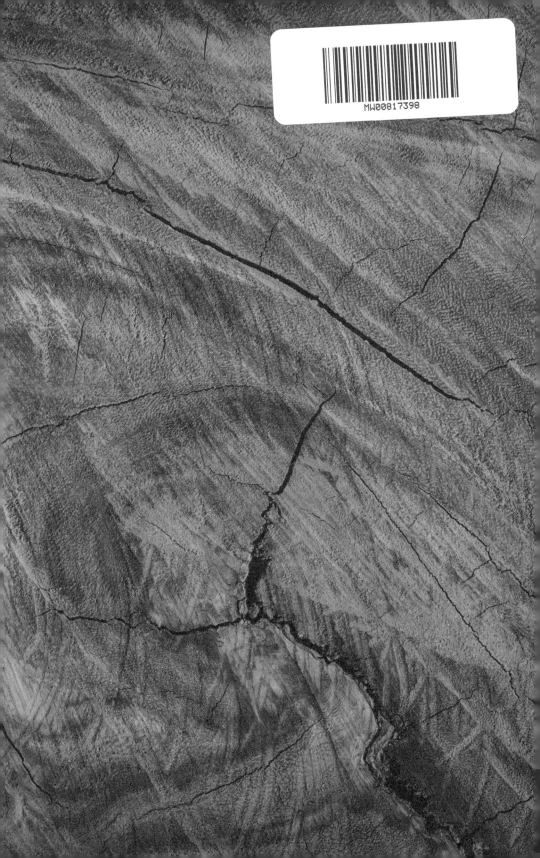

THE LONGBOW,
THE SCHOONER,
& THE VIOLIN

MORE PRAISE FOR MARQ DE VILLIERS

The Heartbreak Grape

"I've lost my heart to a grape! Full bodied, robust, and a fine aftertaste. The best book on wine I've read." John Bear author of *Café Beaujolais*

"A fascinating story, both informative and heart warming . . . Excellent is the word!" Chuck Williams, founder of Williams Sonoma

Down the Volga

"De Villiers has a fine sense of irony and an eye for the absurd, talents that enable him to capture in words the essence of the Russian soul." *The Globe and Mail*

"A rich and deeply sympathetic look into parts of Mother Russia rarely visited by tourists." Kirkus Reviews

Into Africa

"Marq de Villiers takes us on his subject with passion and compassion. . . . [He] writes about what he knows and loves and despises, without apology or polemic." *The Washington Post*

"*Into Africa* is a superbly written piece of authentic African sociology. A work of distinction [this book] is a brilliant and remarkable signature of African history. And a true stunning addition to the human and political archives of our time." *The African Sun Times*

"A deft and fluid intermingling of travelogues with cultural and political history. Rarely is so ambitious a book so resoundingly successful." *Globe and Mail*

Sahara

"A cool book about one of the world's hottest places." *National Geographic Traveler*

"A phenomenal story . . . with this broad perspective, the authors weave together the ongoing life of the desert that is forever changing." *New Scientist*

"Michael Palin may have sexed up the Sahara in the tie-in to his TV programme, but this book is a more satisfying read." *Ireland on Sunday*

A Dune Adrift

"Another finely etched portrait of a strange, romantic place . . ." Kirkus Reviews

"Reading *Sable Island* was like stepping into a big-screen IMax 3D theater where the special lens brings us to places where nature really misbehaves." Portland (Maine) *Press Herald*

"*Sable Island* [is] as delightful to experience in words as it is difficult to experience in actuality . . . Sable Island is that bane of the reviewer's trade, a book so completely of itself, that tells its inherently compelling tale so competently, that it leaves little ground for criticism." *Chicago Sun Times*

Windswept

"Wind is simple. It is nothing more than air moving between zones of high pressure and low pressure, traveling in a straight line until deflected by the rotation of the earth. Unfortunately, things get very complicated after that, as Marq de Villiers explains in *Windswept: The Story of Wind and Weather*, his lively, engaging treatise on wind and the weather it makes." *The New York Times*

"*Windswept* is [an] informative nonfiction about wind and weather. One reason for this book's excellence is De Villiers's careful attention to weather happenings, reinforced by his penetrating insights into nature." CHOICE of the American Library Association

Witch in the wind

"*Witch in the Wind* boasts fishing scenes worthy of Melville." *Canadian Geographic*

"Poignant and often profound, *Witch in the Wind* shows the tone and texture of a seasoned journalist, peppered with distinct Maritime flavor . . ." The *Globe and Mail*

"*Witch in the Wind* is an evocative journey into the previously untold backstory of the Bluenose, exploring the place that built her, the men who sailed her and the industry that gave rise to her. De Villiers is a master storyteller." The Prince Rupert *Library News*

Timbuktu

". . . fascinating glimpses into one of the world's most famed, yet least-known cities." The Montreal *Gazette*

"*Timbuktu* is a fascinating and intimate look at the African city's spectacular past and its daunting present. Drawing from a wide variety of sources, including centuries – old documents and interviews with Tuareg nomads, city residents and officials, the work [bring] the region back to life." Stephen Clare in *The Daily News*

"Written in an appealing, casual style . . . In a time of supposed monolithic Islam, *Timbuktu* still has a lesson to teach." Roger Miller in the St. Louis *Post Dispatch*

Dangerous World

"Marq De Villiers' scary and exciting new book . . . is at its heart, a personal quest to find the social capital and workable plans to signal a clear way forward for us humans who are often blind to the fact that we are living in a frightfully dangerous time. No hectoring, just historical record and a clear narrative analysis that anyone without an ideological ax to grind will find beautifully presented." The Chicago *Sun Times*

"De Villiers finds a great deal to appreciate in the chaotic workings of the planet and the cosmos. His even tone and humor make what could've been the most depressing story ever told oddly inspiring, finding something like hope in life's struggles to continue in the face of the worst of everything. It'd be a bit much to call the book inspirational, and De Villiers doesn't underplay the calamities that lurk around every statistically improbable corner. Instead, [this] is a satisfyingly clear-headed assessment of the state of things that neither talks down to its readers, nor wastes its time mongering fear." *The Onion A.V.*

"De Villiers takes a virtual flight around the globe to examine the natural threats to our existence, from earthquakes to tornadoes to plagues. It's a mix of sobering facts enlivened by historical anecdotes." *Time*

Our Way Out

"Marq de Villiers has earned the right to be bold, and, whether you agree with him or not, he should be lauded for daring to say, in a clear, well-researched argument, what many don't wish to hear." *Quill & Quire*

"The best thing about *Our Way Out* is that Marq de Villiers seems to have no vested interest in fixing the world other than his decent sense of humanity and writing one heck of a book." Mike Landry, in the Saint John *Telegraph Journal*

Back to the Well

"This book will ruffle some feathers as well as open some minds, but for anyone who cares about the earth's most precious resource, it is worth the read." *Publisher's Weekly*

"Marq de Villiers is an expert guide to the vast and contentious terrain of water management, and in *Back to the Well* he steers skillfully past ideological excess and careless hyperbole to provide a clear and thorough account of the state of the planet's water today. This is a provocative and engagingly written book that strikes a welcome balance between hard-eyed truth and buoyant optimism." Chris Turner, author of *The Leap and The War on Science*

THE LONGBOW, THE SCHOONER, & THE VIOLIN

WOOD AND HUMAN ACHIEVEMENT

MARQ DE VILLIERS

SUTHERLAND HOUSE
TORONTO, 2022

Sutherland House
416 Moore Ave., Suite 205
Toronto, ON M4G 1C9

Sutherland House and logo are registered trademarks of The Sutherland House Inc.

First edition, May 2022

If you are interested in inviting one of our authors to a live event or media appearance, please contact sranasinghe@sutherlandhousebooks.com and visit our website at sutherlandhousebooks.com for more information about our authors and their schedules.

Manufactured in Canada
Cover designed by Lena Yang
Book composed by Karl Hunt

Library and Archives Canada Cataloguing in Publication
Title: The longbow, the schooner, & the violin : wood and
human achievement / Marq de Villiers.
Other titles: Longbow, the schooner, and the violin
Names: De Villiers, Marq, author.
Identifiers: Canadiana 20220165793 | ISBN 9781989555590 (hardcover)
Subjects: LCSH: Wood—Social aspects. | LCSH: Woodwork—Social aspects. |
LCSH: Technology and civilization. | LCSH: Material culture. |
LCSH: Technology—Social aspects.
Classification: LCC GN434.7 .D4 2022 | DDC 306.4/6—dc23

ISBN 978-1989555590

Contents

Introduction

You can't see the forest for the trees.
You can't see the trees for the forest.

Both clichés are valid, in context. Except, in the real world, you *can*.

That's what this book is about. To see the forest, to see the trees, to explore the long and entangled history of *homo sapiens* and wood, and to speculate a little.

It is also about the many uses we have found for wood. About the trees that yield the wood. And the fate of those trees. Now, and then.

The story is told in two threads. There are deep dives into the three iconic wooden artifacts of the title, the longbow, the schooner, and the violin, which to me exemplify the inventive ways our species has employed this most extraordinary of substances. The three were chosen with care. All are caught at the absolute pinnacle of their craft. Hand-powered projectile weapons have been speculatively dated back to 64,000 BCE, but none surpassed the Welsh and English longbow in terms of accuracy, speed of fire, and deadliness. Wooden vessels date to the earliest dugouts and coracles, but none in their long history showed the combination of versatility, brute utility, and elegance of the schooner and the schooner's apotheosis, that rakish beauty the clipper ship. Stringed musical instruments are almost as old as human culture but the violin of post-medieval Europe is arguably more expressive, more emotional, more beautiful, than those that came before. These three artifacts are all connected by a thread: the tension string of the longbow, the halyards and sheets of the sailing ship, the strings and bow of the violin, all devices designed by human cunning to give wood its voice and its power.

These studies are surrounded by and embedded into short essays that are intended to explore one aspect or another of our long history with wood. Each essay can be read independently, but there is some merit in reading them sequentially, because they are roughly presented in three clusters.

The first concerns the origin of forests and the trees they contain, with a look at some of the evolutionary puzzles that trees represent, some sense of the extremes to which that evolution has gone, an exploration of the community of life that forests represent, and an examination of the provocative notion that trees might just be communitarian (might have a life beyond the merely passive reaction to sunlight—not sentience, exactly, but something analogous).

The second addresses contemporary forests, the wood they produce, and the uses to which that wood is put, together with a look at the people who live their lives in the forest, even now.

The third considers the future of forests, the hazards they face and the opportunities they present. Forests are endangered in many ways, and forest fires are a constant menace, but this cluster considers how forests can properly be managed, considers the future of trees, and reviews what role wood will play in our ongoing material culture, with a look at "engineered wood," a modern substance with an ancient provenance.

* * *

Forests are the key, and forests are . . . complicated. This much is obvious. Complication has been built into human responses to the mere existence of forests. By contrast a desert, as T. E. Lawrence once wrote, "is a place without nuance, only of light and dark in their eternal opposition"; in a desert journey's long timeline nothing really remains but the heat; "deserts are places where *nothing* is *everything*." Forests, however, are all nuance, places where distinctions are multiple but hidden, boundaries blurred, dark and light manifest together; they are damp, with mould and decay and growth and exuberant fecund life jumbled and tangled. In almost every culture where forests exist, in almost every time but ours, they have been places of hidden ritual, home to totemic creatures, impenetrable groves hiding bottomless waterholes, sacred stones, cave labyrinths, keys to the mysteries, *queerness*. Thus forests in history have been both awful and awe-full. They are splendid, even majestic.

At the same time, in folk memory evil spirits live there, soul-stealers and torturers. Forests are the natural habitat of witches, being secretive and dark places, dangerous for the unwary. In the traditional lore of west Africa, those ancestors who had been solid citizens lived where they died, forever part of the community into which they were born; but the malevolent and the criminal lurked in forests, spiteful, bound on malice.

Forests have also been havens for fugitives from injustice, a redoubt from which corruption can be fought. Sherwood Forest, of course, became a refuge for heroes or a lair for robbers, depending on your perspective. Robin Hood dwelled in Sherwood in some versions, Barnsdale Forest in others, but always in the greenwood somewhere; as we will see, he tricked the Sheriff or murdered him, depending on the version. Before Robin, there were others. Hereward the Brave fought against William the

Conqueror from his secret forest base, where he hid the looted treasure from the monastery at Ely; Baron Fulk Fitzwarin harassed King John and his minions in a guerrilla campaign to restore his just rights—enemy of a law perverted, victim of corrupt justice.

Of course, you can make things from forests: implements, weapons, sculptures, buildings, fortresses, barricades, beautiful objects, utility without limit. Millions of practical people live and have lived in forests—or, rather, among the trees, and have taken their axes and saws to those trees to produce the wood on which their lives and livelihoods depended: practical people doing practical things. In the end, forests did yield to need. It is the human way. This book shows that, too.

Most of the folk tales collected by the indefatigable Grimms were set in or near forests, often the deep forests of the German Hunsrück, beyond the bounds of the familiar world. Some of the forests of Tolkien's Rings cycle had semi-sentient trees consumed with envious malice for all moving things (though the treeherds he called Ents were, on the whole, a benign force, and kept their unruly wards in check). Little Red Riding Hood, alas, wandered into the forest to seek her grandma, and grandma most definitely lived deep in the endless woods, as did the wolf, the imposter. *The Epic of Gilgamesh*, world literature's first known saga, is mostly about death and immortality, but it does contain a magical forest of cedars, guarded by the monster Humbaba. Not to forget Baba Yaga, the grotesque witch of Russian folklore, with her menu of roasted children, who lives deep in the forest in a hut that spins continually on birds' legs, so that nothing escapes her predatory notice.

Forests housed *les hommes sauvages*, wild men, unkempt, untamed, like Enkidu of the Gilgamesh saga, domesticated through the ministrations of a harlot (no symbolism there!), or Orson of the medieval epic *Valentine and Orson*, who learns virtue at the stern hands of a knight but then returns to the wild as a holy hermit:

The forests doughty Valentine prepared to trace,
To find the man who'd laid the country waste;
With sword of steel and shield of glittering brass
He sallied forth, and saw wild Orson pass,
Who swift as stag advanc'd, and fought the knight;
Long, dubious, and conflicting was the fight.

And, much later, Tarzan and his mighty thews (a very Edgar Rice Burroughs word) lived in the "jungle" in the company of a tribe of tree-swinging great apes with a rudimentary language and a curiously modern code of quasi-military honour. These great apes were purely imaginary beings, and Burroughs's portrayal of their "mighty roar as they proclaimed their kill" corresponds poorly with beleaguered vegetarian gorillas in their ever-shrinking habitat, more intent on finding tasty shoots than drawing blood. In the Arthurian cycle the *veray parfait gentil knight*, Lancelot himself, loses his sanity on four separate occasions and takes to the forest, no more than a beast, at least for a while. In the *Iliad*, Aeneas finds himself in a dense forest at the entryway to Hades. So did Dante, in the opening passages of the *Divine Comedy*: "In the middle of life's path I found myself in a dark forest, where the straight way was lost." Thus he finds himself in the shadows, hidden from God's moral law. Virgil went further: woodland places were once the home of fauns and nymphs, "together with a race of men that came from tree trunks, from hard oak," and that's where Rome began:

In that first time, out of Olympian heaven,
Saturn came here in flight from Jove in arms,
An exile from a kingdom lost; he brought
These unschooled men together from the hills

Where they were scattered, gave them laws, and chose
The name of Latium, from his latency
Or safe concealment in this countryside

Tristan and Iseult find refuge in the lush Cornish forest of Morrois, where the cuckolded king Mark finds them, asleep with a naked sword between them. Renaud de Montaubon and his brothers, in the time of Charles the Bald, take to the forests to evade prosecution. Despite being brigands, the legend is sympathetic. Poor put-upon pillagers! Who could blame them? Where else could you find refuge? The forests were eternally "forid," outside, home of outcasts, the mad, illicit lovers, brigands, hermits, saints, lepers, the *maquis*, misfits, the persecuted. The Church was endlessly suspicious of what went on in the deep forests—bestiality, the fallen, errancy, perdition—no one could know the depths of forest depravity, everything was secretive, *hidden*. Dark impulses in the Church wanted to burn it all down, scorch out the last vestiges of paganism. There was biblical precedent: in Deuteronomy, Moses orders his people to destroy the groves of the gentiles.[1]

In western Gabon, near the coast and close to the Congo River, lies the sacred Tchebila forest of the old Loango kingdom. The Loango kings were venerated as gods, perhaps not surprising when you consider what they had to go through to succeed to the kingship in the first place: a king could only be confirmed in his stewardship after an arduous seven-year probation, during which time his reign had to be considered exemplary by the kingdom's elders. After that, in the eighth year, he had to make a one-year journey of celebration to every part of his forested kingdom. During this year-long pre-coronation voyage a "delicious young virgin" shared his bed, but he was not allowed to touch her, his abstinence being a symbol of his will and force of character. On return, he still had to demonstrate his physical prowess: he was obliged to tour the deep woods of Tchebila on one foot, and to climb a tall palm tree using only his hands and one leg. If he failed any of these tasks, he could not be crowned. After coronation, everything changed. The king was confined to the royal compound and could only venture out for the reception of notables from away, or to hunt leopards, the royal animal. It was at his investiture that he took on the real power and responsibility of kingship: to control the rhythms of the seasons, and to decide on the abundance of the harvest and of the fishery. He was the intermediary on earth for Nzambi, the supreme god, the ancestors, and the spirits. Obviously, he couldn't be allowed to wander at will around the countryside. His responsibility was too great. And so was the terror of meeting him: coming face to face with God's representative was more than people could bear.

In Slieve Gullion Forest, County Armagh, lived the giant hunter-warrior Fionn mac Cumhaill (a.k.a., Finn McCool), his exploits told in the poems and stories of the Fenian Cycle. He gained his wisdom by eating a morsel of the Salmon of Knowledge, was able to kill Aillen, the fire-breathing fairy, and built the Giant's Causeway in County Antrim. To allow proper contemplation of these deeds, the county has now pushed a two-kilometre trail through mature woodland of oak, ash, birch, beech, sweet chestnut, and horse chestnut, places where Finn took his leisure.

There are such stories everywhere humans congregate.

The English word *savage* is derived from the Latin word *silva*, meaning woods. It was progress, indeed, when humankind moved from the forest to the field, from the unruly to the orderly, or so European folklore would have it. And then back again: Simon Schama, in his splendid essay *Landscape and Memory*, recounts how often penitents, from Ireland in the west to Bohemia in the east, fled from the temptations of the world into the woods, where "in solitude they would deliver themselves to mystic transports or prevail over the ordeals that might come their way from the demonic powers lurking in the darkness." Saints and hermits, very often the same person, frequently made the deep forest their home. Saint Fiacre cleared much of a small forest in the Brie area of France; Saint Diel did the same in the Vosges mountains. Disciples of Robert d'Arbrissel took as their "theatre of asceticism" a forest northeast of Fougères.[2] Robert himself collected so many acolytes that he had to send them into many a far-flung forest, where they had room to be alone with their impulses. He himself lived the life of a penitent hermit in the forest of Craon, before going on to found the splendid, and splendidly opulent, abbey of Fontevraud near Chinon on the Loire. He later named one of its houses after Mary Magdalene, and in monastic lore Robert is famous for his preaching to prostitutes. In a text attributed to Baldric of Dol, a twelfth-century abbot, Robert visits a brothel in Rouen and preaches of sin to the inmates there. "Enraptured, they walk away with him into the wilderness," an unlikely fancy.

Further east, the same flight to the forest happened in the great wilderness of Russia. Many times over the centuries, as peasants revolted against the wretched excesses of the Russian nobility, dissidents melted into the immensity of the Volga's adjacent forests, where they could scarcely be followed, let alone found. The religious, too: many a time, monks split from their urban monasteries and disappeared into the great Russian forests, there to found new communities, some of them living in the hollowed-out boles of forest giants, praying and scavenging. Fanatics and heretics appeared everywhere; out of the forest wilderness came the Skoptsi, a sect of castrated fanatics who called themselves the Holy Eunuchs; they believed sin came into the world through the carnal lust of Adam and Eve, and vowed to root it out by ripping out the genitals of men and severing the breasts of women. They lived in communes in the deep forest clearings, dressed in white. They spent their days gardening and their nights in prayer, snatching sleep when they could. (They also believed, since humans are apparently capable of believing anything, that if the number of castrati reached 144,000, Christ would be induced to come back to save us all, one last time.) There's a marvellous painting in Moscow's Tretyakov Gallery by the nineteenth-century artist Vasilii Surikov that shows white-garbed men, haggard but proud, being dragged off to the gibbet in Red Square in Moscow. In the foreground, women and children (presumably not their own, unless pre-castration) weep in front of the carts to which the men are lashed; off to the right, standing with the commanding officer of the militia, is the Orthodox Metropolitan, calmly supervising the executions. The chaotic opulence of the domes of Saint Basil's in the background is echoed by the seething mobs of peasants who surround the martyrs.

There was always another side to all this. Forests were more than just refuge or trap. In Europe they also came to be a locus of miracles, a place for spiritual awakenings; and the forest itself was held to be a form of primitive church or temple. The first temples in Europe were said to be forest groves, subsequently replaced with temples made of wood, and then stone. For centuries masses were celebrated in front of the *arbre de fées*, the fairy tree, that had existed in Joan of Arc's day near Domrémy; the gospel oak in the forest of Orleans contained a carved shrine and was visited by pilgrims.

There is a famous poem, clunky to modern ears, by William Cullen Bryant, the American romantic poet, that started . . .

> *. . . The groves were God's first temples.*
> *Ere man learned*
> *To hew the shaft and lay the architrave*
> *And spread the roof above them—ere he framed*

The lofty vault, to gather and roll back
The sound of anthems; in darkling wood
Amidst the cool and silence, he knelt down,
And offered to the Mightiest solemn thanks
And supplication . . .[3]

And so forth and so forth, many stanzas offered to the Mightiest, a monotone of humbleness.

It was no accident that Buddha was alone in his forest, sitting under a peepul tree, a sacred fig, when he attained enlightenment and was given the four great truths; that tree was renamed the Bodhi tree and though the living thing itself has long perished its location remains a place of pilgrimage.

Sarah Laird, in an essay she called "Sacred Groves," lists a few iconic instances: the Tree of Life in Mesopotamia and India brings fertility by linking death with life (the birds visiting its branches are the souls of the dead). The cross on which Jesus died grew into a tree on Mount Golgotha. The fig tree opened for Mary to seek shelter for the infant Jesus from the soldiers of Herod. The date palm yielded the staff of Saint Christopher, which helped him to carry the weak and small across a raging river. "The birch in Scandinavia, larch in Siberia, redwood in California, fig in India, and iroko in West Africa are widely revered and respected . . ."[4]

In Belavezhskaya Pushcha, Europe's lasts remaining stand of primeval forest, there is a six-hundred-year-old oak with healing powers. The sick must lay their cheek against its rough bark and project thoughts that are pure, a nice hedge; nearby is a five-foot boulder whose cracks are thought to be the footprints of prehistoric men. King Jagellon of Poland declared the forest a refuge for bison, auroch, and tarpan. That was in the fourteenth century, and only the bison remain, the auroch and tarpan long extinct.

In Ghana, the sacred grove called *Al-gâba* was used by the Soninke people for religious rites: sacred groves are home to dwarves and *sasabonsam*, prime causes of human woe. In New Zealand's Waipoua Forest stands a hundred-fifty-foot, two-thousand-year-old tree called Tane Mahuta, so sacred that it is forbidden even to touch it. The Ife people of modern Nigeria used to sculpt fine terracotta heads of their rulers, bury them at the foot of a giant tree for spiritual safekeeping, and dig them up for sacred occasions, or whenever a crisis needed to be confronted. In China, the Dai people in the extreme south of Yunnan, who still hold to a curious mixture of Buddhism and polytheism, protect sacred forests, where it is forbidden to cut trees, or even to trespass, a purely conservationist ethic; even the modern inclination for "sustainable forest management" is met with suspicion and, mostly, rejection. The Osun Osogbo sacred forest in western Nigeria, one of the last remnants of primary forest in the country, is also (or so devotees of the fertility goddess Osun believe) one of the last remaining places in which the spirits, or orishas, can feel free to reveal themselves. The most famous sacred forest in ancient Greece was at Dodona, an important oracle; and just outside Athens was another sacred grove, this time of olive trees, remembered in the cliché as the Groves of Academe. Shinto in Japan has always been tied to forests, basic to the reverence for nature. In Celtic Europe, fairies often made their homes in oaks, and touching their holes with a diseased limb was a surefire way to heal. In Scotland, mistletoe growing on the Oak of Errol was a potent charm against glamour and witchery.[5]

But we grow up, at last. By the time of Shakespeare, the savagery has largely disappeared, even from the deep woods, and henceforth resides instead in the corrupt hearts of kings and men. Much of the mystery goes, too. In the French *Encyclopédie*, that self-proclaimed "reasoned dictionary of sciences, arts and crafts," edited in the eighteenth century by Diderot, the word *forêt* is reduced to meaning the manicured groves of Versailles. The forest is tamed.

And today? We live in more prosaic times, and our legends are less demon-ridden but also more mistily sentimental. In the climate-change era, forests have become a lazy synonym for unspoiled; see, for example, the tree-hugger campaigns to save the old-growth forests of the American northwest, and James Cameron's parable of imperialism in his movie *Avatar*, in which forest people are a countervailing force against invading human rapacity. Still, that trees have morphed from a trap (or refuge) to a prodigious crop and then to something that should be preserved for planetary health and our own well-being is surely a good thing. So, too, that sacred forests have transformed into repositories of bio-diversity is an advance for secularism, if not so much for romance.

So we arrive at the modern synthesis. I argue, in all this, that despite the fecundity of "materials science" with its bewildering panoply of made-up chemicals, we need wood more than ever. Wood has more uses than ever (even, as we shall see, to form low orbiting satellites). Trees have more benefits than ever. Forests are needed more than ever—*we* need forests more than ever.

Dead trees are wood, if we're careful. And wood is good (a woodworker's credo). Wood can be both beautiful and utilitarian (a woodworker's operating credo).

So we need to cut down those forests, from time to time. Then take care to make sure they grow, again. And again.

Because nature makes no guarantees.

PART 1

The Longbow

Heracles was, as Amphitryon said,
Master of the bow-string's deadly music

—Euripides

At my side put my bent bow which hath ever made sweet music for me

—Robin Hood, on his deathbed

CONSIDER KING PHILIP VI's formidable French army at Crécy in 1346, a crucial early battle in the folly that came to be called the Hundred Years War. Somewhere around 25,000 soldiers, self-described as the flower of French chivalry, had travelled with the king to the battlefield (the number somewhat uncertain because the muster lists have been lost), only to be hemmed in by ill-chosen terrain and mired in post-downpour muck and mud. Across the way was Edward III's greatly outnumbered invading English army, 2,500 men-at-arms (knights and nobles, heavily armoured), 3,000 *hobelars* (light cavalry), 3,500 spearmen, and 5,000 longbowmen.

Then consider those bowmen. Edward, who knew what they could do, deployed them in an enfilade position, massed on two flanks of the front lines. In preparation, he had brought along on his invasion 10,000 or so longbows and more than three million arrows, bundled into 130,000 twenty-four-arrow sheaves. When things went well each bowman could fire a sustained barrage of six arrows a minute, and sometimes one every five seconds; there were many reports of a new arrow nocked before the previous one had reached its target. For the French across the battlefield that meant a hail of 30,000 in-flight arrows every minute of the brief but bloody battle, each arrow deadly enough to kill a horse, pierce leather armour, and even, at shorter range, chain mail.

For the French, the losses were catastrophic. More than 16,000 died in just a few hours before the rest fled, led by the king himself.

The battle was more than just a famous victory: there were to be many victories, and many losses, in the violent calendar of the Middle Ages. This one was different. Almost two hundred years later, in 1545, Roger

Ascham, a Cambridge don and sometime tutor to the young Princess Elizabeth, put it laconically: "King Edward III, at the battle of Cressy, against Philip the French King, as Gaguinus [Robert Gaguin] the French historiographer, plainly doth tell, slew that day all the nobility of France only with his archers."[6] The victory marked a change in the nature of European warfare: the peasantry plus yeomen of England, conscripted for the war, had demolished the assembled chivalry of France. Or as an awed Victorian historian, John Richard Green, put it, "the churl had struck down the noble; the bondsman proved more than a match, in sheer hard fighting, for the knight. From the day of Crécy, feudalism tottered slowly but surely to its grave." A bit overwrought, especially that "sheer hard fighting" and "tottering" stuff, but the point is right.

The consequences went deeper. A popular medieval saying asserted that "you can train a pikeman from nothing, but to make a master swordsman you have to start with the father, and to create a bowman, you have to start with the grandfather." These English (and Welsh) longbows were the most powerful hand weapons ever produced. Few modern archers would be able to draw a full-sized medieval longbow. A modern equivalent has a "draw force" of around 60 pounds-force, or 270 newtons.[7] No bows survive from Crécy, but medieval bows recovered from the wreck of the *Mary Rose*, which sank in 1545, needed a draw force of 150–160 pounds-force (better than 650 newtons), or nearly two and a half times as much as a modern bow, and a few needed as much as 860 newtons. As a consequence, archers had to be "thick" and immensely strong. Obligatory weekly training from childhood produced bowmen with significant skeletal deformation. Archers' bodies were easy to pick out on battlegrounds, with deformed forearms and massive bone spurs.

That such bows were hard to shoot had its own consequences. Precisely because the longbow demanded lifelong training, a monarch was obliged to encourage archery among his subjects. Longbow shooting became a common sport in England, and laws were brought in to encourage and even mandate regular practice. It was a way for the authorities to cheaply and easily prepare many men to take up arms, without paying them (war was expensive enough as it was). Some medieval English kings banned all sports except archery on Sundays, and men who missed archery practice were fined. Edward III, flush from his army's successes in France, issued a proclamation in 1363: "Whereas the people of our realm, rich and poor alike, were accustomed formerly in their games to practise archery—whence by God's help, it is well known that high honour and profit came to our realm, and no small advantage to ourselves in our warlike enterprises . . . that every man in the same country, if he be able-bodied, shall, upon holidays, make use, in his games, of bows and arrows . . . and so learn and practise archery." As a result, English longbowmen were the first ordinary soldiers, as opposed to knights, to be mythologized as folk heroes, tapping into (and then mutating) the Robin Hood legends.

Elsewhere in Europe rulers often feared their peasants more than they did their neighbours, and hesitated to train them in violence. They therefore lost in battle, a lesson that took a long time to unlearn. By contrast, the English kings essentially armed their peasantry. When war came, the kings could ask their peasants to put down their scythes and take up their bows and, again, these ordinary soldiers were celebrated, their exploits told in stories.

Anyone could be a hero. That was new.

Of course, it wasn't as straightforward as that. Arming the populace didn't jump-start democracy nor radically change society; medieval England remained a deeply aggressive, unequal, and violent place. As Hilary Mantel discovered when she was researching her trilogy about Thomas Cromwell, the idea of the English that we associate with the stiff-upper-lip clichés of the Victorian era was far from the way sixteenth-century Europeans viewed them. "They thought the English were . . . berserkers: first of all, they spoke a barbarous language that no one could understand; and then they were really impious and they were extremely violent."[8] Nor did the peasants willingly march off to war, hurrah: they were often reluctant conscripts who made surly soldiers, and malingering on the practice grounds was common enough. The Peasants' Revolt of 1381 was a cautionary tale for the nobility, as we shall see. The longbow could be used for crime as well as battlefield honour, for rebellion as well as conquest.

* * *

In some ways a bow is a simple device, just a bendy stick with a string. But a real longbow needs good wood from scarce trees, with unique properties and a proper relationship between heartwood and sapwood, bendable but not breakable, and sometimes incorporating gristle and bone and gut and horn in sophisticated ways. To derive the Welsh and English longbow took many thousands of years, and there were missteps and prototypes and often-formidable iterations along the way, but it was the supreme weapon of war in its time and, albeit briefly, as suggested above, it gave a nudge to the changing geopolitics of empire.

Simple bows go a long way back, deep into human history. Of course, it can't be known, even to the millennium, when the bow was developed, or exactly where, but the evidence strongly suggests an origin on the same southern African plains where, it is now known, modern humans developed and whence they set off on their epic expansion.

The earliest hunters didn't use bows. The very first way of killing decent-sized animals was what the anthropologists call "persistence hunting," which simply meant running down your prey and clubbing it to death. For obvious reasons, that wasn't efficient.

The spear was the earliest projectile weapon, and it was useful at close range or with smaller and slower prey animals. But it was limited in range, depending as it does on the strength of the human arm, and its "reload factor" was pretty close to zero.

The next development in the early arms race was a device called an atlatl. At its most basic, this is a stick, usually less than a metre long, with a handle on one end and a hook or spur on the other. A light spear, somewhere from one to two metres long, is laid against the hook and held parallel to the atlatl. The launch is rather like throwing a ball, with a flip of the wrist to impart extra energy. This flip propels a spear much faster and further than it could be thrown by hand, easily reaching 100 metres at speeds of 160 kilometres an hour, the same range as a fifty-pound-draw longbow. In modern competitions the world record atlatl throw is more than 250 metres.[9] It was a decent weapon. There is some evidence that the woolly mammoth and the mastodon were hunted to extinction through atlatl use, but it had its drawbacks: hunters couldn't easily carry bundles of spears, so its reload capacity was limited. Better than a spear, but not by much.

The bow was the solution.

The bows of the elder days no longer exist; the oldest complete bow, the elm Holmegaard bow from Denmark, is a youngster at only 9,000 years old. Even so, arrowheads exist, and sometimes their bindings. The oldest so far was found in Sibudu Cave in the northern part of KwaZulu-Natal province, where anthropologists from the University of Johannesburg and the University of the Witwatersrand uncovered stone tools dated to 64,000 years ago, believed to be the earliest direct evidence of human-made stone-tipped arrows. The artifacts, discovered by a team under Marlize Lombard, matched the date of an earlier discovery, a bone point that could have been an arrow tip. Close inspection of one such arrowhead yielded remnants of blood and bone that were clues to how it was used.

Its shape, Lombard suggests, indicated where it had been impacted and damaged, and how it was hafted. "This showed that the pieces were very likely to have been the tips of projectiles rather than sharp points on the end of hand-held spears." There were also traces of glue: a plant-based resin that the scientists think was used to fasten them onto a wooden shaft, which "implies that people were able to produce composite tools— tools where different elements produced from different materials are glued together to make a single artifact, an indicator of a cognitively demanding behaviour." The discovery pushes back the development of bow-and-arrow technology by at least 20,000 years.[10]

Because these ancient bows have long rotted away, we can't be certain how they were made or what, exactly, they looked like. Still, there are hints, from cave drawings and a few leftover fragments, and the bows of the few remaining hunter-gatherer societies are very likely close, or close enough, to the very earliest bows. I once had a chance to handle one of them, owned by a pygmy hunter, a member of the Baka tribe of Cameroon. I wasn't looking for bows, or weapons, but had become curious about how the pygmies lived in the rainforest, and had hired a guide, a member of the Fang tribe named Clement, because he said he spoke their language fluently and could introduce me properly. Their home was near the Cameroon–Gabon border, and we reached them by travelling up the Sanaga River, whose course curves away from the coast to the east.

We banked our pirogue in a small cove. It looked like hundreds of others, a small clearing in the blank face of the jungle, but Clement said the band he knew was close by. At mid-morning Clement held up a hand and brought us to a halt. Silently, a small figure glided out of the bush, intent on a spot about twenty metres from where we had stopped and, judging from the angle of his head and the tilt of the arrow already nocked in his bowstring, a good deal over our heads. The hunter was small, but not tiny, wizened, but muscular. Just then he loosed his arrow, and it flew true: there was a solid thunk and a porcupine fell to the earth.

Back at his family encampment, five huts arranged in a semicircle around a clearing in which one large tree had been left standing for shade, our new friend showed me the tools of his trade. He hunted with snares, a spear with a fifteen-centimetre blade honed to a fine edge, and his bow. The bow was only about a metre long, perfectly straight when unstrung, made of a wood that felt damp and was springy to the touch. It looked fragile, but our host strung it for me and let me pull, and it wasn't nearly as easy as I had thought. The string was hairy, fibrous, but clearly tough enough. The arrows were feathered but without added tips, just the sharpened wood with a spiral groove. They didn't look very deadly, but they obviously did what was needed. Our host sensibly wouldn't let me fire one.[11]

Probably such bows were invented in multiple places at different times, in multiple shapes with multiple materials, and with varying success. Whatever the exact dates and origins, by the end of the last glacial period, around 15,000 years ago, use of the bow and arrow had spread to every region on earth except Australasia and parts of Oceania. By 13,000 years ago, it was already a developed and efficient tool. Fragments of a hunting bow dating back at least that far were found in the Trois Frères cave in Montesquieu-Avantès, in the Ariège department in southwestern France. More fragments were found in Germany, at Mannheim-Vogelstang, dated 17,500 to 18,000 years ago, and at Stellmoor, dated 11,000 years ago. Near Grotte du Bichon, Switzerland, the mummified corpses of a bear and a hunter were found together, with splinters of flint buried in the bear's backbone: teeth and claws against arrowheads, a technological draw.[12]

* * *

The very earliest bows were used for killing game, as these were. But soon archers turned the bow to what would become its other historical uses: homicide and warfare. A human skeleton from Turkana county in northern Kenya has obsidian fragments embedded in its skull and throat. This ultimate cold case has been dated to around 10,000 years ago. Whether the perp was ever punished is, of course, unknown.

Pace Roger Ascham, military and criminal use of a bow and arrow goes back to the legendary passages of the Old Testament. In his survey of archery, Ascham quotes Nicholas of Lyra the first prominent medieval biblical exegetist (he produced the earliest printed biblical commentary), as asserting that "Lamech killed Cain with a shaft." Which seems dubious: even amateur perusers of the Bible will know that Lamech was a sixth-generation descendant of Cain's, the son of Methuselah and the father of Noah. Still, they all lived for centuries in those days, so I suppose it is possible that a youngster could kill his still vigorous great-great-great-great-grandfather. The Bible also indicates that other eminences favoured the bow, for "King David's first act and ordinance was, after he was King, that all Judea should learn to shoot."

Legends aside, the first people known to have regularly used bows and arrows were the Egyptians, who adopted archery for both hunting and warfare in the closing days of the Old Kingdom, somewhere around 3000 BCE. Tomb frescoes show a variety of weapons in use by the Egyptians:

spears, clubs, maces, and daggers (though not swords), as well as bows. In the pre-dynastic period, the commonest bow seems to have been made of horn; two pieces of antelope horn were joined by a central piece of wood. They had a double curvature (the tips of the horn segments curving away from the archer), the bowyers using the natural curve of the animal horn. By the start of the Old Kingdom, these artifacts had been abandoned in favour of the "self-bow," a single piece of wood with a gentle curve, usually about two metres long and tapering at each end, strung with fibre. They were harder to pull than the double-curvature bows they replaced, and with a longer draw, but they were easier to make and considerably more powerful.

Somewhere around 2500 BCE, the restless nomads of the central Asian steppe made a technological breakthrough. Since they raided on horseback, a two-metre bow was cumbersome to carry and deploy. To solve the problem, they constructed bows as a composite, layers of wood, sinew, and horn that could be bent much further than even the most flexible wooden bow, and could thus be shorter, more convenient for use from the back of a horse. The sequence was horn on the inner curve facing the archer, wood in the middle, and sinew on the outer curve. These bows were carried into Egypt by the invading forces of what historians were wont to call "Asiatic Hyksos," who were actually from Palestine, an aggressive culture whose armies conquered the Middle Kingdom. They were then widely adopted by the pharaohs of the New Kingdom and continued to be deployed through to the Islamic period. Most of the weapons were imported from Palestine and Babylon, then the home of most "modern" armaments. When they were made by local bowyers they were often of imported materials.

Archery in China dates back at least as far as the Shang dynasty (1776–1027 BCE), but composite bows were not used until somewhere around

300 BCE. The Greeks of the time of Homer used bows, too, some of them self-bows and some composite. The Persians, for their part, were supposedly skilful in archery, and Persian coins reliably contained images of bows and arrows. Indeed, King Darius the Great, who died in 486 BCE, had these lines carved on his tomb:

> *Darius the King lieth buried here,*
> *That in shooting and riding had never peer.*

Darius's grandson Xerxes (also self-styled the Great) put together a polyglot army, most of whom used the composite bow. Herodotus in his *Histories* asserted that of the many nations making up the Persian army, almost all used the bow, though the Scythians and the Parthians were the most celebrated archers in the East. Among the Greeks, the Cretans were acknowledged as the master bowmen. Indeed, the Cretans frequently served as a separate assault force in Greek armies, as they did later among the Romans.[13] The Scythian and Parthian bows were generally shaped like a half moon, whereas the Greek and Cretan bow proper was double-curved, like Cupid's.[14]

* * *

Partly because archers tended to be "foreigners" in classical Greek armies (even Cretans were so defined), and because foreigners were by definition shifty, use of the bow itself was sometimes scorned. The distance killing it made possible didn't go down well with classical commentators huffy about manly traditions, who thought close combat the honourable way to kill and die. In his play *Heracles*, Euripides captures the sentiment well. He has Lycus, the usurper king of Thebes, sneer at Heracles's wife, Megara, and his "father," Amphitryon, suggesting that (a) Heracles will never return from Hades and (b) he is not such a hotshot after all.

> *. . . You, Megara*
> *Styling yourself a hero's wife! What were they, then,*
> *These marvellous exploits of your husband Heracles—*
> *Destroying the swamp serpent or the Nemean lion?*
> *That lion he said he strangled with his hands; in fact*
> *He snared it with a trap. Are such performances*
> *Your weighty arguments for sparing his sons' lives?*
> *Heracles won his fame by fighting animals;*
> *In other matters he was no hero—he was nothing!*
> *His left arm never held a shield; whenever he faced*
> *An enemy's spear. He used a bow—the coward's weapon,*
> *Handy for running away. The test of courage is not*
> *Skill with a bow, but the firm foot, the unflinching eye*
> *When the spear drives its hurtling furrow through the ranks.*

This is a bit rich for someone who has usurped the kingdom by murdering his predecessor. In any case, Amphitryon, Heracles's putative father (really Zeus was his father) is dismissive:

> *". . . and then you sneer*
> *At that superb discovery, the bow! Listen:*
> *I'll teach you a little sense. A man with a spear and a shield*
> *Is slave to his own arms. Suppose, to right or left,*
> *The next man loses courage, he himself gets killed*
> *Through others' cowardice; if he breaks his spear-shaft*
> *How can he defend himself? He's lost his one resource.*

While a skilled bowman has two great advantages;
First, he can shoot a thousand arrows, and still have more
To defend himself with; secondly, his fighting's done
Well out of reach—he wounds a watchful enemy
From perfect safety, with invisible stabs . . ."[15]

Later, Heracles is going to Athens from Thebes after killing his family, an anguished parting . . .

My bow! Which I have loved and lived with, and now loathe
What shall I do—keep it or let it go? This bow
Hung at my side, will talk: "With me you killed your wife
And children; keep me and you keep their murderer!"
Shall I then keep and carry it? With what excuse?
And yet—disarmed of this, with which I did such deeds
As none in Hellas equalled, must I shamefully
Yield to my enemies and die? Never! This bow
Is anguish to me, yet I cannot part with it.

Even the gods were sometimes sniffy about the bow. Paris, "the pretty wife-stealer," was thought to be cowardly, as godlings go, for the bow is his weapon. "No bowman would ever have been made Best of the Greeks, no matter how skilled he was."[16]

The bow could also be "treacherous" in another way, as Herodotus once put it. It could kill through chemistry, not just from force, but from poison amplifying its already wounding power.

As recounted above, the bow I was shown during my sojourn with the Baka pygmies of Cameroon had looked puny and not at all dangerous, but that was misleading. It had a hidden advantage: since the arrows were poisoned, a light puncture was enough to do the killing. I remember gingerly feeling the tip of our host's spear, having asked whether it was poisoned, but he said no, only the wood-tipped arrows were; the spiral I had noticed at the tip of each arrow was designed to better retain poison. He showed me the leaves from which the poison was made—they looked like ivy and oozed a black sap when crushed. It was an arrow dipped in this poison that had finished off the porcupine we ate later for dinner; I had thought the blow itself had done the trick, but apparently not. It never occurred to me to ask how you could eat poisoned meat without becoming ill yourself, but it seemed you could, for we took no ill effects.

In the same way, in many societies through history, early bows became incrementally more deadly with the widespread use of poison, in legend and in fact. Heracles, in his mad fit, killed his children and wife "*adrift in a storm of insanity . . . his arrows dipped in the hydra's blood.*" The hero remembered: he had earlier killed the centaur the same way, with an arrow dipped in the poison of the ruined hydra's blood, a teachable moment—from this killing came the term *toxic*, from the Greek word *toxikon*, meaning "arrow poison." It wasn't just Heracles. Homer had Odysseus poison his arrows with hellebore (lately a trendy pot plant in North American horticultural circles). Both sides used poison in the Trojan War. In the Norse sagas, Baldr was killed by a poisoned arrow.

In history, too, not just in myth. Herodotus provides a number of useful recipes for poisons, as does Hesiod.

The poison used by the Baka, it turns out, was from a plant called *Strophanthus hispidus*, a five-metre-tall liana with elegant yellow lobes spotted with red and brown. They called their poison *onaye*, and those who have studied such things say it contains a cardiac glyceride called strophanthin which acts to increase the output force of the heart and increase its contractions. In the woollier regions of folk medicine, it is sometimes recommended for counteracting "hardening of the arteries and for high blood pressure," but you'd be hard pressed to find a real physician cheerfully dispensing such advice. In South America, famously, curare is the poison of choice; in west Asia the venom of the Russell's viper does the trick. The black-legged dart frog is a source of poison for some western Colombian tribes (the toxin of one species of dart frog, sensibly called *p. terribilis*, is so strong that it is enough to prick an arrowhead in the back of the frog without killing it). Still, the easiest manufacture of poison is to leave the body of a man to rot in the sun, collecting the resulting putrefaction in a shallow bowl in which the archer dips his arrowheads. Tetanus is the result.[17]

Strabo, the gossipy Greek geographer, noted that the people of Ethiopia dipped their arrows in the gall of serpents, although he did not say which kind. He also reported that a poison used by the Suani people of the Caucasus region was so noxious that the smell alone was enough to overthrow an enemy. The Scythians, a nomadic people of Siberia, went one better: they mixed viper venom with human blood and animal dung, causing shock, necrosis, suppuration, and then gangrene and tetanus—nothing like tripling down, using three poisons where one would have sufficed. Ovid, in his *Tristia*, reported the recipe with, seemingly, a mix of horror and relish.

* * *

Modern military bows, which means bows from the Crusader period onward, had no use for poisons. The English longbow was deadly enough on its own. Poison was finicky and dangerous to make, and hardly useful in a battle—where to keep tubs of the stuff? In any case, despite what moviemakers have to say, very few poisons were instantaneous, and a poisoned enemy could wreak more havoc than you would want before he eventually expired; a poisoned horse would trample you before taking any harm. Brute force was better, and the English longbow delivered that and more.

What were they like, these English longbows? Of what were they made? How did they pull? What damage could they do?

What of the bow?
The bow was made in England:
Of true wood, of yew wood,
The wood of English bows;
So men who are free
Love the old yew tree
And the land where the yew tree grows.[18]

They were made from yew, preferably, and yew was slow-growing, strong, flexible, somewhat poisonous, rare, carefully rationed, occasionally sacred. Yew was preferred because it possessed the best available combination of flexibility (in our jargon-driven days called the "modulus of elasticity") and strength (the "modulus of rupture"). Put more simply, the best bows needed to bend easily and not break, and yew was the best available wood for that. Where yew couldn't be found, wych elm made a decent substitute, as did ash and regular elm, with osage orange and mulberry cheaper and less effective substitutes. The thirteenth-century Welsh archdeacon known as Giraldus Cambrensis, or Gerald of Wales, once recorded seeing elm bows in the southwestern Welsh region of Gwent, and he wasn't impressed: "They are made neither of horn, ash nor yew, but of elm; ugly unfinished-looking weapons, but stiff, large and strong, and equally capable of use for long or short shooting."[19]

If yew trees were scarce, it was partly because of demand, but also because the Druids, the mystics of southwestern England and Wales, jealously guarded their small groves.

In the cosmology of the Druids, many things were held sacred, and the yew was preeminent among them. They had long been aware of the tree's longevity and its ability to regenerate: branches of old yew trees can droop to the ground and take root, and so yews came to stand as a symbol of death and resurrection. Sometimes, indeed, new shoots can sprout from apparently dead wood, even from beams in ancient buildings. Possibly the world's oldest surviving wooden artifact is a yew spearhead, found at Clacton-on-Sea, in Essex. It is somewhere around 450,000 years old, easily predating the Neanderthals.

The Druids used yew for other purposes. The tree's needles are toxic enough to cause death to the vulnerable and unwary. (Didn't Hamlet brew up a poison made of "slips of yew, silvered in the moon's eclipse"?) Yews were commonly planted on the graves of plague victims to protect and purify the dead; they were sometimes symbols of immortality, but also omens of doom. At least five hundred English churchyards still enclose yew trees older than the buildings themselves; the church was built where the yew was found, the yew a ward against evil.

At the other end of Britain, in the Scottish county of Perthshire, in the churchyard of the village of Fortingall, is likely the oldest tree in Britain, and possibly one of the oldest in Europe. The Fortingall yew is certainly at least two thousand years old, and may be as many as nine thousand years old (experts differ, and growth rings of yews cannot be counted because the heartwood eventually rots from the inside). A popular tale recounts how Pontius Pilate played in its shade as a young boy; he had apparently accompanied his father on a diplomatic mission to visit a Pictish ruler. Even more fanciful was the notion that Pontius had actually been born under its spreading branches.[20]

In the Celtic myth of the beautiful Deidre, so lovely that she was destined to cause wars and many deaths, a yew tree grew from her bones after her suicide, and spread across the country until its branches found another yew, which had grown from the bones of her lover, Naoise.[21]

There weren't many yew groves in Scotland, but enough that Robert the Bruce ordered bows made from the sacred grove at Ardchattan Priory, which were then triumphantly used in his victory over Edward II at Bannockburn in 1314. The clan Fraser had a yew sprig as its clan badge.

You couldn't make very many bows from a yew tree, which weren't very large to begin with. You would need a piece of the bole or a heavy limb two or more metres long without knots or burls or blemishes. It then had to be carefully cut so that a single stave would include a layer of heartwood, for strength, and a layer of sapwood, for flexibility. The side of the bow facing away from the archer would be sapwood; yew sapwood had good cellular memory and would spring back to straight after being bent many hundreds of times. The sapwood layer was usually flat, and about a third of the total; the full staves would be either circular or D-shaped in cross section. This naturally layered structure made the longbow similar to the composite bows of the East. The finished bow would end up somewhere between 1.6 metres (5.5 feet) and 1.8 metres (six feet). Generally, an archer would match a bow to his own height, for maximum draw. Earlier and shorter bows had a shorter draw (distance of travel in the bend); archers generally drew such bows to the chest, or "to the paps" as medieval writers put it, whereas longbow users drew at least to the chin.

Because the trees grew slowly, and it was not easy to find straight and unblemished pieces of yew, mass production was difficult. Even when available, the wood needed to be dried for up to two years or more, while being carefully worked throughout that time. Later, as the battles of the

Hundred Years War created an ever-greater demand for bows, shortcuts were found, such as submersing the wood for a period before working it.

Complicating the supply, there were not always enough English yew trees to be had, even counting those of the prickly Druids, and yew bowstaves had to be imported to England, starting in 1294. In 1350, Henry IV violated landowners' rights by ordering the royal bowyers to enter private land and cut whatever yews they could find; it turned out there weren't many. He reluctantly allowed archery practice to be held with bows made from ash and hazel, saving the yew for serious killing. Eventually the demand for yews was so strong and the supply so weak that Parliament passed the Statute of Westminster in 1470, which required each ship trading in English ports to pay four bowstaves for each tun of goods imported, a number later increased to ten. By the sixteenth century, yew forests no longer existed in northern Europe, and bow materials were brought in from Spain when geopolitics made it possible.

Arrows were easier. They didn't demand yew. They could be made of many woods, and even of reeds. Herodotus, in his recounting of the exploits of Xerxes the Great, asserted that the army's arrows were reed. Mind you, Herodotus, ever one to recount fanciful tales, told of a Nile beast called the "water horse" (presumably a hippopotamus), from whose dried skin the Egyptians made arrow shafts. The arrows of India were also of reed, as were those of the Lycians (those were a marvel, apparently, flying true without feathers).

But not all woods would do. Some were too hard and dense, and "such-like make dead, heavy, lumpish, hobbling shafts," as Roger Ascham put it. They would fly true, but ordinary archers could not send them far enough to be useful. Other woods were too light. These make "hollow, starting, studding, gadding shafts," which would not fly true and sometimes not even reach their target. "And although I know that some men shoot so strong, that the dead woods be light enough for them, and other some so weak, that the loose woods be likewise for them big enough, yet generally, for the most part of men, the mean is the best." Only one stash of medieval arrows has survived, from the 1545 wreck of the *Mary Rose*, about 3,500 of them, made variously of poplar, ash, beech, and hazel.

There were arrow manufactories wherever there were forests, which is pretty well everywhere in medieval England, for demand was insatiable and ever-escalating (as recounted earlier, the invading English took a million and a quarter arrows to France, for use at Crécy and elsewhere). Judging from those found on the *Mary Rose*, arrows came at various lengths, depending on the reach of the archer, but they averaged about seventy-five centimetres. Indian arrows, if medieval accounts can be believed, were even longer: "a yard and half long, and therefore they gave the greater stripe; but yet, because they were so long, they were the more unhandsome and less profitable to men of Inde, as Curtius doth tell." Very long arrows still exist in obscure parts of the world, for specialized uses. Pictures from North Sentinel Island (one of the Andamans in the Bay of Bengal) show Sentinelese fishermen shooting fish from a dugout canoe; their bows are slender and very long, a good deal taller than the archers, and their arrows are even longer, spears really. An archer can carry a sheaf of such spears, maybe a dozen or more.

Armorers experimented with multiple materials for arrowheads, ranging from the flint of the ancients through the brass or horn of the classical period, to the iron and steel of the medieval arrows. The aboriginal tribes of the American southeast sometimes used alligator gar scales as arrow tips.

There were dozens of designs for arrowheads. Some were broad, to make a wide cut. Some were barbed, to make extraction harder. Some had forked heads, such as the swallowtail, though the real purpose of those has been lost. Some had homely names: the dog arrow, the wolf arrow, the Welsh arrow, the Scottish arrow, the broad arrow. Some designs worked best on unarmoured infantry, some were designed to grievously wound horses, and a few (the straight bodkin, shaped like a stiletto) were purpose-made for cutting through armour. Occasionally arrowheads were interchangeable according to circumstances, and could be carried to the field of battle in a bag. Others carried a smear of pitch, the theory being that they could be set alight and so set fire to the defences; these seldom worked as planned. The great yarner Herodotus attributed this invention to Xerxes: "He made his archers bind their shaft heads about with tow, and then set it on fire and shoot them; which thing done by many archers, set all the places on fire, which were of matter to burn; and, besides that, dazed the men within, so that they knew not whither to turn them." Some armies experimented with these in the Hundred Years War, but they mostly failed and were soon abandoned.

The other end of the arrow is "fletched," usually with feathers, three or sometimes more. Arrows can be fired unfletched, but they are less stable and seldom fly true. The fletching creates wind drag, a disadvantage, but also imparts spin, which makes arrows stable in flight and more accurate (modern rifles, whose barrels are "rifled," do the same thing with bullets). In medieval times, fletchers argued endlessly and vigorously about which feathers were best, how they should be installed, and how cropped. As Roger Ascham rather windily put it:

> there is no one thing in all shooting [that provokes] so much as
> the feather. For, first, a question may be asked: whether any other
> thing beside a feather, be fit for a shaft or no? If a feather only
> be fit, whether a goose feather only or no? If a goose feather
> be best, then whether there be any difference as concerning the

feather of an old goose and a young goose; a gander or a goose; a fenny goose or an uplandish goose? Again, which is best feather in any goose, the right wing or the left wing; the pinion feather or any other feather: a white, black, or grey feather; Thirdly, in setting on of your feather, whether it is pared or drawn with a thick rib or a thin rib, (the rib is the hard quill which divideth the feather), a long feather better or a short, set on near the nock or far from the nock, set on straight or somewhat bowing; and whether one or two feathers run on the bow? Fourthly, in couling or sheering, whether high or low, whether somewhat swine-backed or saddle-backed, whether round or square shorn? And whether a shaft at any time ought to be plucked, and how to be plucked?

The final piece of the working bow was the humble string. Humble, but critically important, for it does, after all, launch the arrow. If the string breaks in battle, the archer is lost, his weapon useless. He can carry a spare, but in the press of battle would have scant time, and scant room, to bend the bow to notch the string. Archers also needed to pay attention to the length of the string, and its weight. Too short, and the bow must be bent too far to notch it, with the risk of breaking. Too long, and the bow will have to be drawn too far in the shooting, again with the risk of breaking. The weight of the string is important, too. Heavier strings are slower, but surer. Lighter strings make the bow easier to use, but risk breakage.

Armourers all advised careful attention to the string. "When the string beginneth never so little to wear, trust it not, but away with it; for it is an ill saved halfpenny, that costs a man a crown. Thus you see how many jeopardies hangeth over the silly poor bow, by reason only of the string. As when the string is short, when it is long, when either of the nocks be naught, when it hath but one wap, and when it tarrieth over long on."

What the strings were made of depended on the resources to hand. There is some evidence that even the Neanderthals, recently rescued from their unkind designation as *homo stupidus*, made woven fibre strings, though whether they were ever attached to bows is not known; fragments found in France dating to around 50,000 years ago were attached to a stone tool, or flake, so it is possible. The fibres in this case were made from the inner bark of a conifer, twisted and re-twisted into cord.[22] The Greeks of Homer's time used "the thermes [intestines] of bullocks," twisted together in the way ropes are made. Sometimes horse-tail hair was used, sometimes even silk. Diverse cultures variously used linen, hemp, and other fibres such as the inner bark of elm or cherry, sinew, and rawhide. The Dakota Americans sometimes used the necks of snapping turtles. Almost any fibre could be used in emergency, although many plant fibres tended to come unravelled if not kept under tension. By the fourteenth century, hemp was the most common bowstring. The most important qualities were a light weight, strength, resistance to abrasion, and resistance to water. At Crécy, for example, the strings of the Genoese crossbow archers failed entirely, having stretched in the heavy rain that preceded the battle.

Strings were usually secured to the bow by a timber hitch (still used by farmers and fishermen); sometimes called a bowyer's hitch, it can securely grasp even a round post, but is easy to untie. The so-called Flemish string was made with a loop at each end, which made the bow easy to string and unstring, but it was never popular because it was finicky to make.

* * *

How far, and how hard, did medieval arrows fly?

It's not known, not for certain. Much depends on the draw weight of the bow itself, the type of arrow, and the strength of the shooter.

Three hundred paces was common on the medieval practice fields, and four hundred was theoretically possible. But no one thought this plausible on the battlefield. Sustained shooting, particularly the six-a-minute rate of battlefield shooting, took its toll; so did the enervating life of constant campaigning, not to mention the terrors of a charging enemy (or one that was firing back). The English writer and retired soldier Barnabe Riche, whose most engaging work was the delightfully titled *Riche his Farewell to Militarie Profession conteining verie pleasaunt discourses fit for a peaceable tyme*, suggested in a tract published thirty years after the sinking of the *Mary Rose*, that if a thousand English archers were mustered, then a mere hundred would be able to shoot further than two hundred paces after a week's campaigning.

Before battle, each archer would be given around six dozen arrows. Depending on the terrain, they generally stored their arrows point down in the ground in front of them, for easy reloading. At some battles, resupply was possible, youngsters running quivers of arrows to those who seemed to need them. The firing rate of five to six a minute seems rapid, but a fast-advancing enemy could get seventy paces nearer between arrows, so haste was important; once they were on you, bows were useless and flight the only option.

Even at the reduced rates of fire on the battlefield, they were murderously effective weapons. Gerald of Wales, quoted earlier on the Welsh longbow, was vivid in his description of its brutal power. Describing a Welsh attack on the Norman castle of Abergavenny in 1182, he saw a man-at-arms struck by a Welsh arrow. The arrow penetrated his thigh, pierced the chain armour called *chausses*, went right through his leather tunic, passed through his saddle, and cut deep enough into the horse below to kill it.[23]

A bodkin-tipped war arrow could penetrate four inches of solid oak at two hundred paces. At shorter range, a similar arrow could pierce not only chain mail but also wrought-iron armour; only Damascus steel would withstand it but, even then, the steel would be dimpled and its wearer bruised so badly that he was usually unhorsed. (That the front rank of the French army at Agincourt, nobles who could afford steel, took fewer casualties than lesser ranks may be owed to steel plate backed by a generous layer of padding.)

The wounds, as described, could be grievous. Given battlefield conditions and the state of medieval surgery, no wound was a trivial one. There is a curious small dialogue in Roger Ascham's *Toxophilus*, where Toc., as the protagonist is called in the book (*toxophilus* means "lover of archery"), is discussing war wounds with the scholar Phi. (for philosopher). The philosopher wonders whether a broad arrowhead is better against enemies because it makes a wider hole. Toxophilus demurs: "when a man shooteth at his enemy, he desireth rather that it should enter far, than stick fast. For what remedy is it, I pray you, for him which is smitten with a deep wound, to pull out the shaft quickly, except it be to haste his death speedily? Thus heads which make a little hole and deep, be better in war, than those which make a great hole and stick fast in."

If the wound was a flesh wound only, and didn't terminate on bone, the technique was to tie a water-soaked cloth to the protruding end and push the arrow through the wound to the other side. Where bone was the problem, early physicians devised an ingenious array of implements to deal with them. Hippocrates's successor Diocles invented what he called the *graphiscos*, a thin tube with hooks on the end and long-handled forceps to extract embedded arrows.

One of the most famous battlefield surgeries describes just such a deep wound. At the Battle of Shrewsbury, the sixteen-year-old Prince Henry (Prince Hal to Shakespeare) was shot in the face, the arrow entering beside the nose. When the royal surgeon Thomas Bradmore arrived at the scene, he saw that others had attempted to pull out the arrow, which was embedded fast in the back of the skull, a wound a good six inches deep. The shaft had come free, but the arrowhead remained behind. Other physicians had tried to remove the head with potions, with predictably meagre results.

In Bradmore's own journal, he describes what he did:

> First, I made small probes from the pith of an elder, well dried and well stitched in purified linen [made to] the length of the wound. These probes were infused with rose honey [as antiseptic]. And after that, I made larger and longer probes, and so I continued to always enlarge these probes until I had the width and depth of the wound as I wished it. And after the wound was as enlarged and deep enough so that, by my reckoning, the probes reached the bottom of the wound, I prepared anew some little tongs, small and hollow, and with the width of an arrow. A screw ran through the middle of the tongs, whose ends were well rounded both on the inside and outside, and even the end of the screw, which was entered into the middle, was well rounded overall in the way of a screw, so that it should grip better and more strongly . . . and by moving it to and fro, little by little (with the help of God) I extracted the arrowhead.

After that, Prince Hal being still conscious, Bradmore had to clean and close the wound. This he did in stages. First, he poured white wine into the cavity, along with a probe smeared with barley, flour, honey, and flax. For twenty days he repeated the process, each day making the probes thinner and thus the hole smaller. This allowed the wound to heal naturally and eventually close.

Hal survived. But it is worth nothing that pre-wound, he had been known as a libertine. Post-healing, he became pious, an ascetic. Not a great surprise.[24]

* * *

Before it was turned against the French, the longbow had an extended history of purely British killing.

It seems to have been first deployed by the Welsh. The earliest death (or first recorded killing, at any rate) by a longbow was in 633, more than five hundred years before the weapon was adopted by the English. The victim was Osfrid, the son of the king of Northumbria, Edwin. The Mercians, as the folk of central England were then called, fought a series of sixteen inconclusive wars against the Welsh, the result a dispiriting stalemate for both sides. The chronicles don't record the nature of Osfrid's wound; a laconic entry simply records that he was killed at Hatfield Chase, in Yorkshire. Whether the Welsh won that particular war is not known.

The first major deployment, still by the Welsh, was against the invading army of Edward I, who conquered and annexed Wales between 1277 and 1283. The Welsh lost that one, but their archers were so effective that Edward adopted the longbow for his own military, and it remained the principal weapon of offence for the next three hundred years.

By 1298, when war broke out between Edward II and the Scots (the First War of Scottish Independence), the longbow had already become a mainstay of the army, and helped Edward defeat the forces of William Wallace at Falkirk. Wallace survived, but his own sense of his worth did not; he was so discouraged by his defeat that he resigned as Guardian of Scotland shortly after the battle.

Robert the Bruce took over as commander of Scotland, and after a famous victory at Bannockburn in 1314, led a raid deep into England and went on to besiege the castle at Carlisle in 1315. But his siege engines got bogged down in the mud from the River Esk (Eden), and his scaling ladders were easily toppled; he was driven off with heavy casualties. Roger Ascham recorded the victory: "The fear only of English archers hath done more wonderful things than ever I read in any history, Greek or Latin, and most wonderful of all now of late, beside Carlisle, betwixt Esk and Leven, at Sandysikes, where the whole nobility of Scotland, for fear of the archers of England, (next the stroke of God), as both English and Scottish men that were present told me, were drowned or taken prisoner."

Even so, the longbow was not yet famous. It took on its fearsome reputation in the many battles of the 116-year-long Hundred Years War, including, as we have seen, the victory at Crécy, in which bowmen from the conquered principality of Wales fought for the first time alongside English archers to inflict a devastating defeat on the French.

The proximate cause of the war lay in internal dynastic squabbles in England. King Edward II began the process, through his marriage to Isabella of France, daughter of France's Philip IV, but also through sheer fecklessness. He gained a reputation as a particularly feeble ruler after he lost to the Scots at Bannockburn; but instead of attending to matters of state or to securing his military, he spent much of his time promoting those who caught his fancy at court, including the egregious Hugh Despenser the Younger, who had been "collecting" towns and castles in England, most of them illegally; his love affair with Edward didn't do anything to improve the king's reputation. Edward also royally ticked off his wife, Queen Isabella, who had left him in disgust and decamped to France, where she took up with Roger Mortimer, the Earl of March, who was in France at the time. In 1326, the queen's patience finally ran out and she invaded England with Mortimer and several other powerful barons; it was this episode that earned her the sobriquet She-Wolf of France. The king was forced to abdicate and was locked up in Berkeley Castle, where he was murdered in 1327, by means of a red-hot poker, or so legend has it. Although Edward III was crowned as the new king, he was only fourteen, and Mortimer became de facto ruler of England. Not for long, however. Just three years later, the young Edward led a successful coup against Mortimer, after which he ruled England for the next fifty years. Isabella was put out to pasture but not otherwise punished.

In 1337, Edward declared himself the legal heir to the French throne, which caused a predicable uproar across the Channel. This declaration was not, however, unprovoked; French forces had been sniping away at his continental territories, such as Guyenne and Gascony, for decades, and had been winning more skirmishes than they lost. Edward's claim turned on a fine legal point. Under French law, known as Salic law, property could only be inherited through the paternal line. Under English law, however, property could also be inherited by male heirs through the maternal bloodline; the English argued that the blood of kings ran true to the firstborn male, whether from mother or father. This gave Edward his argument: his mother was a French royal, and in his view his lands in France allowed him to extend English law more broadly than the French allowed. The French, naturally, disagreed.

The long war went through several phases. The first was the sudden and unexpected dominance of the English—the longbow again.

The weapon's first test against the French was not on land but at sea. Before Edward could even contemplate an invasion of France, he needed to control the Channel. French ships, assisted by pirates from Genoa and Castile, had been raiding English ports. Portsmouth and Southampton were sacked in 1338, Dover and Folkstone burned the following year, while pirates were nibbling away at English imports. In 1340, Parliament reluctantly raised money for a counterattack. The English fleet was still tiny, and Henry was obliged to press merchant vessels into service, most of them "cogs," broad, sturdy single-masted vessels steered by oar. By the time the combined fleet set sail, it numbered somewhere between 120 and 200 vessels, of varying capacity and capability, some of them tiny. The French had assembled a flotilla of 180 ships, berthed at the Belgian port of Sluys, the sea outlet for Bruges, where they were tasked with heading off an invasion through Flanders.

The chronicler Jean Froissart, who was there, gave a colourful account of the voyage across, and the battle. He described Edward crossing the channel on the deck of his cog, *Thomas*, while Sir John Chandos, "a bold and strong knight," entertained him by singing German songs, accompanied by minstrels. (Bold and strong Chandos may have been, but in a later battle, at Poitou, he tripped on his long robe and fell upon a lance that pierced his brain and killed him.) An engaging piece published on an Australian naval history website gives a few more details: "The object of the expedition was firstly to . . . set-up a royal court in Flanders and secondly to convoy an invasion force. A number of high-born ladies were being shipped—'embarrassant, mais essentielle,' to quote Froissart, it being those times of chivalry when knights indulged in jousts wearing the talisman of their favoured ladies—the cult of courtly love. It was Edward, after all, who instituted the Order of the Garter (leading, no doubt, to the contemporary courtesan couplet: "Here's to the knight with his hand on my garter; he hasn't gone far but he's a jolly good starter").["25"] Froissart, although French, was then in the service of Queen Philippa, Edward's wife.

In any case, in a go-right-at-'em tactic later mimicked by Lord Nelson at Trafalgar, Edward's fleet essentially sailed headlong into the still-moored

French vessels, and subjected them to withering fire from longbowmen on deck, along the gunwales, and even in the sail tops. They overwhelmed the crossbowmen among the French, after which they lay alongside and mercilessly slaughtered the French crews. All but a score of the 180 French vessels were captured, and of those that escaped, most were sunk. In a letter to his son, the Black Prince, Edward, said that of the 35,000 men at arms on the French vessels, 5,000 escaped and the rest "are lying dead in a great many places on the coasts of Flanders."

Arthur Conan Doyle, in his novel *The White Company*, captured the slaughter: "Wilder was the cry, and shriller still the scream, when there rose up from the shadow of those silent bulwarks the long lines of the English bowmen, and the arrows whizzed in a deadly sleet among the unprepared masses upon the [French] decks. From the higher sides of the cog the bowmen could shoot straight down, at a range which was so short as to enable a cloth-yard shaft to pierce through mail-coats or to transfix a shield, though it were an inch thick of toughened wood. One moment Alleyne [Doyle's protagonist] saw the galley's poop crowded with rushing figures, waving arms, exultant faces; the next it was a blood-smeared shambles, with bodies piled three deep upon each other, the living cowering behind the dead to shelter themselves from that sudden storm-blast of death."

Then Crécy, whose results we know. Afterwards, the English invaders marched overland to Calais, where they set siege to the French garrison. French armies tried several times to lift the siege, but were beaten off each time. The whole thing lasted a year before the town succumbed, after which Calais became an English base for further incursions deep into French territory. They held on to the city until 1558.

* * *

The year following the siege, the Black Death came to England. Even before plague, there had been grumblings in England about Edward and his war-making. The landowners and the Parliament fretted about the cost, and the taxation required. Among yeomen and the peasantry, the mutterings were more personal, and angrier; they were the bowmen, after all, who were called away from their fields to kill the French, and they didn't like it one bit (the calling-away part, not the killing). At the start of this essay, I quoted several historians as saying that Crécy and the other battles of the Hundred Years War changed everything, in that the yeomanry of England defeated the chivalry of France, which made folk heroes out of peasant bowmen. I suggested that the action of arming the peasantry to produce a corps of cheap and ready bowmen had shifted, even if only slightly, the odds in favour of political democratization. I also noted that the peasantry were often surly and reluctant soldiers. If there was malingering, and there was, it had more to do with resentfulness than idleness. Plague laid bare the grotesque inequalities of English society, and the class resentment that inequality generated, and then the fury that class resentment generated in turn.

The Black Death was a pandemic of bubonic plague. It reached England in June 1348, spread by an infected sailor arriving from the English province of Gascony. By the fall, it had reached London, and by the following summer it had infected the whole country, in the end killing somewhere between 40 and 60 per cent of the population. One geopolitical consequence of the plague was to bring the whole edifice of English conquest of France to a rapid, if temporary, halt. Within England, it caused widespread panic, and with the panic came anarchic uprisings and localized violence, exaggerating the existing deep resentment of the established order.

The population crash caused by the Black Death upset what order remained. After the population stabilized and the plague receded, land was suddenly plentiful and workers scarce. Inevitably, this meant upward pressure on wages paid to labourers and rapidly deteriorating profits for landowners. The peasantry met opportunities as never before, including practising skilled trades from which they had been excluded. The gentry had previously been able to prevent their serfs from leaving; not anymore.

The response was predictable: repression and suppression. The Ordinance of Labourers and the Statute of Labourers were passed as early as a year after the plague began to recede, the first in 1349 and the second a year later. The intention of both statutes was to fix wages at pre-plague levels and to criminalize the refusal to work. When the fines the laws imposed failed to halt desertions, penalties were increased, including branding and jail time. Still no luck. Wages continued to rise, and as they did the lower classes started to buy goods and services they had not been allowed before. Parliament then passed what were called the Sumptuary Laws, forbidding workers from buying things that previously only the elite classes could own. That didn't work either. Resentment simmered, barely beneath the surface.

Meanwhile Edward III, still obsessed with his "right" to the French throne, reinvigorated his French campaigns after a six-year hiatus and resumed pressing peasants into his armies and bullying the gentry into paying more taxes.

Once again, the bowmen picked up their weapons and boarded an invasion fleet headed for French shores. There were a few battlefield successes. Edward's son, the Black Prince, raided France in 1356, and was met by King Jean II of France outside the city of Poitiers. The French attacked first and were beaten back, although it was a near thing. What followed, once again, was disastrous for the French, as English longbowmen stood off and did their deadly work. "Such like battle also fought the noble Black Prince Edward, beside Poictiers [sic], where John the French King, with his son, and in a manner all the peers of France were taken, beside 30,000 which that day were slain, and very few English men, by reason of their bows." King Jean and two thousand nobles were taken to England, and the English demanded a ransom equivalent to a third of the French economy for his return.

There was another success eight years later, in 1364, with both sides fighting for the control of the Duchy of Brittany. English forces besieged the town of Auray. French troops were sent to break the siege, but the attack was repulsed and the town surrendered. The leader of the French army, Bertrand du Guesclin, was captured and later ransomed.

But the initial successes were followed by indecisions and inconclusive battles, and when Charles V ascended to the French throne his armies began cross-Channel raiding. By the 1370s, the English garrisons in France were running out of funds and Parliament kept attempting to raise taxes to support them. In 1372, French troops had regained Poitou and Brittany, and the same year a fierce naval battle took place offshore of La Rochelle, in the French southwest. The English navy was defeated and the French took control of the Channel, making it impossible for the English to reinforce Calais. Parliament was balking, again, at the ruinous cost. In 1376, a new poll tax was reluctantly raised in England, its intention to spread the tax burden to a wider base, including the newly richer working classes. Once again, it did not go down well; the new tax was widely hated and widely evaded.

A year later, Edward died and was succeeded, sort of, by his grandson, who became Richard II (Edward's son, the Black Prince, had already been killed in battle). The new king was just ten, and "his" government was made up of his grandfather's officials and his uncles, led by the formidable (and formidably arrogant) John of Gaunt, otherwise best known as an early patron of Chaucer. So the war, which they could have ended, continued, and continued to go badly. Yet more money was needed, and more taxes were levied. None of that solved the fiscal problem and in 1380, Parliament was called together once more. The new chancellor, Simon Sudbury, the archbishop of Northampton, warned the Commons that the crown might have to default on its debts.

More poll taxes, more balking, more tax evasion, more severe enforcement, more unrest. London, with its politically active guilds and fraternities, was seething. Xenophobia flourished. "Foreigners," mostly Flemish weavers, were widely suspected of stealing jobs. Animals seized from yeomen as punishment for transgressing the ever-shifting codes were seized back, sometimes violently, and sheriffs were harassed. In the countryside, the peasants continued deserting.

Often, they took their bows with them. They were more dangerous now than they had been, because angrier.

* * *

It was at this time, around 1380, that William Langland wrote his epic poem, *Piers Plowman*, one of whose themes was to praise those peasants who stuck with their masters and to rail against shirkers and malingerers.

"By the Lord," said Piers, bursting with rage. "Get up and go back to your work! Or you will get no bread when famine comes! You can starve to death and to hell with the lot of you." Then the shirkers were scared, pretended to be blind, or twisted their legs askew, as these beggars can, whining to Piers to have pity. "We're sorry, master, but we've no limbs to work with!" Said Piers, "I know quite well you are shirking. If anyone really is blind or crippled or has his limbs bolted with irons, he shall eat wheaten bread and drink at my table,

till God in his goodness sends him better days. But as for you, you could work for Truth well enough if you wanted . . . The fact is you would rather have a life of lechery, lying, and sloth, and it is only through God's mercy that you go unpunished."

Bizarrely, this anti-worker jeremiad was later adopted by the leaders of the Peasants' Revolt as an inspirational text.

Matters became so bad that Parliament fretted that were the French to invade, all but the small circle of gentry around the king might take their side. It was no longer just the peasants that had "bitterness in their hateful hearts."

Into this buzzing mass of resentment came new iterations of the legend of Robin Hood. Nowhere to be seen in these versions are the Merry Men and the brotherhood of the forest. Nowhere is any fealty shown to the Crusader Richard Lionheart over his perfidious brother, John Lackland. Nowhere is Robin an aristocrat in forest exile, but instead a yeoman turned out of his home and forced to flee. Nowhere is Maid Marian to be found, nor feasts on the greensward, nor Friar Tuck. However, the antipathy to the Sheriff of Nottingham and the established Church is very much there, standing in for resentment against authority in general. Also present is the notion of stealing from the undeserving rich.

These tales of Robin Hood were much less sanitized, and considerably angrier, than the version in Sir Walter Scott's 1820 romance, *Ivanhoe*. They matched the mood of the times. A perfidious monk was caught in the forest and ripped apart, his head impaled on a stick. As collateral damage, his servant was killed, too, despite his evident innocence. Robin was skilled with a longbow, able to "thrice split a slender willow wand" at two hundred paces, but hc was also considerably more violent. In the *Gest of Robyn Hode*, Robin shoots the sheriff with his bow:

Robyn bent a full goode bowe,
An arrowe he drowe at wyll;
He hit so the proude sherife
Upon the grounde he lay full still.

And, then, to be doubly sure, Robin cuts off his head:

And or he myght up aryse,
On his fete to stonde,
He smote of the sherifs hede
With his bright bronde.

A somewhat later version of the story has Robin engaging with another of his villains, Guy de Gisbourne. Sir Guy shows up in the forest (Barnsdale, in this case, not Sherwood). Not recognizing Robin, Sir Guy asks him for directions through the wood and tells him he is hunting for the outlaw Robin Hood. Robin suggests that they have an archery contest and then bests Sir Guy before revealing his true identity to him. The two men brandish knives and fight. Robin kills his adversary, sticks his severed head on the end of his bow, and disfigures the face with his knife. "There you stay, good Sir Guy," he says, and then he disguises the dead man's body in his own clothes of green.[26]

The bow and Robin's prowess with it is meant, clearly, as a stand-in for a peasantry newly armed and becoming conscious of its latent power; the Sheriff of Nottingham, in turn, stands in for the hated gentry. Class warfare had become the whole point. As J. Rubén Valdés Miyares put it in *National Geographic*, "Robin Hood takes on a role as an administrator of justice for the underclass . . . When Little John consults his leader for guidance on whom to beat, rob, and kill, Robin Hood provides him with a code divided along the lines of rich and poor. No peasants, 'sturdy yeomen,' or virtuous squires were to be harmed. On the other hand, the outlaws were allowed to beat and bind bishops, archbishops, and, above all, the loathed Sheriff of Nottingham." The definition of legitimate target widened to include pretty well everyone more or less unsympathetic to the lower classes, whether merchants, certain yeomen, gentry, knights, or rulers.

Finally, it all boiled over in the Peasants' Revolt, a.k.a. Wat Tyler's Rebellion, a.k.a. the Great Rising, a.k.a. the Uprising of 1381. The precipitating event was yet another effort to collect poll tax, a radical increase from one groat per head to three.

The revolt began in the city of Brentwood in Essex, where the would-be tax collector, a hapless noble called John Bampton, was severely beaten, his offices ransacked, court records seized and burned, jails broken open and their residents freed. Under Wat Tyler, a band advanced on London, demanding the end of serfdom and the sacking of the king's senior officials. A delegation from the king met the rebels at Blackheath. Richard III himself, then just fourteen, took refuge in the Tower of London. On June 13, 1381, the mob entered London and was joined by a raucous crowd of Londoners. The city's jails were opened, and John of Gaunt's London home, the Savoy Palace, was burned to the ground along with the law library and buildings in the Temple. The following day, Richard essentially bowed to their demands, even including the abolition of serfdom. While the parley was going on, another mob broke into the Tower of London, where it caught the Lord Chancellor, Simon of Sudbury, and cut off his head. One of the ringleaders, the person who ordered the killing, was Johanna Ferrour. The same Ferrour ordered the beheading of the Lord High Treasurer Robert Hales; and she was present, too, at the sacking of the Savoy, from which she purloined a chest of gold and carried it off.

A little later, another female leader, Katherine Gamen, beheaded the chief justice John Cavendish. (In the more militant regions of early feminism, these women were lauded for their exploits, and celebrated as feminist heroes. Just so, the revolt itself was later celebrated in socialist literature, and was widely cited by the opposition to Margaret Thatcher's poll tax in the 1980s.)

In the end, the revolt was put down without much further ado. A military sortie under the boy king Richard met Tyler at Smithfield, where the rebel was wounded, stabbed by a king's squire. Smithfield's mayor made his way to Saint Bartholomew's hospital where Tyler had been taken, dragged him back to the field, cut off his head, and stuck it on a pike. That was that.[27]

* * *

On the battlefield in the years after the revolt, the French gradually began to claw back lost territory. A truce was signed and extended for twenty-eight years in 1390. Even so, the year after Wat Tyler was killed, in 1382, the Scots attacked England, and attacked again in 1389. Both times, they were armed and reinforced by the French. Meanwhile, Charles VI of France went raving mad. In 1396, Richard II married seven-year-old Isabella of Valois, Charles's daughter, in an effort to make peace, but a few years later the French landed an army in Wales to support a rebellion there. Richard was deposed and murdered by his cousin, Henry of Bolingbroke, John of Gaunt's son, who became Henry IV. In 1412 Jeanne d'Arc was born. Henry died the following year from some unknown "wasting disease."

In 1415, the English went at it again. The new king, Henry V, took up the earlier claim to the throne of France, and at the battle of Harfleur defeated an army twice his size, but his own forces were reduced, many of them ill with fever. There followed the third major land battle in which the English longbowmen were decisive, that at Agincourt. Crowed Roger Ascham: "King Henry V, a prince peerless, and most victorious conqueror of all that ever died yet in this part of the world, at the battle of D'agincourt, with seven thousand fighting men, and yet many of them sick, being such archers, as the chronicle saith, that most part of them drew a yard, slew all the chivalry of France, to the number of forty thousand and more, and lost not past twenty-six Englishmen."

But the tide was turning against the English. The Siege of Orleans was the turning point. The English general Thomas de Montacute was killed by a cannonball, and thereafter Jeanne d'Arc and her vision from God led the reinvigorated French armies to repeated victories. By 1463, the port of Calais was the only English possession on the mainland.

One hundred years of bloodshed and repeated futility was over. Only the memory of the English bowmen survived the consequent disillusion and cynicism.

* * *

Even so, wars in which the longbow remained critical persisted in England itself. Roger Ascham recalled the recent (for him) Wars of the Roses, the bitter thirty-year civil war between two cadet Plantagenet branches, the House of Lancaster, whose emblem was a red rose, and the House of York, who adopted the white rose as its insignia. "The bloody civil war of England betwixt the house of York and Lancaster, where shafts flew of both sides to the destruction of many a yeoman of England, whom foreign battle could never have subdued, both I will pass over for the pitifulness of it, and yet may we highly praise God in the remembrance of it, seeing he, of his providence, hath so knit together those two noble houses, with so noble and pleasant a flower."

The phrase "the destruction of many a yeoman of England" was no exaggeration. In one battle alone, the Battle of Towton in Yorkshire in 1461, more than 50,000 men engaged in battle in a late-winter March blizzard, serried ranks of English longbowmen against serried ranks of English longbowmen, and when the day was over almost 30,000 of them had perished, dying the way so many of them had killed.

* * *

The last hurrah for the longbow was the Battle of Flodden, sometimes called the Battle of Branxton Moor. It is widely celebrated as the last battle to have been fought in England with the bow as the principal weapon but this is somewhat misleading: the battle was supposed to be an artillery duel; the reason longbows were decisive was that cannons in the field turned out to be useless.

Flodden was fought in September 1513 between an invading Scottish army under James IV and the defending army of the English king Henry VIII, under the command of the Duke of Norfolk. The term *invasion* is somewhat pejorative: Scotland was just honouring its alliance with France, and the raid was retaliation for Henry's invasion of the French mainland. Roger Ascham, in his English toadying best, put it this way: "The excellent prince Thomas Howard duke of North-folk (for whose good prosperity with all his noble family all English hearts daily doth pray), with bow men of England, slew King Jamie with many a noble Scot, even brant against Flodden Hill; in which battle the stout archers of Cheshire and Lancashire, for one day bestowed to the death for their prince and country sake, hath gotten immortal name and praise for ever."

Many a noble Scot indeed: perhaps 10,000 Scottish soldiers were killed, to somewhere around 1,500 English.

Both sides used cannon, to poor effect. The Scots brought thirty of them, seventeen "very large," requiring four hundred oxen and twenty-eight horses to draw and deploy. Their powder was unreliable and malfunctioned often. They also used solid cannonballs instead of grapeshot, which did little damage except to the hapless individual soldiers who took a direct hit. In addition, the Scots were firing downhill, and most of their balls sailed harmlessly overhead. By contrast, the English archers were firing uphill, an easier task, and they did their usual damage.

Cannon, on the evidence, were useful mostly for sieges and breaching fortifications, not for battlefield deployment. Muskets, on the other hand, were getting steadily better and more reliable. At first, they were less effective than bows. They took longer to reload, came with unreliable shot powder, and were not accurate over distances, being more or less useless at ranges much longer than ninety metres. But even the early guns had advantages longbows couldn't match. They were simpler for untrained soldiers to use, even not very muscular ones: that was the tipping point. The velocity of their shot was such that plate armour was easily penetrated. They steadily became more reliable. Shot was easier to carry and store than arrows. By the 1580s or so, the longbow had become, if not obsolete, at least supplanted. The English navy stopped using bows in 1585, although they remained in service in the army throughout the sixteenth century and into the seventeenth. The longbow's last deployment was at the battles of Bridgnorth, Shropshire, in 1642, in which English Royalists surrendered to Oliver Cromwell after he reduced the town to ashes, and Tippermuir in Scotland in 1644, which revived the Royalist cause in Scotland in the Wars of the Three Kingdoms. Even so, muskets saw much of the action.

In the aftermath of the long wars, as the Peasants' Revolt receded, as the longbow's military hegemony evaporated, the Robin Hood stories mutated again. In the new versions, Robin was reconciled with the king; those on whom he preyed were not part of officialdom but were corrupt and deserved his predations. Then he morphed again into an exiled nobleman. His thefts had been only for the purpose of succouring the poor ("if he be a pore man, of my good he shall have some"), and his violence was softened into little more than pranks. By the early 1500s, Robin had so much changed that his story was absorbed into May Day festivities, in which revellers would dress up as Robin Hood and his Merry Men and play tricks on the crowds. Robin could still split a slender willow wand with his arrows at two hundred paces, but mostly for show, in friendly exhibitions. Maid Marian made her first appearance, and the jolly friar, Tuck. Henry VIII and his wife Catherine took part, too; two hundred of the king's men dressed in green led the royal couple to a banquet. There is a story, possibly apocryphal, that an eighteen-year-old Henry, newly married to Catherine, dressed up as Robin and burst into her bedchamber, to entertain her with dancing and ballads, among other activities.[28]

You can take this two ways: as a sign that the nobility had prevailed and the peasants had been suppressed (the version preferred by Labour historians), or that English society was beginning to blur its rigid stratification (co-option and conciliation rather than repression, playing peekaboo with democracy, the view preferred by establishmentarians). In either case, the longbow was no longer a weapon but now a plaything.

The longbow had one more outing in battle, or so it was said. Its very last deployment was in the Second World War. The archer was one Mad Jack Churchill (full name John Malcolm Thorpe Fleming Churchill, no relation to the more famous W.), a British commando who fought in several battles in France and Italy with a longbow, broadsword, and bagpipes in his kit, earning himself a Distinguished Service Order along the way. ("Any officer who goes into action without his sword is improperly dressed," he was wont to declare.) In May 1940, the story goes, Mad Jack and a few fellow troopers ambushed a German patrol in the Pas-de-Calais. Churchill gave the signal to attack by waving his claymore (the Scottish broadsword, not the mine) over his head and promptly shot a German soldier with his longbow.

Alas for romance, he later admitted that an army truck had crushed his longbow several days earlier, and that he had made the story up.

Thus the longbow ended its days in braggadocio and buffoonery.

PART 2

The Invention
of Trees

Before forests

THE WORLD'S EARLIEST KNOWN TREE, cautiously dated to about 385 million years ago, give or take an eon or epoch or two, is neither in the place it first rooted nor in one of the world's leading natural history museums, where it should surely be given star billing. It is not, in fact, anywhere particularly special or exotic. It is on display in the New York Power Authority's visitor center in Schoharie County, New York, about midway between Long Island Sound and Lake Ontario, near a place now called Gilboa. The petrified tree was found in the scars caused by power shovels excavating a new supply dam. The workers first uncovered the upright stumps of fossilized tree trunks, which had grown near the coast of what had once been an inland sea covering much of New York and Pennsylvania. Most of the relics the shovels uncovered were just stubs less than a metre tall, but then, in 2007, geologists from the New York State Museum and from the UK found the jackpot: an intact tree more than eight metres tall.

True, it didn't look much like a tree, but that was the point. It was a not-yet-tree, a primitive-looking thing, obviously enough: a series of branches, frond-like, somewhat resembling an overgrown fern or primitive palm. It had no "leaves," only smaller and smaller branches. Still, it was already "vascular," which means it had the means to transport water and nutrients from the soil, which in turn meant it had the ability to grow massively, because only vascular plants can support the weight needed for an internal plumbing system.

If you want to be technical about it, the thing that they uncovered was a *Wattieza*, itself an *Eospermatopteris*, part of the Cladoxylopsida class, "big vascular plants with spectacular morphology," as the scientists put it in their excited way. They are entitled to their excitement: this is a leftover part of the first greening of the earth; it had a major impact on the planet's climate, carbon cycling, and, ultimately, on what kinds of animals evolved in the ecosystems they created and protected. It was the original afforestation of the planet, the beginning of the three trillion or so trees we acknowledge today.

Popular cartoons often show fish creeping out of the ocean and sprouting legs, thus evolving into what the scientists blandly call "terrestrial fauna." No one thinks cartoons mimic life, but had any water-based creature ventured onto land, it would have been given a nasty surprise—there would have been nothing to eat, just rock, unweathered into soil. No plants. Current thinking suggests that "life" appeared on land somewhere around 1,200 million years ago (mya in palaeontologist jargon). Organisms, nature unknown, already capable of photosynthesis, seem to have been established by then; microbial fossils dating back a billion years have been found in freshwater lake deposits. Land plants evolved quite a bit later, somewhere around 470 mya, during the Ordovician period, when ocean life was diversifying rapidly. Their immediate ancestors were a group of green algae, skinny branched things with long filaments, living in shallow coastal waters—*that's* what crept out onto land, their nether parts still trailing in the water.

By the start of the Devonian period, 420 mya, there were already proto-trees, but they were tiny, a few centimetres tall, and the landscape was dominated by massive spires poking up from the rock, some of them eight metres high and a metre in diameter. They were called *Prototaxites*, and by the turn of this century they were still a puzzle. No one yet knew what they were—surely not giant fungi? Perhaps they were really just huge mats of liverwort that had somehow been rolled up, mechanism unknown? Finally, in 2007, scientists, including Francis Hueber at the Smithsonian National Museum of Natural History in Washington, DC, concluded that they were, indeed, fungi. Kevin Boyce, a geophysicist at the University of Chicago, admits that "a six-meter fungus doesn't make any sense. This gets my vote for being one of the weirdest organisms that ever lived."[29]

Indeed, Google *Prototaxite* and you'll come up with headlines like "Humongous fungus!" and "Mushrooms as big as trees!" and "When mushrooms covered the earth." Fish with legs suddenly didn't seem as interesting.

By the Middle Devonian, the time of the Gilboa fossil, the giant fungi had vanished, supplanted by *Wattieza* and its cousins. These proto-trees still reproduced with spores, not seeds, which came later. They didn't have real wood, either, just a fibrous interior, and those tiny branches, likely tipped with green for photosynthesis, in place of leaves. They did well, spreading from small groves clinging to the water's edge to extensive forests covering much of the planetary landmass.

Christopher Berry, a specialist in early trees, from Cardiff University, was euphoric about the Gilboa find. "This . . . has allowed us to recreate these early forest ecosystems. Branches from the trees would have fallen to the floor and decayed, providing a new food chain for the bugs living below . . . [it was] a significant moment in the history of the planet. The rise of the forests removed a lot of carbon dioxide from the atmosphere. This caused temperatures to drop and the planet became very similar to its present-day condition."

Global cooling brought us here. With any luck, global warming won't take us back.

* * *

Even so, from a planetary perspective these new trees were a mixed blessing, and from some perspectives were a blight. Sure, the earth now had forests, and the presence of forests paved the way for more diversification of life forms in the microclimates and climatic niches they allowed, and helped create the rivers and muds that built the soils. But there was a bad side, too. Fungi, mosses, and lichens had no massive impact on land, but trees did. The astonishing spread of vascular plants, early trees, ferns, and flowering plants, is thought to be a prime cause of the Devonian Extinction Event, a massive change in the earth's biosphere that essentially choked the oceans and killed nearly everything that lived in them.

How so? A 2012 report in *Nature Geoscience* described the process: "Before the era of plants, water ran over Earth's landmasses in broad sheets, with no defined courses. Only when enough vegetation grew to break down rock into minerals and mud, and then hold that mud in place, did river banks form and begin to channel the water. The channelling led to periodic flooding that deposited sediment over broad areas, building up rich soil. The soil allowed trees to take root. Their woody debris fell into the rivers, creating logjams that rapidly created new channels and caused even more flooding, setting up a feedback loop that eventually supported forests and fertile plains."[30]

These new river channels, in turn, washed newly released minerals and nutrients in massive quantities into the oceans, proving deadly for the creatures that already lived there, which were the majority of creatures, to that point. By the time the Extinction Event was over, somewhere between

80 and 90 per cent of all life had been extinguished, one of the worst mass extinctions in the planet's history. The Devonian had been the Age of the Fish; by the end of the Devonian and the beginning of the Carboniferous, only a few fishes had begun the slow climb back to viability. To the fish, trees were deadly pollutants. As a piece in *Devonian Times* put it, "Ironically, the development and maturation of terrestrial environments fostered by the expansion of terrestrial plants may have wreaked havoc on the oceans from which life first arose."[31]

Trees did something else, too. By sucking massive quantities of carbon dioxide from the air, they went much further than just moderating the climate: they rapidly cooled the planet and caused a brief period of intense glaciation. As the journal *Nature* put it, "The expansion of . . . land plants accelerated chemical weathering and may have drawn down enough atmospheric carbon dioxide to trigger the growth of ice sheets."[32]

When Snowball Earth finally warmed, "trees" went on evolving. Club mosses, which are now small creeping things, were once much larger, pencil-shaped plants that could reach thirty metres and more, with curious whorled leaves that made them look like giant bottle brushes (in Adam Dimech's phrase).[33] With a group of early trees grouped under the name *Lycopods*, they dominated earth's forests for millions of years. They were prolific, and spread rapidly: they seemed almost purpose-built for spreading—each cone on a tree could be almost seventy-five centimetres long and could release over 8 billion spores. Alongside them were the horsetails, which grew to substantial size, again unlike their modern counterparts. They eventually fell victim to another episode of climate change: when the swamps in which they lived began to dry, they eventually disappeared, at least as large plants. Ferns, too, appeared early in the Carboniferous era, many of them ten or twelve metres high. The massive coal beds laid down during the Carboniferous were generally made of these tall, spare, almost frondless "trees" that kept falling over because their roots were rudimentary. They piled up, and kept piling up, for millions of years, compressing into peat, then lignite, then bituminous coal. Nothing ate them. The bacteria that decompose trees in modern forests had not yet appeared.

Trees continued to evolve as the Devonian transitioned into the Carboniferous. The fossil record shows more or less continuous improvements (or at least modifications) in the morphology of trees. They began to develop a "stele," a central core, a not-yet-trunk. Lignin, the organic polymer that gives strength and rigidity to wood, began to appear, allowing trees to grow taller. They evolved the ability to grow in girth through the development of cambium (technically, the layer that allows secondary growth after the first season and results in an increase in the trunk's thickness). The veins of the tree improved, allowing for more efficient transport of water and minerals. Spores changed into seeds, a major advance that eliminated the requirement for external sources of water for sexual reproduction of plants . . . It also provided better protection and a nutrient source for the developing embryo. Broader leaves appear, bringing shade to the forest floor and changing forest ecosystems. Pollen shows up in the record. Here and there, small pockets of these primitive flowering plants still cling to life, more or less unchanged, although sidelined from the main evolutionary track. Australia's *Idiospermum australiense* (a.k.a. the idiot tree) is one of them, still found in parts of Daintree forest.

The first "real" tree that accumulated all these advances (with the possible exception of seeds) was called *Archaeopteris*, for which, curiously, no one has yet coined a less technical name, possibly because the thing has been extinct for far longer than hominids have existed. In turn, the *Archaeopteris* was a member of a class of plants called Progymnosperm, themselves precursors of gymnosperms proper (defined as non-flowering plants that produce cones or seeds, a.k.a. conifers).

Surviving *Archaeopteris* fossils showed they reached somewhere around twenty or twenty-two metres tall, and had trunks made up of lignin and cellulose, just like modern trees. In structure, they rather resembled modern conifers, except they had leaves rather than needles, which were large and webbed, creating dense shade. Their roots were much deeper and wider than had been the norm, which allowed them to colonize drier areas away from floodplains. They were deciduous, but whether seasonally or continuously is not known.[34] There are two other curiosities about *Archaeopteris*: one is how thoroughly they dominated the ancient forests (the diversity of the time was not very diverse); and the second is how rapidly they went extinct. Just as the planet transitioned into the Carboniferous age, *Archaeopteris* abruptly disappear from the fossil record, and so did forests themselves. Ferns like the *zygopterids* and horsetails and low-growing seed plants dominated the plant world for multiple millennia after that. The "forest biome" simply disappeared. Trees didn't become prominent again until much later in the Carboniferous.

True gymnosperms were among the first trees to reappear following the extinctions. They are still odd-looking, by modern standards. "Gymnosperms are . . . the surviving prehistoric cousins of the new, young, and dynamic species that have colonised much of the world since the Cretaceous, and must appear to an apple or cherry tree in magnificent bloom something like a primitive coelacanth appears to us." Thus Justin Smith, in an essay called "Do Trees Exist?"[35] Arizona's petrified forest is made up of these early conifers, some species of which survive in more or less unchanged form even now: tropical cycads and monkey puzzle trees, also known as the Chilean pine, are among them, and so are the dawn redwood and the Wollemi pine. The ginkgo tree, its leaf extract a staple of Chinese traditional medicine and more recently beloved of faddish herbalists, also made its appearance at this time, and still thrives in small and protected areas, and as an ornamental.

The last tree type to make its appearance came much later, in the early Cretaceous, a mere 150 million years ago. This was the *angiosperm*, in its tree form more familiarly known as the hardwood, which appeared more or less at the time the earth's single continent, Pangaea, split apart into Laurasia and Gondwanaland, an early iteration of our present continental layout.

Angiosperms, the family of plants that produce flowers and bear their seeds in fruits, make up the vast majority of all known living plants, from oaks to wildflowers and water lilies. They arrived late, and mutated and proliferated very quickly, a matter that puzzled and upset Darwin; he couldn't understand how such plants spread so far, so fast, while leaving very little in the fossil record in the way of intermediate species. Indeed, he called this flowering an "abominable mystery," and long feared that if he couldn't explain it, it would throw his entire theory into disrepute. Perhaps, he speculated, they arose on some as yet undiscovered island or continent? (It is fair to say that science has yet to solve this mystery; Richard Buggs, an evolutionary biologist at Queen Mary, University of London, says, "One hundred and forty years later, we still don't know. Of course, we've made lots of progress in our understanding of evolution and in our knowledge of the fossil record, but this mystery is still there."[36])

In any case, hardwoods rapidly diversified and spread throughout each new continent, pushing the conifers to the higher latitudes or to higher elevations. Fossils of magnolia, laurels, maple, oaks, and sycamores are commonly found from this period, instantly recognizable, easily identified, geographically widespread, and as modern as a modern lumberyard.

There weren't always trees. They have come, and sometimes they have gone. As I said in the introduction, nature makes no promises.

Trees, root and branch

WHAT IS A "TREE"? Does a tree need a single large stalk? In which case alder thickets are not trees. Must a tree be woody? In which case bananas and palms are not really trees—they have fibres, not wood. Must a tree increase in girth over time? Many early trees did no such thing. Is height a defining factor? Many shrubs reach ten metres or more, and some trees are not that tall.

Or is it more obvious than all that?

"A tree is a big plant with a stick up the middle," writes Colin Tudge in his book *The Tree*.

Tudge was (partly) joking, but that will serve as a working definition: a tree is any plant that has a single stem, reaches significant height, and supports branches and leaves (or needles) above ground. Generally, trees grow in two ways: primary growth from the "growing tip," and secondary growth from accreting wood and thickening each growing cycle. There is speculative evidence that the "woodiness" that results from this secondary growth evolved multiple times in multiple places, a logical evolutionary solution for herbaceous plants. A tree has roots, a trunk, and a crown.

A decent-sized tree can have more than forty kilometres of roots with as many as five million root tips, and many more root hairs, which do most of the work. Functionally, roots serve two broad purposes: they promote growth and they support the tree structurally, holding the thing upright and bracing it against wind damage. They also fuel growth by taking up water, oxygen, and minerals from the soil, their own activity fuelled by the sugars and starches the leaves produce during photosynthesis. Roots thus serve as a transport system, feeding nutrients to the trunk, and absorbing the sugars they need to do their work. Using these sugars requires oxygen, which the roots find in the interstices between soil particles.

Roots differ from above-ground parts of the tree in that they contain no pith and fewer fibres, but more food-storage cells, and, obviously enough, they don't need light and are rather more water and rot resistant. The take-up from the soil is done by so-called absorbing roots, together with the fungi and the root hairs. These feed into conducting roots, which do the transport of nutrients back to the trunk. Conducting roots, in turn, merge into brace roots, which finish the transport and also keep the tree upright.

This intricate network extends laterally, but how far laterally depends on a number of factors: competition from other trees, the availability of water, the height of the water table and its seasonality, barriers such as rocks, and the permeability of the soil. It is a common misconception that a tree's root system extends to the area covered by the tips of the branches, an error still conveyed by some gardening advice books which urge homeowners to water to the drip line of the tree.[37] Roots do require water, and where the soil is moist will grow faster and branch more than they would in dry areas, but they don't go wandering in search of it: they are opportunistic, but not adventurers. A root system in undisturbed soil will commonly extend twice the width of the tree's canopy, and sometimes more, mostly in the top metre of soil; in clay soils oxygen barely exists more than a metre down.

The trunk of a tree is its main structure, and partly what defines it. The trunk is the woody bit, which is what makes the tree resilient and helps its longevity. The bole of the trunk is the section between the upper brace roots and the lowest branches. The trunk serves to elevate the leaves above the ground, above standing water, and into the light, which they need to photosynthesize. Trunks are also the main transport system between the leaves, the crown, and the roots, carrying water and nutrients upward and food (sugar and starches) downward.

The outer bark is the tree's defensive perimeter. It's no longer alive (it consists of formerly inner bark cells pushed outward by the tree's increasing girth) but it does a number of jobs. It is a moisture barrier, keeping rain out and in dry times preserving moisture inside the trunk. It is a barrier, not always successful, against boring insects and birds like woodpeckers. It insulates the tree from debilitating heat (and may serve as a fire retardant in some cases).

Bark is also an easy way of identifying tree species. Some barks are smooth, like that of the American beech, while some are deeply pitted, like that of the white ash or northern red oak. Even these pits and ridges vary by species. Ridges on the white ash, for example, intersect, while the oak's ridges are continuous. Some pines and spruces have overlapping scales; the black birch has what look like small plates. Some barks are thin, others can be six inches thick, as in the cork oak, the primary source for wine corks and the interior of cricket balls. All barks have "lenticels," tiny pores that move oxygen and carbon dioxide through the bark. They are not always easily seen, but they are always there, and come in different shapes, sizes and colours—diamond shapes in the aspen, horizontal lines in the yellow birch. Sometimes bark peels off from the tree, like a cat shedding, which means that the tree is growing faster than the bark can stretch; the paper birch is a well-known example, its bark was used for centuries for birchbark canoes and as kindling. Bark colours vary. The smooth-boled beech is a light grey, cherry's the colour of well-steeped tea, black walnut is, well, pretty black. Tree bark can also be distinguished by its smell. Oddly, the ponderosa pine smells deliciously of butterscotch or vanilla. Other pine trees smell less like dessert and more like turpentine, while yellow birch smells like the shrub wintergreen, widely brewed by indigenous Americans as a tea to cure headaches, sore throat, and rheumatism. Sassafras bark smells like cinnamon (of course, so does cinnamon bark, but that's harder to come by outside spice shops, since cinnamon trees hardly grow beyond Sri Lanka or Zanzibar).[38]

There is also an inner bark, called phloem (from the Greek word for bark, go figure). Unlike the outer bark, phloem is not dead, though it lives only a short life before perishing and becoming one with its outer-bark cousin. While it lives, it is important. It is one of the two major transport routes trees have invented. In this case, the transport is downward, transporting food (sugars and starches) that the leaves have created and turned into sap and sending it back down the trunk, and on to the roots. It is a one-way traffic lane. The phloem itself is not simple. It is part of the tree's "vascular bundle" and is made up of sieve tubes (hollow cells placed end to end, like a long straw); companion cells (which the botany books, rather winningly, admit has an uncertain function except to work nicely with its adjacent sieve); parenchyma, whose main function seems to be to store starch crystals produced by enzymes acting on sugar, which crystals can then be used to help trees respond to injury (and there is some evidence they may help produce natural fungicides); and finally fibres, whose function is to be, well, fibrous and hold stuff together.

Inward from the phloem is the cambium layer. This is where trees bulk up, adding heft and girth, like a bodybuilder scarfing steroids. Cambium grows two ways, inward and outward: outward to create new bark; inward to create new wood. Generally, a tree will add a new cambium layer each growing season, producing the growth rings that, when felled, allow lumbermen to reckon a tree's age. The outward growth activity is important. It allows a tree to heal minor injuries and isolate pockets of rot that would otherwise put the tree at risk of disease and possibly death. The cambium layer grows through ingesting hormones called auxins, which are concocted by leaf buds and the tips of branches and then sent down to the cambium via the phloem, together with food from the leaves, a potent chemical cocktail. This makes the cambium one of a tree's three meristematic zones, which means it contains cells capable of division and growth; the other two such zones are the root tips and the buds at the ends of twigs, both of which allow the tree to grow upward.

Inside the cambium is the main event: wood.

But even wood is not so simple. The outer layer of wood, the sapwood, is also known as xylem, from the Greek word meaning wood (go figure, again). Xylem is young wood, lighter in color than heartwood. Xylem is the other major transport vector in trees. While the phloem moves stuff downward, the xylem moves sap upward, from the roots to all branches and the crown. Like the phloem, the xylem has three main forms of cells: thick-walled tubes running parallel to the trunk or branch (which carry the water and minerals from the roots); ray cells, called medullary rays, that transport lesser amounts of sap from the inner bark to the centre of the tree; and the same parenchyma warehousing cells found in the phloem, which hold bundles of manufactured starches. An evolutionary curiosity of xylem is that the cells are already dead when they become functional, zombie cells that nevertheless work just fine. Why this is so remains a matter of speculation; in any case, when xylem cells cease work, they darken and become heartwood.

Heartwood is the strong stuff that gives strength to the tree. It consists of dead xylem cells, but will nevertheless be protected from decay by the previously listed layers.

At the centre is the spongy stuff called pith. Pith, also called medulla (the Latin word for bone marrow), helped start the whole growth process; it was the initial caregiver for saplings before they grew much in the way of roots or branches. It is therefore the tree's oldest wood, and in a way resembles old folk with osteoporosis; its cells are thin-walled and prone to cracking. Nevertheless, the pith and the first few growth rings are often called the tree's juvenile wood.

Finally, the crown, where the leaves and the branches are. You might say the crown is the whole purpose of the thing, and the leaves the crown jewels.

Trees don't really have purpose, but they do need light and space, so the leaves can do their photosynthetic thing, which in turn sets the whole engine in motion. To do this, a tree needs to get its head above its neighbours', and to catch as much sunlight as it can. Hence the "big stick" at the heart of Colin Tudge's definition of a tree: a tall single trunk with lateral branches is the most efficient way to achieve height and width and give the leaves the sun they need. As a by-product, the crown does other duties: the leaves and twigs filter the air of dust and debris, they collect and distribute rainwater, they cool the air by producing shade, and fallen leaves add to the humus on which so many other creatures depend.

Branches grow from twigs, which grow from buds, which themselves are meristemic, or capable of reproducing themselves. The meristems in the cambium continue to divide, thickening the twig into a branch, tied into the trunk by a swelling called the branch collar.

On the growing branch grow more twigs, and leaves. Depending on the species, leaves come in all shapes and sizes and types, broad or needle-shaped, whorled, waxed, lobed, hairy or smooth, delicate or fibrous.

Varying shapes and sizes and textures, yes. But they are all green. That would be chlorophyll. Chlorophyll enables photosynthesis. And without photosynthesis most life would be impossible.

Extreme trees

THE OLDEST TREE IN THE WORLD IS DYING.

Maybe. Probably. Partly. And "tree" might not be quite right. And, in any case, its age is just an educated guess. But still. There are aspens pretty well everywhere in the temperate regions of North America, pretty trees with light bark and leaves that turn a brilliant yellow in the fall. We have a few on our little plot of land in Nova Scotia, mixed in with beech and wild apples. Locally, they are often called white poplar, or popple, and they make a decent flooring, although rather soft. They are also the only tree that you can identify by sound alone: even in the slightest breeze, the leaves rustle and rattle, they quiver, as though afraid. Which is no doubt why they are called trembling aspen, or sometimes quaking aspen, and occasionally trembling poplar, for they are members of the poplar family. The botanical name is *populus tremuloides*, for obvious reasons.

The leaves tremble because their individual stems are a curious oblong shape, which makes them strong in one axis but weak in the other. Why they evolved this way is not known, but speculation is that the quaking maximizes the fresh supply of carbon dioxide near the leaf surface, where it is used in photosynthesis. The quaking also seems to minimize insect damage; the constant movement may just piss the pests off. Also, aspen's soft bark is rich in salicylates, an effective poison for parasites and other invaders (phytocide, a potent herbicide, is derived from aspen bark).

But the truly curious thing about *populus tremuloides* is its ability to produce genetically identical "offspring" through offshoots from the root system. In effect, the tree grows and spreads by asexual cloning, meaning that what appears to be a grove of aspens is actually one tree with many trunks and a shared root system. In this way the tree can colonize large parcels of land and still maintain its shared identity. And grow it does: the aspen (or aspens) in Fishlake National Forest near Richfield, Utah, spreads over forty-three hectares and consists of 47,000 apparently discrete stems. It weighs approximately 6,600 tons, making it by far the heaviest living thing on the planet. The whole "forest" originates from a single male parent, each new trunk sharing an identical genetic makeup, and has been cloning itself for thousands of years. This clonal tree has been dubbed Pando, Latin for "I spread."

How old is Pando? You can't count the tree rings, for each bole is relatively slender and only a few decades old. Even so, arborists have come up with credible estimates ranging from a low of 80,000 years to a high of "around a million," based on plausible circumstantial evidence: how its genome differs from aspens born in the modern era; that a climate shift 10,000 years ago meant that few if any aspen seedlings could any longer be generated in their current location; that males grow more slowly than females; and that aspens grow more slowly at higher altitudes (Pando is at nearly 2,750 metres); and its sheer size.

Even if it isn't that old, it is old enough. But it may now be dying. Mapping over time and a seventy-year history of aerial photography has shown the tree declining in size gradually over the past few decades, with a much slower rate of regeneration of new stems. The blame, predictably enough, falls to humans. Cattle and mule deer are allowed to graze freely among the boles, and feed on new shoots and leaves. An informative piece by Trevor Nace in *Forbes* has found several other human traces: there are campgrounds, power lines, hiking trails, cabins, and other signals of human development. On the positive side, fences protecting limited areas of the aspen grove have been successful: in those areas the aspen was able to rapidly grow and reproduce.[39] So maybe there will be a new growth spurt, with a little help from its friends.

Another clonal giant, a Palmer's oak, is found in the Jurupa Mountains of California. Not very impressive to the eye (it is rather drab and is stunted for a tree, at about a metre tall). Still, its roots have produced around seventy clusters of stems spread over 185 square meters, and its estimated age (again based on plausible circumstantial evidence) is around 13,000 years. A curiosity about this "tree" is that it depends on fire for reproduction. It only grows new sprouts from the base of burned stems. "It has opted out of the Darwinian struggle for existence," as an admiring botanist put it.[40]

Before scientists dated the Jurupa oak or the Utah aspens, a Norway spruce on Fulufjället mountain in Sweden was widely thought to be the world's oldest tree. "Old Tjikko" is a mere 10,000 years old, and is, yes, another clone, although it operates rather differently. It isn't a colony but regrows in the same spot on the same roots when the previous trunk expires, usually after a speedy six hundred years or so.

No doubt the geneticists are right, and these are single ancient trees and not groves, but they look too ordinary. You can lay your cheek alongside a Pando sapling and it feels neither old nor particularly venerable; the same would be true for the Jurupa oak or the Norway spruce. The oldest surviving (persisting) single-trunk tree is a bristlecone pine in Inyo County, California, dated at about five thousand years old. Another bristlecone called Prometheus in Nevada was almost as old (maybe 4,900 years, some five hundred years older than the date for Noah's flood, if you happen to be a creationist) but it died in 1964, murdered at human hands; and yet another dubbed Methuselah, in the White Mountains of California, is just a few years younger. All three were adults when the first of the great pyramids of Egypt were being cobbled together. Bristlecones are unattractive as trees go, stumpy and with meagre foliage as they age. But they are long-lived and resilient, surviving for centuries in harsh conditions.

Other oldsters would include Chile's two-hundred-foot-tall Patagonian cypress called Gran Abuelo, at 3,646 years; Iran's Mediterranean cypress called Sarv-e Abarkuh (or Abarkuh cypress), somewhere around four to five thousand years; and the Llangernyw Yew in Conwy, Wales, also between four and five thousand years, which has a folkloric association with the Recording Angel. I have already mentioned the Fortingall yew in Scotland, fancifully linked to the boyhood of Pontius Pilate, which is somewhere between two and nine thousand years old (you can't really tell with yews).[41] An olive tree in Ankara was apparently planted by early Iron Age Greeks about three thousand years ago, and has been producing oil ever since.

Longevity is interesting in itself, but it isn't everything; bushes can live a long time, too, as Tasmania's 43,000-year-old King's holly can attest. And longevity is "wholly unsatisfying," as botanist Richard Lanner once put it, "in the search for a unified treeness of trees."[42] Longevity is also sometimes slippery of definition. Date trees growing on an Israeli kibbutz are only a few years old, but they germinated from seeds recovered from ancient archeological sites, including the famous siege of Masada from the first century BCE. At least some of those seeds have been lying dormant for two thousand years and more. Is the tree they then produce old or new?[43]

There are other extremes than age. Girth, for one. The sequoia called General Sherman is generally reckoned the world's biggest tree at 83.8 metres tall, 10.9 in diameter, the lowest branch forty metres off the ground. It's not the fattest tree, however. That would be the Montezuma cypress called the Tule tree, in the Mexican village of Santa Maria del Tule, which is 11.5 metres in diameter and has a circumference of fifty metres. Sherman isn't even the tallest: that would be the Hyperion redwood in Redwood National Park, currently 115.54 metres tall. On the lower end of the tree scale, girthwise, forester Peter Wohlleben described how,, "On a journey to Lapland, I stumbled upon completely different ambassadors of the tree family that made me feel like Gulliver in Lilliput. I'm talking about dwarf trees on the tundra, which are sometimes trampled to death by travelers who don't even know they are there. It can take these trees a hundred years to grow just 20 centimetres."[44]

A list compiled by Oishimaya Sen Nag for *World Atlas* includes these oddities: the tree with the largest crown is a eucalyptus in Queensland's Neuragully Waterhole, 72.8 metres. The tree with the deepest roots is a fig tree growing in the Echo Caves, near the town of Ohrigstad in South Africa's Limpopo province, 122 metres deep. The fastest-growing tree is the foxglove of China, which grows thirty centimetres in three weeks, and can reach almost six metres in a year. The most suicidal tree would be the Tahina palm of Madagascar, which flowers only once, decades after its germination, but the fruit it produces uses up all available nutrients, and the tree collapses and dies. The most dangerous tree would likely be the manchineel tree of the Florida Everglades, whose sap can cause human skin to blister, and blindness if it reaches the eye.

The world of trees has endless oddities. How about the rainbow gum, a.k.a. the rainbow eucalyptus, *Eucalyptus deglupta*? It's tall (up to seventy-six metres), and is the only gum growing in moist rainforests (Indonesia,

Papua New Guinea, Philippines), but its real attraction is its bark, which it sheds prolifically and frequently, although not all at once. The first layer of inner bark is bright green, which slowly transforms itself into a painter's palette of colours: maroon and orange, blue and purple, a range of greens. Because the outer bark is shed in patches, all of these colours can appear on the same tree at the same time, bits ageing into different colours over time. The purpose of this colourful display? Unknown.

And the walking palm, the nearest thing to John Wyndham's Triffid, though without that creature's malevolence? Like all the oddities in this list, *Socratea exorrhiza*, the walking palm or *cashapona*, a native of the Central American rainforests, has evolved its own solutions to problems no one yet understands. In this case, the oddity is in the roots, which grow in a way that holds the tree up on stilts, so the bottom of the trunk is actually in the air. One theory is that such roots allow the palm to grow more easily in flood conditions. Another theory is that the root structure is a hedge against accident; if a more mature sapling falls on the seedling and knocks it over, it can then grow new vertical roots away from the fall, allowing the first set of roots to rot away. In this fashion, the tree will slowly move from its original point of germination. More likely is that the movement is a way to avoid debris. No one knows. In any case, "walking" is something of an exaggeration. But the tree can and does move, albeit at a pace that makes a tortoise greased lightning.

The dragon blood tree, Dracaena cinnabari, is an evergreen native only to the Socotra archipelago, a granite plateau that is politically part of Yemen. It very much resembles an opened umbrella, a straight trunk with "spokes" radiating upward toward the leafy canopy. But it is mostly known for its sap. When wounded, the tree oozes a bright red resin that looks unnervingly like blood. Local legend has it that the tree was created from the blood of a dragon vanquished in battle by an elephant, although there is some evidence that the story was recently concocted to increase the sap's perceived value among the credulous. Certainly, the colour has attracted users from many arts and traditional sciences. In homeopathy it treats a variety of high-profile ailments, from ulcers to loose bowels. Occasionally it has been used in toothpaste and cosmetics, as a dye, as a pigment, and even for varnishing violins.[45]

The tree called *Hura crepitans* has a number of names: Jabillo in the Amazon rainforest, where it is native; the monkey no climb tree in Tanzania, where it is regarded as a noxious invader; the sandbox tree, for no apparent reason; and, occasionally, the dynamite tree, for an excellent reason. The Jabillo can grow to more than thirty metres, and has both male and female flowers. The female is a delicate reddish pink; the male, growing on the bole, is a nasty spiky thing, like a grenade planted on a prison wall. Its fruit are small, gourd-like globes. When they ripen, they explode. And they don't just burst, either. The flat hard seeds within the fruit explode outward at the speed of a category-three hurricane, and over a radius of twenty metres. Oh, and the sap is toxic, raising nasty welts on the skin and threatening blindness. No one can remember who took the thing to Tanzania, or what the hell he was thinking.[46]

The kapok tree, native to the American tropics and also found in parts of west Africa, is very large (up to sixty metres tall) and fast-growing (two metres a year). It is an aggressive colonizer, and is often the first to move into areas logged and damaged by fires. It has pretty white and pink flowers that are renowned for their stink. Apparently, bats find the odour enticing, and flit from flower to flower doing bees' work. One theory is that the seeds made their own way to west Africa from the Americas. Unopened kapok seeds float, and it is plausible that some hitched a ride on the eastward-flowing south Atlantic current, itself fed by the Brazil current, a fraction of which reaches the African coast before merging with the cold north-flowing Benguela current. Perhaps they washed up on the pristine beaches of Cameroon. There are worse fates.[47]

The banyan tree of south Asia is neither toxic nor projectile-prone. Instead, refreshingly, it is entirely benign. Benign, but big. The most impressive specimen is in Kolkata's Acharya Jagadish Chandra Bose Botanical Garden. It looks like a forest, but the apparently 3,600 separate trees are actually the aerial roots of a single banyan. The tree covers a little more than two hectares, about the size of a Manhattan city block.[48]

The Wollemi pine is another "dinosaur tree," also dating back to somewhere around 200 million years ago. There is only one grove left on earth, a mere two hundred trees, in a gorge in the Blue Mountains about two hundred kilometres north of Sydney. During the Australian wildfires of 2019, firefighters went to extraordinary lengths to save the grove, with tankers dropping fire retardant and firefighters being winched into the gorge from helicopters. The trees were discovered in 1994 by David Noble, a ranger with the NSW National Parks and Wildlife service, when he noticed a stand of unusual trees and took a fallen branch for identification. The species had previously been believed long extinct. The trees once formed vast forests across Australia, New Zealand, and Antarctica.[49]

And one more. The kokerboom or quiver tree of the Kalahari Desert has evolved over many centuries to cope with the extreme conditions in which it finds itself. Its branches are smeared with a white powder that reflects back much of the sunlight it receives. It is a natural refrigerator: the fibrous tissue of the trunk has a cooling effect as air passes through, and both branches and trunk are filled with a soft fibre that stores what meagre water exists. In particularly severe droughts, it seals off its branches from its leaves to further conserve moisture. The bark is razor sharp to deter predation. The San of the Kalahari hollow kokerbooms to store material that needs to be kept cool. They make quivers from its branches for their arrows.

Finally, two sad tree stories. Sad, in any case, if you like to anthropomorphize just a bit.

A little over a hundred years ago Uchter John Mark Knox, 5th Earl of Ranfurly, then the Governor General of New Zealand, visited one of the most remote southern islands, Campbell Island, for a purpose now forgotten, except that it *was* owned by New Zealand. When he was there, he planted a tree. It was a Sitka spruce, and it was the only tree on the island. It is still alive, still growing vigorously, and is still the only tree on Campbell Island, in deference to the Maoris now called Campbell Island/Motu Ihupuku. The nearest tree is 222 kilometres away on one of the Auckland Islands. The Campbell Island tree has left a small marker in history: a core sample taken in 2013 showed a peak in radiocarbons within the annual growth ring for 1965, from radiation released during nuclear testing in the 1950s and 1960s. Some scientists suggest this event marks the real beginning of the Anthropocene epoch.[50]

Then you have the *pennantia baylisiana* tree, a variant of New Zealand's elegant little kaikomako, which is surely the rarest, and loneliest, tree on the planet. In 2019, only one specimen survived, living out its solitary life on one of the thirteen uninhabited Three Kings Islands. She's a female, and needs a male to reproduce, but there is none.

Life in the forest

T REES *ARE* THE FOREST, but they are far from the only living thing found there. A forest is a single biome, in the jargon of the planetary sciences. While each biome is different according to its geography, all forest biomes are similar in design if different in detail. In the dispassionate language of the ecologists, forests are repositories of 80 per cent of the planet's terrestrial biodiversity, or, to put it more plainly, four-fifths of earth's creatures live in forests. And those creatures, as the Bible would say, are legion.

Trees and plants, of course. The greater fauna, yes, including the photogenic subjects of nature documentaries, the forest elephants, the wild boar, the remaining mountain and lowland gorillas of Africa, the wolves and wolverines of Canada, the black panther of India, and the jaguar of Brazil, the evil-tempered pygmy hippopotamus, the anacondas and constrictors (who hasn't seen a beady-eyed anaconda in a cheap jungle movie?), the terminally cute slow loris of Java, and the rest. But most of forest life is secretive and very small: bacteria, lichens, fungi, and insects, creeping things and burrowing things and biting things and poisonous things and helpful things, parasites and symbiotes, feeders on the dead and predators of the living. As the forester Jim Drescher has said, any forest biosphere remains constant when left in equilibrium, but also changes all the time. Death and renewal are constants, old age and fire the agents of change, insects, fungi, and mould the executors. Decay is essential to life, precursor to regeneration.

In most cases the creatures of the biome form a sympathetic and cooperative whole, having learned to live in proximity through eons of evolution. But evolution is competition, too, and the various parts of this community are often at war with each other. Death can mean life, just as decay can.

An elegant example is the endangered yellow-eared parrot of Colombia, which nests only in the equally endangered wax palm. The problem is, those palms must be dead for the parrot to survive. An environmentalist's dilemma.

* * *

Animals are important, clearly and obviously. Insects are *very* important.

There are a lot of insects, many more insects than trees. Current estimates count three trillion trees on the planet, which sounds like a lot but is a trivial number by insect standards: an admittedly speculative estimate suggests there are more than ten quintillion crawling, hopping, or flying insects alive at any one time, and the number of insect species could be anywhere from two million to thirty million. A Panamanian study found 955 species of beetles in just nineteen trees, and that's not individual beetles, that's beetle *species*. Every hectare of forest, by extrapolation, could host hundreds of millions of individual insects.

FiveThirtyEight.com, Nate Silver's statistical organization, which is usually devoted to extrapolations from polls to predict elections, has occasionally turned its attention to less political matters and has come up with this somewhat outré comparison: all the humans on earth, more than seven billion of us and counting, weigh approximately 287 million metric tons; but the mass of just those beetles eaten by spiders in one year amount to somewhere between 400 million and 800 million metric tons.[51]

All kinds of insects, then, all over. Ants, of various persuasions. Bees, bumble and otherwise. Sawflies, with their sharp little cutters. Wasps. Murder wasps. Hornets. Beetles and weevils (Coleoptera, the omnivores of the insect world) and true bugs (Hemiptera, plant feeders and heavy drinkers). Cicadas, aphids, and scale insects (also Hemiptera, but sap-suckers who dribble froth and make a mess). Flies (Diptera), horseflies, crane flies, fruit flies, botflies, blackflies, blowflies, tsetse flies, and mosquitoes—120,000 species and counting. Butterflies, moths, and skippers, which are basically fat furry butterflies. Cockroaches of course. Damselflies and dragonflies. Earwigs. And no, ticks and spiders are not insects but arachnids, but who's counting? Insects serve as pollinators, herbivores, carnivores, decomposers, and as food.

In the forest they serve many purposes. And, as per the above, they suck life from the living and give life to the dead.

* * *

Take a newly expired tree. If you kick at a fallen trunk it may resist, being still mostly wood. But it may crumble a little, the damp bark peeling away, and if you look closely, you will see a multitude of small scurrying things. These are called pioneer insects, technically saproxylics. They eat bark or wood, drilling small holes to access their meal better. The chippings they produce, and the bugshit they excrete, can then be digested by microorganisms that would find actual wood difficult. These saproxylics are mostly beetles, the various bark beetles, longhorn beetles, jewel beetles, and more. They loosen the bark and tap into the underlying wood, sometimes taking fungal spores with them to speed things up. Wood wasps do much the same work. A tree will generally lie there for two years or more while this work goes on, at first showing little sign of the decay beginning inside.

Stage two begins after the newly exposed wood begins to decompose, and twigs and branches break off. At this point another crowd of insects elbows into play. Still mostly beetles of one sort or another (anobiid or powder-post beetles, stag beetles, click beetles, and darkling beetles, one of the insect world's preeminent scavengers) but also flies and midges, which accumulate in the detritus left by their predecessors, attracting, in their turn, other insects for whom they are the prey. Bacteria and fungi come into play here, too, hastening the rotting. The same happens to cadavers on the forest floor, only faster. Blowflies and carrion beetles are very efficient rotting machines.

In stage three, the final phase, the wood gradually decomposes into soil. Ants, flies, maggots, and mites take up residence in what is left. Worms and snails enter into the picture, and begin the final decomposition of the cellulose and lignin of what was once wood. This ex-wood is now formally humus, pre-soil; it is in the rich organic matter in which new saplings take root. There would now be nothing for you to kick at in your stroll through the woods. The old has gone, and has yielded to the new.

Beetles can kill the living, too, as foresters have learned to their chagrin. In a "wild" forest with good species diversity, this can be beneficial. Weak and dying trees are eliminated, which in turn elevates the overall health of the forest and its resistance to disease. As with selective cutting in a managed forest, this allows light into the forest so that pioneer trees, such as red oaks in the Acadian forest, can find new vigour.[52]

At the same time, many of these insect species are themselves prey to birds such as woodpeckers and tits, or to mice, bats, shrews, and salamanders (nature really is quite efficient). What goes around comes around, a lot.

Another important citizen of the forest is the fungus family.

Fungi, like insects, are pretty good at decomposing stuff. They recycle carbon and minerals to other creatures, and transport nitrogen, potassium, and phosphorus from logs into the resulting humus. They are built for that: fungi are made of tiny tubes called hyphae, which serve as extensive nutrient-transport systems in the soil. But there are fungi everywhere in the tree, not just the roots: in the foliage, the wood of living trees, the bark surface, the roots, litter, soil, and deadwood—the catalogues show about a million species, but there are likely many more. There are even fungal spores high in the atmosphere, sometimes causing rain showers when droplets coagulate on them, spawning more droplets and then rain. Some fungi, such as the brutally named heart-rot fungus, are also efficient killers. They can sharply reduce, or even eliminate, plant species and open gaps in the canopy that can contribute to forest diversity. Some are purely beneficial. Some are efficient destroyers of wood lignin, which is otherwise hard for insects to digest. Down in the soil, certain fungi are mycorrhizae, in a symbiotic relationship with tree roots (a tree's "rhizosphere") which allows a more efficient uptake of water and soil nutrients in exchange for the carbon that the fungi crave. Fungi are also food for many creatures, including humans—truffles are a fungus, after all, and so are chanterelles, boletes, and morels.

Downed trees are important to fungi. Forest management practices that clear up the forest floor or haul away "debris" are destructive to fungi generally. Fungi need downed wood to survive, and many learned tomes have been written by modern foresters trying to estimate the amount of dead wood necessary for the efficient functioning of fungal communities, which in turn are needed for the sprouting of seedlings, providing the necessary nutrients on demand. This would argue that proper management of forests would maintain a diverse, not to say thriving, population of dead things.[53] Just as Jim Drescher has insisted.

Supporting players to the fungi are curious creatures with a descriptive name: slime moulds. They aren't fungi and they aren't animals, or not purely either. They are called "fungal animals," Mycetozoa, which is hedging all kinds of bets. Slime moulds are useful: they feed on the microorganisms living in any dead plants, thereby contributing to their decomposition; in turn, they feed on bacteria, yeasts, and fungi. Bizarrely, slime moulds have been found to be "memristors," creatures that can "remember" electrical charges, and there is even speculative science that is considering such moulds as living computers.

Bacteria, those little single-celled creatures that can cause infection (bad!) or fermentation (wine! good!) are also everywhere in the forest, where like fungi they help recycle carbon, nitrogen, and phosphorous, take part in the decomposition of dead wood and plants by encoding plant-cell-wall degrading enzymes, and then, in turn, help decompose dead fungal mycelia. Also like fungi, they can be found pretty well everywhere in the woods, and just as fungi do, they help roots transport nutrients and, more controversially, information. "The high abundance of fungal biomass in forest soils has multiple consequences for bacteria, including . . . an increase in soil connectivity by fungal mycelia that allow certain bacteria to move across the environment."[54] Bacteria, like plants, can perform photosynthesis. They also obtain energy through parasitic or symbiotic relationships with other organisms—fungi again. They can also kill. *Enterobacter agglomerans* is a plant pathogen living in fecal matter and in soil that can cause certain forms of pneumonia in humans; *Escherichia coli* (*E. coli*) lives on the forest floor, in discards from deer, bears, raccoons, and other creatures, and can cause severe illness in humans. *E. Coli* is one reason forest streams are not always safe to drink from.

Anyone who has spent time in a forest will have noticed mosses and lichens clinging to trees (though distinguishing a lichen from a moss is not always simple). A hoary old cliché from Boy Scout days suggests that people lost in a forest can navigate by taking note of which side of the trees moss is growing on. This is, in fact, almost true: moss usually, but not always, grows on the north side of trees, because that side usually gets less sunlight, but in relatively sparse forest with an open canopy that rule will lead travellers astray. (And you should remember that in the southern hemisphere the south side is what you should be watching.) Mosses are a sign of excessive moisture and low light levels, but they are otherwise harmless to trees (and, on the upside, heavy moss cover means the air is very clean, since moss is vulnerable to air pollution).

Technically, mosses are plants, but primitive ones, so primitive that mosses may be the ancestors of all plants existing today. They have rudimentary structures that look, sort of, like leaves and roots. They are "non-vascular" plants, which basically just means they lack the specialized tissues, called xylem and phloem, that help move minerals and water throughout plants like trees and shrubs. One consequence of being non-vascular is that mosses can't grow very large; if they did, they would collapse of their own weight.

Lichens, on the other hand, are not plants at all. They are two things in a symbiotic relationship: a kind of sandwich made up of a fungus and an algae, or a fungus and a cyanobacterium, or sometimes a fungus and both. The dominant partner is always the fungus. There are maybe 17,000 or 18,000 species of lichens. Algae are of another family altogether, neither plants nor fungi, though they can photosynthesize; they are generally aquatic except when they attach themselves to a fungus to form lichens. Seaweed is an algae, even the big stuff like kelp; so is the charmingly named pond scum. Algae blooms in lakes or on the ocean are familiar, and sometimes harmful to other life.

Lichens, like mosses, do the trees no harm. But also like mosses, their presence does signify that not everything is going well. Lichens on a tree is a sign of ill health, caused by pests, disease or old age.[55]

Are trees communitarian?

W HAT OF THE BEGUILING NOTION that trees have some form of intelligence, that they can communicate, even remember and plan? Do they, as British Columbia ecologist Suzanne Simard has asserted, advertise their needs, send each other nutrients, and issue warnings to other trees through a network of soil fungi, filigrees of mycelium called mycorrhizal associations? Do they "converse" through what she and others have dubbed the Wood Wide Web? Do they really use these fungal networks to issue bulletins about environmental change, to search for kin, to establish symbiotic relationships with fellow trees even of other species? Do they transport nutrients to other plants before they die? Do trees really talk to each other, have sex, form friendships, and feel physical pain? Are trees *sociable?*

Or is this all a form of misty sentimentality, driven by an animism moving into the vacuum caused by departing mainstream spirituality and religion? There may be a clue in the adulatory reviews of Richard Powers's mega-bestseller, *The Overstory*, published a few years ago. A much-praised passage in the book involved an anti-logging protest, during which activists occupied the canopy of a giant California redwood named Mimas, sixty metres above the forest floor. "Living up in the canopy for weeks, the protesters trying to prevent Mimas's logging come to know the tree as a living community, a sky city. Animism is the driving force of their activism; a belief in the rights of more-than-human beings to exist, flourish, and naturally evolve." Robert Macfarlane, writing in *The Guardian* late in 2019, called Powers's book "a vast forest of a novel, with animism as its sap. Powers has said that he was trying to resurrect a very old form of tree consciousness, a religion of attention and accommodation . . . that credits other forms of life—indeed, the life process as a whole—with wanting something."[56]

There are two parts to this discussion: whether trees and non-human living beings have rights, aware or not, and whether they are, in fact and in reality, aware. The first is contentious, but not really complicated. The second, it turns out, is *really* complicated. It is tangled up in definitions (of language, communication, and messaging), in folk memory and spiritualism, in wishful thinking, in science, and sometimes bogus science, and in what, to paraphrase an infamous Bill Clinton quote, "the definitions of 'are' are." Evidence-free assertions overlap with scrupulous experiment. This will be an attempt to disentangle them.

What are the facts, undisputed?

Bacteria and fungi are essential to trees and all plants. Beneath the soil, largely hidden from view and just coming into science's purview, is a world as complex, subtle, and all-pervasive as the plant world above it, a network that lives in symbiosis with plants, giving trees access to nutrients, and taking, in turn, the sugars and starches they need to survive.

This network is essential in almost all ecosystems for its role in decomposing plant material; its components contribute to the organic portion of soil, and through decomposition of wood help release carbon dioxide into the atmosphere.

Mycelium is the vegetative part of a fungus, consisting of a mass of slender branching threads called hyphae, which can be microscopic, or kilometres long, or, in the bizarre case of *Armillaria ostoyae*, can cover an area stretching over ten square kilometres, the planet's widest-spread single organism. And slender they are: a teaspoon of soil will contain many kilometres of these filaments. Those hyphae can and do penetrate directly into plant roots, which is why they are called mycorrhizae, a word coined from the Latin *myco*, or fungus, with the Greek *rhiza*, or root.

Mycorrhizal networks, or "associations," can be vast, covering many hectares, and can spread into many plants, not just of the same species, but across species and even across kingdoms. Therefore, most trees in a grove, and perhaps most trees in a forest, are indeed connected to each other.

Nutrients can make their way along these networks. So can poisons. Nutrients and poisons can travel both ways, from one tree to another. The purpose? Only to be guessed. So far. If there is one. Trees can also send out electrical pulses, which other trees can and do receive. So, too, with pheromones and gases. Whether these are "signals" is also unknown.

Sped-up videos of plants show them behaving in complex ways. There are hints, no more than that, of a control system, not based on neurons, that governs such behaviour. Some experiments have tracked oscillations in some mycorrhizal networks. Sometimes pulses, or even nutrients, can go back and forth, sometimes at regular intervals. No one yet knows what this means. An *outré* speculation is that they are coded messages.

* * *

The whole "are plants aware?" debate has come in two discrete waves. The first, now decades distant, can seem to a modern ear shockingly naïve. Not quite on the level of the early-twentieth-century Ouija board / ectoplasm / ghost-hunting New Occultism, but not far off. On a par, perhaps with Erich von Däniken's *Chariots of the Gods* or the healing power of pyramids or, now, the notion that 5G data networks cause viral epidemics.

As Elsa First put it in a *New York Times* piece in 1973, "The recent flurry of experimentation with plants in the psychic research underground has reached *New Yorker* cartoon fame: 'The only thing that seems to be wrong with your plant, Mrs. Jones, is that you've been talking to it too much.' But it hasn't been generally realized above ground that all those plants wired up to oscilloscopes, electro-encephalograms and other devices were hopefully meant to demonstrate Cosmic Consciousness. The idea—in some minds—wasn't just to show that plants appreciated attention. The idea was to show the mystical interconnectedness of all life."

First's irritation was set off by the 1973 bestseller by Peter Tompkins and Christopher Bird titled *The Secret Life of Plants*, which reported, among other things, that plants can "read human minds," "feel stress," and "pick out a plant murderer." The authors also recorded, admiringly, the work of a promoter who named himself T. Galen Hieronymous, inventor of the Hieronymous Machine, which worked on "eloptic" energy, which was half electricity, half light. In any case, his black-box Machine enabled farmers to insert a photo of their fields into the box, smear it with pesticides, and the field itself would miraculously become pest-free. Tompkins was also, predictably, into pyramidology.

Cleve Backster, supposedly a polygraph tester for the CIA, did one widely publicized experiment in 1966 in which, "on a whim, he attached a galvanometer [an instrument that detects electric currents] to a *dracaena*, a tropical houseplant whose name means "female dragon." Backster then imagined that the plant was on fire. The galvanometer flickered, and Backster concluded the plant was feeling stress from his thoughts, reading his mind and flinching at what it found there. In another experiment, Backster had a friend stomp on a plant. Then that friend and five other human suspects walked out in front of a companion plant that had "witnessed" the stomping. Again, the plant was hooked up to a galvanometer. When the killer entered the room, the plant sent out a wave of electricity, thereby identifying the murderer.[57]

The second wave of plant communication researchers, still very much with us, derives from ecologists, botanists, and foresters, and not from pseudo-science. Peter Wohlleben is one who comfortably straddles the worlds of speculative imagining and science. He is a professional forester. He manages a forest in Germany, the subject of his popular book, *The Hidden Life of Trees* (and its 2021 follow-up, *The Heartbeat of Trees*), and he spends his life in close observation of what happens within the wood. His expertise is obvious, even to a non-specialist. Even so, the language he chooses is relentless in its insistence on trees being aware. Here's a representative series of quotes:

Trees are very social beings . . . the mother trees look after their offspring . . . they like to stand close together and cuddle.

Beeches . . . know exactly how to exploit abundance, and they suppress competitors by growing up through the crowns of other trees and then covering the losers with their upper branches.

Any tree that wants to find an ecological niche next to a beech must be ready to practice self-denial in one area or another.

So, let's get back to why the roots are the most important part of a tree. Conceivably, this is where the tree equivalent of a brain is located. Brain? you ask. Isn't that a bit farfetched? Possibly, but now we know that trees can learn. This means they must store experiences somewhere, and therefore, there must be some kind of a storage mechanism inside the organism. Just where it is, no one knows, but the roots are the part of the tree best suited to the task.

When a root feels its way forward in the ground, it is aware of stimuli . . . If the root encounters toxic substances, impenetrable stones, or saturated soil, it analyzes the situation and transmits the necessary adjustments to the growing tip.

The *New York Times* columnist Timothy Egan, an astute observer of matters social and political, has nevertheless absorbed some of this flavour himself. "Trees are sociable, it turns out, and even somewhat selfless, nurturing their drought-stricken or wounded arboreal siblings. They share nutrients. They suffer when a big arm is lopped during the growing season, or a crown is next to an all-night light. Some trees warn other trees of danger by releasing chemical drifts."

Journalist Richard Schiffman is another who has fallen under Wohlleben's spell. "Far from the solitary giants we imagine them to be," he suggested in *The Washington Post*, " trees are highly social creatures that communicate chemically and electromagnetically with their neighbours, warn one another of dangers, and share resources through the tangled network of their root tips underground."

National Geographic, for its part, has even suggested that trees practice social distancing in their canopies, thereby allowing them to share resources and stay healthy. (Hedging its bets, the magazine acknowledged that the gaps between adjacent crowns, called crown shyness, "remain mysterious.")[58]

More whimsically, the philosopher Justin Smith (or Justin Erik Halldór Smith, as per his website *jehsmith.com*), points out that Heidegger "had dismissed even animals as merely being rather than existing . . . *a fortiori*, it is usually assumed, the world of plants must be even poorer, and thus trees are taken as exemplary instances of being without existing . . . [but] looking at the hanging branches of Louisiana oaks, as I am at present, reaching down to the bayou in search of something they want, I wonder if this is true, and it seems to me, at least fleetingly, that I can imagine what it is like to be a tree, that there is something it is like, and that it is weltreich indeed. If it is difficult to grasp this, this may only be because we are limited in our sympathy by the radical difference of time scale that separates their experience from ours. I am fairly certain that if this difference were removed, we would see that trees too have projects, and experience feelings of accomplishment, defeat, joy, pensiveness, and wistfulness."

An influential voice in this burgeoning field of tree communications is the researcher I mentioned above, Suzanne Simard, a British Columbia ecologist and tree specialist, and a professor of Forest Ecology at UBC. It was Simard's pioneering work that first identified the underground fungal networks integral to the theory. "In the early 1990s," she writes as a postscript to the Wohlleben book, "when searching for clues to the remarkable fertility of these Pacific forests, we unearthed a constellation of fungi linking manifold tree species. The mycelial web, as we later discovered, was integral to the life of the forest." For her doctoral thesis, she set out to prove it. Using microscopic and genetic tools, she peeled back the forest floor, as she put it, to trace that mycelial network, and discovered a complex community of mycorrhizal fungal species which were "mutualistic"—that is, they connected trees to soil in a "market exchange" of carbon and nutrients. She also discovered that two unrelated species of trees, the Douglas fir and the paper birch, were intricately connected. Simard's key experiment was for her doctoral project at Oregon State University. She infected carbon dioxide with radioactive carbon isotopes "and injected it into bags installed around pint-size birch trees growing near Douglas fir seedlings. After a little while, she ran a Geiger counter along the Douglas fir trees, and the device beeped like crazy. Moreover, she found that the radioactive carbon could also flow from the Douglas firs to the birches if she planted the bags near the firs. She had discovered that the trees shared carbon via underground networks. Her findings, published in *Nature* in 1997, lit a fire under scientists and the public alike."[59]

As Simard herself wrote, "When the interwoven birches and firs were spiked with stable and radioactive isotopes, I could see, using mass spectrometers and scintillation counters, carbon being transmitted back and forth between the trees, like neurotransmitters firing in our own neural networks . . . I was staggered to discover that Douglas firs were receiving more photosynthetic carbon from paper birches than they were transmitting, especially when the firs were in the shade of their leafy neighbours. This helped explain the synergy of the pair's relationship. The birches, it turns out, were spurring the growth of the firs, like carers in human social networks. Looking further, we discovered that the exchange between the two tree species was dynamic: each took different turns as 'mother,' depending on the season."

"The trees," she exclaimed, "were communicating through the web!" She reinforced this notion in her 2021 memoir, which she titled *Finding the Mother Tree: Discovering the Wisdom of the Forest.* It's a book that received adulatory reviews, not least from those inclined to view her as a brave iconoclast battling the "snickers and heckling" (to use a phrase from a *Washington Post* review by Kate Brown) from her mostly male colleagues.

Still, it's one thing to record how trees form a symbiotic association with below-ground fungi. It is more of a stretch to assert that they form a mutually supportive network, conversing about dangers, sending warning signals, and searching for kin.

Or is it?

It seems true that trees don't just sit there growing. The fungal networks really do seem to convey information. Dozens of experiments have shown that a tree can sabotage unwelcome invaders by sharing toxic deterrents with their neighbours, even neighbours of different species. Trees can defend themselves in many ways: by emitting chemical "flares" that alert others plants through the release of "jasmonate" hormones; by enlisting allies, for example, by attracting wasps that kill caterpillars; by releasing gases toxic to predators; by learning the communication codes of their enemies and subverting them, and so on.[60] Acacias do seem to issue alarms to their fellows, just as Timothy Egan suggested, albeit through the air. As the BBC put it in a defensively jocular piece, "The wood wide web, it turns out, has its own version of cybercrime." (Or cyber policing, more aptly.) Fungal networks also boost their host plants' immune systems. When a fungus colonizes the roots of a plant, it triggers the production of defense-related chemicals, which make immune system responses quicker and more efficient, a phenomenon called "priming." Scientists have occasionally deliberately severed a network of mycelial connections to see what happened; new filaments inevitably appear, heading out in exactly the right direction. Is this "memory"?

* * *

Simard was among the first scientists to prove the existence of free exchange in the mycorrhizal networks, but the idea actually goes back to the 1970s. An American mycologist (he actually sells mushrooms for a living) named Paul Stamets noticed similarities between fungal networks and the early U.S. Department of Defense precursor of the internet called ARPANET; much later, in a TED talk in 2008, he referred to the phenomenon as "Earth's natural internet."

Other scientists have suggested that just like with the real internet, there is a dark side to all this trafficking. It's nice for Wohlleben and Simard and others to suggest a cross-species underground collaborative community, but some suggest that plants use the network to steal from each other, too, and even to poison rivals. Like in other marketplaces, participants in the Wood Wide Web can apparently be cutthroat, competitive, and quite willing to put each other out of the game.

Allelopathy, as it is called, is part of the competition for water and light, and many trees supposedly use the Wood Wide Web to sabotage their neighbours, even to the degree of importing or manufacturing toxins to do the job. The American black walnut, a lovely tree much prized by furniture makers for its wood, is nevertheless a potent allelopath, wiping out many other plants by releasing a poison called juglone, which sounds like a joke but isn't, into the mycelial fungal network.[61] In this darker view, the fungi are as much out for themselves as they are helpful to others. Mycelia, after all, is how fungi feed. As ecologist Merlin Sheldrake put it, "Animals tend to find food in the world and put it in their bodies; fungi put their bodies in the food." They can reward or punish plants, lock away nutrients, and shift, store, or exchange nutrients to maximize their own health. A key scientist taking this view is Toby Kiers, an evolutionary biologist at Vrije University Amsterdam, who has used economist Thomas Piketty's *Capital in the Twenty-First Century* as inspiration, particularly his view that inequality and competition is the driver in human development.[62]

This view doesn't dispute the existence of the network and, in fact, has done much research to acknowledge and support it. What it does reject is the network's benign nature, accusing its proponents of gauzy sentimentality, of being Gaia wannabes. The Kiers people, in turn, are often derided as neo-Darwinist free-market fanatics. The world of botany can be cutthroat. It's worth noting that both sides accept that communication and information are shared through mycorrhizal networks. Both sides even agree that plants have agency. They just don't agree on motive.

Monica Gagliano is another academic researcher who has propounded radical notions of plant intelligence. Gagliano, an associate professor of evolutionary biology at the University of Western Australia, is perhaps best known for her "shameplant experiments," which sought to demonstrate that plants not only learn, but also remember. The shameplant, also known as the touch-me-not, is a pea relative called *Mimosa pudica*, usually grown in pots for its curiosity value: the leaves fold inward and droop when touched or shaken or disturbed in any way, "defending themselves" from harm, and reopen a few minutes later.

Gagliano dropped a bunch of the plants onto a cushioned surface, not far enough to do them any real harm. "The first time Gagliano dropped the plants—fifty-six of them—from the measured height, they responded as expected," reported Cody Delistraty in a *Paris Review* piece. That is, they closed up on cue. "But after several more drops, fewer of them closed. She dropped each of them sixty times, in five-second intervals. Eventually, all of them stopped closing. She continued like this for twenty-eight days, but none of them ever closed up again. It was only when she bothered them differently—such as by grabbing them—that they reverted to their usual defense mechanism."[63] Gagliano's findings were published in 2014 in the ecological journal *Oecologia*. Her conclusion? The plants had learned that a small fall was not harmful, and thus it was not necessary to close up. Not just learned: they actually remembered the lesson. Not for all time, but at least for a month, after which they became nervous Nellies again. "Brains and neurons are a sophisticated solution but not a necessary requirement for learning," she concluded. Gagliano and her team also found that plants could distinguish between the recorded sound of running water and the real thing, and concluded that they had "learned" through acoustic vibrations.

For what it's worth, Gagliano's home page records her signature on the petition about the link between COVID-19 and the 5G network.

Peter Wohlleben quotes František Baluška, a scientist at the Institute of Cellular and Molecular Botany at the University of Bonn, who "is of the opinion that brain-like structures can be found at root tips."[64] Baluška does indeed think so. Here's a passage from a paper of his in the journal *Plant Signalling and Behaviour*:

Recent advances in plant molecular biology, cellular biology, electrophysiology and ecology, unmask plants as sensory and communicative organisms, characterized by active, problem-solving behaviour. This new view of plants is considered controversial by several plant scientists. At the heart of this problem is a failure to appreciate different living time-scales: plants generally do not move from the spot where they first became rooted, whereas animals are constantly changing their location. Nevertheless, both animals and plants show movements of their organs; but, as mentioned, these take place at greatly different rates. Present day results, however, are increasingly coming to show that, in contrast with the classical view, plants are definitely not passive automatic organisms. On the contrary, they possess a sensory-based cognition which leads to behaviour, decisions and even displays of prototypic intelligence.[65]

And then Ren Sen Zeng, of the South China Agricultural University in Guangzhou, found, as he put it, that tomato plants in his lab "can eavesdrop on defense responses [of neighbouring mycelia-linked plants] and increase their diseases resistance against potential pathogens."[66] Plants can even share. Cody Delistraty again: "In a 2010 study, when four *Cakile edentula*, or sea-rocket plants, were put in the same pot, they shared their resources, moving their roots to accommodate the others. If the plants were just acting evolutionarily, it would follow that they would compete for resources; instead, they seem to be 'thinking' of the other plants and 'deciding' to help them."

Neither side has been able to prove that fungi (or trees for that matter) are agents in all this traffic, that they are able to actually process the information that passes through and can act appropriately on it, or whether they are simply an agglomeration of tiny pipes. The language both sides use indicates that they believe it, but real evidence is scant. Peter Wohlleben's fellow foresters are often his most active critics; and two scientists from the Universities of Göttingen and Freiburg have gathered thousands of signatures to protest "[his] conglomeration of half-truths, biased judgments and wishful thinking . . . not based on scientific evidence." Freiburg's head of silviculture, Jürgen Bauhus, declared that "even in the forest, it's facts we want, not fairy tales."

The eminent palaeontologist and geologist Richard Fortey is another who scoffs at the idea of plant intelligence. "It's so anthropomorphized that it's really not helpful," he told *Smithsonian*. "Trees do not have will or intention. They solve problems, but it's all under hormonal control, and it all evolved through natural selection." These magical notions of plant intelligence are worrisome, he says, because people "immediately leap to faulty conclusions, namely that trees are sentient beings like us."

Well, that's the point, isn't it? Whether the conclusions are, indeed, faulty.

In contrast to scientists like Fortey, the proponents of plant communication don't shrink from anthropomorphizing. They think anthropomorphizing is a positive. They hope it can teach humans that they don't need to be Masters of the Universe, that they can live in harmony with other species, that protecting trees is a valuable endeavour in itself, that species interconnectedness is beneficial to all parties.

My conclusion: you can acknowledge the complexity of the above-ground to below-ground relationship, you can admit the intricacy of the networks so created, and you can have reverence for trees. You can admire trees, even love them. But you don't have to believe you can chat with them.

The other side of this search for forest intelligence is to declare natural phenomena "persons" in the legal sense, the same odd legal sense that, in the United States, allowed corporations to be so defined. Lake Erie has already gone through this awkward process, when the citizens of the Ohio city of Toledo issued a Bill of Rights for the Lake Erie ecosystem, declaring it a legal person in law, with all the rights that such matters entail: "The right to exist, flourish and naturally evolve." That didn't go very far. The residents of the equally Ohioan city of Cleveland paid no attention, nor did any other jurisdiction, and any attempt by the lake, or its human interlocutors, to sue offenders has been met mostly with scoffing.

New Zealand has gone further than Ohio. The Whanganui river, the country's fourth largest, has been enshrined as a person by the national legislature. In the particular philosophy of the local Maori tribe, the river was regarded as a tribal ancestor, and in this view if the river were harmed in some way the tribe itself was also harmed, and could sue. It is hardly possible in these post-colonial (and post-colonialist) days to question aboriginal world views, but when a Maori spokesman declared that the river was an ancestor, and that "we can trace our genealogy to the origin of the universe," it is reasonable to be skeptical that such a view should be enshrined in law, even if the effort to get the river declared a person had been in litigation for 140 years.

Ecuador later one-upped New Zealand by declaring that Mother Nature herself, whole and entire, was an indivisible and living whole, and should therefore be accorded the rights of a person too. The benefits of such a declaration have been, it is fair to say, elusive.

Just so, the work of the Australian Multispecies Justice Project, which explores the whole notion of non-human rights, has been derided as "giving votes to wombats." Instead, it is attempting to "explore the relationships and entangled functioning of human and non human systems . . . understanding that humans, other animals, trees, rivers, soil, and more are inter-dependent, and all depend on the viability of ecological systems. It means challenging the traditional western view that human success will be won through neglecting and exploiting other beings' interests, needs, or viability."[67]

That the project and its participants, including the Sydney Environment Institute and philosophers like Dalia Nassar, have been attacked as lunatics by the *Daily Mail* must surely be a sign that they are onto something. (Nassar was the author of a provocative essay in *Aeon*, called "Rooted: What if, rather than mere props in the background of our lives, trees embody the history of all life on Earth?" The *Daily Mail* probably didn't read it.)

What does any of this have to do with forests, or trees? So far, not very much. But the rights-of-nature movement and, with it, the belief that trees are thinking beings, with their own mode of intelligence, brings a troubling undercurrent to the whole notion of forest management, and, especially, to logging. What then? Can a tree (or its surrogates) sue a logger for cutting it down? What then happens if a tree falls on a logger, killing him? Can his estate then sue the forest? Or was it self-defence? How to make sense of the New Animist credo that we should acknowledge and give agency to non-human interlocutors? Or as Amitav Ghosh put it in his lively essay "The Great Derangement," "[we have] stirred a sense of recognition . . . that humans were never alone, that we have always been surrounded by beings who share elements of that which we thought most distinctively our own: the capacities of will, thought and consciousness."[68] Richard Fortey would scoff. Peter Wohlleben, not so much.

PART 3

The Schooner

You can build a boat with wood and a carpenter;
but without wood all you have is a craftsman with nothing to do,
and without a carpenter all you have is forest.

—Anaximenes of Miletus, circa 600 BCE

Heart of oak are our ships, heart of oak are our men
We always are ready, steady, boys, steady
We'll fight and we'll conquer, again and again

—Chorus to Royal Navy march, early 18th century

THE LONGBOW, NO MATTER HOW technically superior to its antecedents, no matter how lethally utilitarian, is nonetheless an uncomplicated creature in relation to a ship, even a simple ship. And the schooner, with its apotheosis and successor, the clipper, was anything but a simple ship. Here's Sterling Hayden, topmast-man turned Hollywood actor, on the vessels that were turned out in shipyards all up and down the Atlantic seaboard: "From roughly 1870 . . . [they] brought to life a wondrous swarm of two-masted two-fisted sweet-sheered vessels calculated to do battle with that malevolent wilderness of waters known as the North Atlantic. Their everyday task was to catch fish, but their niche in maritime history is due in no small part to their incomparable ability to battle to windward in the teeth of living gales. To say nothing of their capacity to heave to and ride out some of the most daunting weather and infuriate conditions to be found rampaging around on the surface of the Seven Seas . . . They were also beautiful. Now we're getting down to it. Working craft around the world usually have sea-keeping qualities. But beauty? Soaring, mind boggling beauty? Now that is something else . . ."[69]

Schooners were called "able handsome ladies" in the parlance of the coast. *Able* was for their ability to beat to windward, even in a gale; *handsome* meant the set of the spars, the flawless proportions, the sweep of the hull, the balance of rig and gear; and *ladies* . . . well, maritime lore called all vessels ladies, able or handsome or not. The clippers, though, left a little to be desired in the able department, as we shall see.

Indeed, the clippers weren't true schooners. They were post-schooners, really, and usually square-rigged and multi-masted instead of having the fore and aft rig of a true two-masted schooner. But they were in very much the same tradition. The first of them, the Baltimore clipper, sprang directly in sensibility (and good looks) from the classic working schooners of Gloucester and Essex and Lunenburg.

The *Ariel*, built in 1865 in Greenock, on the Clyde in Scotland, was just such a rakish, clipperish vessel. A bow that swept forward by almost fifty degrees gave her a lean and eager look. She had a very narrow beam for her length, and three tall masts capable of carrying a cloud of sails in the heaviest weather. Below the waterline she had a knife-edge stem, narrow "foreparts," a long flat run aft to the rudder, and a sharp rise, the hull angling outward from the central keel. Her master, John Keay, was besotted with her. "A perfect beauty," he called her, "a beauty to every nautical man who saw her; in symmetrical grace and proportion of hull, spars, sails, rigging and finish she satisfied the eye and put all in love with her without exception. Very light airs gave her headway, and I could trust her like a thing alive in all evolutions." *Ariel* was the fleetest vessel of her time; carrying the astounding total of more than 26,000 square feet of canvas, she could reach speeds of sixteen knots, faster than the early steamers. There were sails everywhere: each mast on the *Ariel* carried a lower course sail, double topsails, single or double topgallants, and above those a royal and a skysail. Keay sometimes crammed small sails known as moonrakers at the very tip of each mast, and added supplementary staysails and studding sails off to the side of the yardarm, as well as fancy racing canvas such as water sails close down along the waterline. In favourable conditions, she could set thirty or more sails.[70]

One of the best-known, not to say notorious, vessels built in maritime Canada was the *Marco Polo*, a substantial three-masted clipper, 185 feet stem to stern on deck, with three decks of eight-feet clearance, constructed of hard-pine beams, hackmatack, oak, and other woods. Her story was recounted by Frederick Wallace, journalist and gadfly and celebrated author of the 1924 classic *Wooden Ships and Iron Men*: "The ship had a clipper-ish bow but the bilges of a cargo carrier. She was built at Marsh Creek on the Bay of Fundy near Saint John, the most godforsaken hole possibly discovered, considering the fine ships that had been built there. At low tide the place was a marshy creek with little or no water." It didn't start well: while still under construction the ship's skeleton was scattered about the shipyard by a passing hurricane and had to be reassembled. "The *Polo* was so big it was decided to wait until the spring tides to launch her, but even then the launching went awry and she careened right across the creek and burrowed into the mud on the other side. When the tide went out she fell over, and it was feared she was ruined, but two weeks later after much excavating, she floated off undamaged." The *Polo* could carry 22,000 square feet of canvas on her three masts, and introduced a few technological marvels: she was fitted with a rolling reefing system, which meant the sails could be reefed from the deck rather than the crew climbing the rigging and onto the yards in a heavy sea.

She was bought by English merchants for the Australia run, and the *Illustrated London News* was gushy:

> Her timbering is enormous. Her deck beams are huge balks of pitch-pine. Her timbers are well formed and ponderous. The stem and stern frame are of the choicest material. The hanging and lodging knees are all natural crooks and fitted to the greatest nicety . . . On deck forward of the poop, which is used as a ladies' cabin, is a home on deck to be used as a dining cabin. It is ceiled with maple, and the pilasters are panelled with richly ornamented and silvered glass, coins of various countries being a feature of the decorations . . . A sheet of plate glass with a cleverly painted picturesque view in the centre, with a framework of foliage and

scroll in opaque colours and gold . . . the saloon doors are panelled in stained glass bearing figures of commerce and industry from the designs of Mr. Frank Howard.

But it wasn't just her pilasters or her reef-rollers that impressed. Her skipper on the Australian run was James Nicol Forbes, the "Bully Forbes" of fo'c'sle legend, who took her into the roaring forties for her easting where she covered 2,162 kilometers miles in four days. He was not a man with many scruples. To ensure that his crew wouldn't skip for the Australian gold diggings, Forbes trumped up charges of insubordination against them and clapped them in irons for the duration of their stay in port. Even so, the crew mutinied after the captain thrashed the third mate, attacked another member of the crew, and challenged every man jack to a fight. Seventeen crewmen deserted when the captain was busy firing his cannon in port.

The *Polo* went out to Australia and back in five months and twenty-one days, and as she lay in the Salthouse Dock in England, she flew a banner proclaiming her *The Fastest Ship in the World*. Bully Forbes boasted to whoever would listen: "Ladies and gentlemen, last trip I astonished the world with the sailing of this ship. This trip I intend to astonish God Almighty."

* * *

The very earliest boats probably never astonished anyone, never mind the Almighty; they kept their passengers dry, mostly, and that was astonishment enough. They have all long rotted, and their construction and materials can only be guessed. The oldest "boat" still extant is a youngster, a dugout called the Pesse canoe, an oddly square artifact about three metres long by half a metre wide, an old pine scraped hollow with flint; it would have been a two-person craft, at most, and not very stable. It has been dated to the beginning of the Mesolithic period, also called the Middle Stone Age, somewhere around 10,000 years ago, and you can goggle at it in the Drents Museum in the Dutch city of Assen. But boats like it, and better, or at least larger and more elaborate, predate the Pesse canoe by many centuries.

The Gobustan petroglyph in Azerbaijan, two thousand years before Pesse, shows a boat made of reeds manned by twenty paddlers, its purpose and fate unknown; scattered remnants of just such a boat were found in Kuwait. There is speculative evidence that describes leather kayaks in Europe around 11,500 years ago. There is even a controversial theory that very early humanoid migrations from Bali to what is now the island of Flores must have been by boat (land bridges would not have existed at the time of the supposed crossings, and more than a hundred kilometres of open water surrounded Flores). If it is true that sea voyages were necessary, which is far from certain, then they would have been made very shortly after *homo sapiens* evolved, somewhere around 200,000 years ago,[71] and this would have been before tools to hollow out logs had been invented. Best guess, if these journeys really took place, is that they would have been made on bamboo rafts, lashed together with vines. Whether early *homo sap* ever really made such boats or undertook such voyages remains unknown. It is merely prudent to be skeptical. [72]

The largest known ancient boat is the "solar barge" built by the pharaoh Khufu, and buried with him at the foot of the Great Pyramid at Giza. It is not clear whether the vessel ever actually took to the water, but even so, it was remarkable—and remarkably large, 43.4 metres long and 5.9 on the beam, made of Lebanon cedar planking using unpegged tenons of a wood that later came to be called Christ's-thorn, and lashed together with halfah grass. It was sealed into its pit around 2500 BCE. Whether the pharaoh ever clambered into it is not known.

Small boats developed in many places. In Europe, especially the British Isles and especially Wales, riparian people built small round boats called coracles. They were generally wickerwork frames covered either with leather or cloth sealed with pitch, and unstable, modern ones being tippier than a canoe. In North America, familiarly enough, the aboriginal people developed framework canoes covered with birchbark and sealed with hot pine or spruce resin. The Inuit made kayaks over driftwood or whalebone and coated with whale fat; umiaks were the cargo equivalent, open sealskin boats used to transport people and goods.

The renowned Viking longboat, sharp at each end like the umiak, was built for exploring the northern isles, in sometimes wild weather, and for raiding wherever raiding was profitable. In due course, those longboats took Viking raiding and trading parties as far southeast as Russia's Volga river (they raided downriver, past Tver, past Kazan, until they met with Arab traders at Samara, who reported their astonishment at the sight of golden hair and fierce blue eyes, and tried to barter for the women of the Golden Race to take back to Baghdad to amaze the sultan), and of course it took them to Iceland, Greenland, Vineland, wherever that really was, and certainly to what is now Newfoundland.

Longboats were lightweight, infinitely manoeuvrable, and sturdy, made of shiplapped oak planks nailed together (so-called clinker construction) and caulked with tarred wool and animal hair. Julius Caesar was impressed. He came across longboats in his conquest of Britain and northern Gaul and imported the design to Rome, but despite his urging they never really caught on.

Other far-farers travelled the African littoral, and may have gone much further. One of them was Abu Bakari the Second, known as the Voyager

King, master of the Empire of Mali in its fourteenth-century heyday. Abu Bakari had travelled the length of his growing empire and had spent, or so the griots say, too many hours staring out over the Atlantic, which he came to see as a barrier to his more or less infinite expansion. "Therefore," said his successor, Mansa Musa, "my predecessor sent a preliminary reconnaissance fleet of four hundred ships towards the unknown and shadowy horizon. Only one returned, but that one told stories of a mysterious river in the middle of the ocean."

Fishermen still go out every day from Dakar, the Senegalese capital, which is almost certainly where Abu Bakari's astonishing fleet departed for their great adventure. Like the boats of the Niger, the fishing pirogues of Senegal are huge, pieced shiplap fashion from thick planks hewn from the giants of the rainforests; it takes a dozen men to drive them through the surf to the smoother ocean beyond. Their single masts are lateen rigged, like boats all up and down both African coasts, flexible, manoeuvrable, seaworthy, rugged. Every day they disappear over the horizon and return, nets bulging with fish. But four hundred vessels! Lost in the middle of the great ocean, caught in the oceanic currents that . . . what? Drift across to the Americas? Indeed, the Atlantic South Equatorial Current joins the Guinea current and, yes, swings across equatorial waters to Brazil.

In any case, that story of the river in the middle of the ocean was enough. For Abu Bakari, his fate was decided. "Not in the least discouraged," Mansa Musa said, "the emperor ordered the building of two thousand more vessels, a thousand for the men, a thousand for supplies." When the fleet was ready, he led his entourage once more down to the coast. There, he placed himself in the lead boat. "He assigned to me his authority and power until such day as he should return, but to this day no one has ever seen him again."[73] Abu Bakari the Second set sail for America somewhere between 1310 and 1312. Did he ever get there? On this subject, the griots are, of course, silent. Historians of the Americas are similarly silent, and except for a few African-looking statues in fifteenth-century Mexico, and a few Spanish texts describing "black men from Ethiopia" near the Darien isthmus in 1513, which may or may not have anything to do with any of this, Abu Bakari's hubristic journeying has vanished from memory.

* * *

The increasing use of iron tools made it possible to hew longer planks, and planks made possible ever-larger vessels.

Phoenician and then Roman ship design used carvel construction, long planks butted on edge and not overlapped, caulked with horsehair and subsequently oakum, which was tarred fibres, usually from unravelled old ropes. It was the Phoenicians who first developed the three-deckers called triremes and took them to Greece, at least according to Thucydides, who would have known. Some of the Roman ships were big enough to carry even a five-hundred-man army cohort; the trireme, a warship with three decks of a hundred oarsmen each, could be forty metres and more long and six wide. The largest boats in the Roman merchant navy could be even bigger than that; the very largest could have had as many as ten banks of oars. Biremes and triremes were the supply lines of empire, a kind of early just-in-time commerce that kept Roman industry humming.

Despite all this, the most advanced wooden vessels in the world, from the start of the Christian era until well into the nineteenth century, were made and sailed in China. They were called junks, a word that doesn't play well in English, with its connotations of being rubbish. Instead, the word is derived from the Malay-Javanese word *ajung*, which in turn is derived from the Mandarin word *jung*, meaning floating house.

Junks were very solid vessels, their planking thick, heavy, dense. Unlike Western boats, whose planks were fastened to a ribbed skeleton, junks used solid walls of wood running from side to side and fore and aft, dividing the interior into twelve or more separated compartments, providing rigidity and strength to the whole, and offering insurance if part of the hull was ever holed. Junks were also the first vessels to be provided with a rudder instead of a steering oar. They were big, too, sometimes with five masts.

Just how big is uncertain, since accounts of the treasure voyages of the Ming dynasty admiral Zheng He are almost certainly exaggerated. Some non-contemporaneous accounts of Zheng's ships suggested that the largest, which set off from China in 1403, were 135 metres by fifty-five metres, which would make them among the largest wooden vessels ever built and twice as long as the largest European ship. More likely, they were around sixty metres. A Zheng-era inscription puts the vessels at five hundred tons, which makes the smaller dimension more plausible, despite the contrary fact that an eleven-metre rudder has been unearthed in an old shipyard in Nanjing, which would be ungainly on a smaller vessel. Whatever their size, there were a lot of them. A Ming-era history claims the first voyage consisted of sixty-two treasure ships supported by a flotilla of 225 more, collectively carrying 27,000 men.

* * *

Oared vessels continued to be employed long after sails became standard gear. Warships, particularly, needed to be able to pivot on command, without relying on the vagaries of wind. But for longer voyages, or for vessels where cargo was more important than fighting men, sails were essential. Most early boats had a single square sail hung from a crosspiece nailed to the mast, later called a yard, and a single bank of oars. Until the thirteenth century, this single sail on a single mast, usually without the oarsmen, was the standard rigging. It was inflexible, and worked only when sailing before the wind, that is, with the wind coming from the stern. Eventually the mast, or a second one, as things developed, was fitted with a newly invented device called a lateen sail, a triangular sail on a long yard, or boom, attached at its top or its middle to the mast, and able to swivel. This gave these boats unmatched manoeuvrability. For the first time it became possible for a boat to catch the wind on either side of its sails, enabling the tactic called tacking, which in turn enabled the vessel to head almost-but-not-quite into, as opposed to away from, the wind, and to move forward in a zigzag pattern.

Lateen-rigged vessels, usually called dhows, were still being made in the twentieth century for the coastal trade on Arabian and African shores. The felucca, a small lightweight version with a single lateen sail made of homespun cotton, has been the workhorse of the Nile for centuries, and it still is.

The flexible lateen rig was further developed by the Dutch in the fifteenth century into what they called fore-and-aft sails (sails arranged on an axis of stem-to-stern, as opposed to square-riggers, whose sails were athwart). A substantial advantage was that the fore-and-aft sailplan required only a small crew, and not the many brawny persons required to lift and reef the sails on a large square-rigger. A four-masted schooner of the nineteenth century could operate with only eight hands, a nice savings for her master.

Most ocean-going vessels through the age of exploration and well past the Napoleonic wars used a combination of square and fore-and-aft sails, giving them both manoeuvrability and speed. By this time square sails were also designed to swivel somewhat, allowing them to cut closer to the wind, as close as sixty degrees, in skilled hands. A tactic called "backing" allowed one or more sails to catch the wind against the forward side rather than the aft side, holding the sail tight to windward, thus acting as a sort of brake; the manoeuvre was used to good effect by skilled commanders in the British navy in its wars against France.

* * *

The schooner, the vessel that plied the waters of what were to become one of the world's most productive fisheries, grew organically from the many variants of sail and mast and hull that preceded them, in turn modified for the conditions and weather they sailed in. Their immediate predecessors, vessels with the same bones, were shallops and ketches. The shallop, a proletarian name for a humble craft, was a little double-ended thing driven by manpower or by a single simple sail. Because they were open to the sea, without any deck, they were only good for close-to-shore work, and that only when the weather was good, for they were not seaworthy in Atlantic waters. The much more versatile ketch was usually rigged with two masts, the larger mainmast forward, and had a single deck and a round stern. They were larger than shallops and a good deal more weatherly. From the ketches came the New England "pinky," a little thing "with her kittiwake-tail stern raised as pertly as a pinky finger." Pinkies were the predominant vessel by the 1830s, still common along coastal waters throughout the nineteenth century, and survived as a fishing vessel into the early twentieth century. Ports in Maine, Massachusetts, and Nova Scotia built scores of these popular vessels. During the 1840s the "sharpshooter," a hull with a straighter keel and a modified schooner rig mostly supplanted the pinkies.[74]

The first true schooner (the word referred more to the rig than the hull shape) was popularly supposed to have originated in New England around 1700, the name deriving from the Scottish word *scoon* or *scon*, meaning to scoot along the water. More probably, the schooner rig came from England, whose sailors may in turn have derived it from the Dutch. Many seventeenth-century Dutch illustrations show small two-masted vessels, commonly with square sails but sometimes with a spritsail/lateen combination on both masts. A spritsail is an ungainly thing, a four-sided fore-and-aft sail supported at the top by the mast and a diagonal spar called the sprit; it can sometimes be stretched by a boom, but more usually just by its sheets. Karl Heinz Marquardt, an historian of sail, has shown that in the third decade of the seventeenth century an innovation began to appear on small cargo vessels, a half-sprit that came to be called a gaff. Why this happened is unknown. Marquardt suggests it might have been the result of an accident, a broken sprit hoisted up to sail home in an emergency, the half proving more efficient and not as cumbersome as the full thing. By 1700, these so-called gaff-rigged vessels had been adopted by the American colonists, where poor roads and great distances demanded efficient ships. "Besides," as Marquardt slyly points out, "gaff rigs had proved their superiority over square rigged vessels in the confined waters so preferred by smugglers."[75]

By definition, a schooner is a sailboat with at least two masts, the foremast being a little shorter than the mainmast, a rig that proved more efficient and easily manageable than masts of comparable height. Schooners can have more than two masts—the tern schooner popular after about 1880 had three, and some schooners had four, and at least one had seven. Some of these masts carried square sails. For a period in the middle of the nineteenth century, four-masted schooners were popular, on the theory that spreading the same amount of canvas over more masts would be easier on small crews, who worked without power-driven winches. (The longest wooden ship ever built was the schooner

Wyoming, constructed as late as 1909; she was 450 feet (137 metres) long and could carry six thousand tons of cargo. She also leaked like a sieve. Her wooden planks were constantly breaking, because she was just too big to be made out of wood. She was eventually lost with all hands in a storm near Cape Cod.)

Still, most of the Grand Banks working schooners stayed with two masts and a fairly standard set of canvas: on the foremast, a foretopmast staysail (jumbo), a jib, a jib foresail, a fore gaff topsail, and a foresail; on the mainmast, the main gaff, the main gaff topsail, the mainsail, the fisherman's staysail, and a storm sail. In heavy weather, and sometimes in winter, schooners would sail without a topmast, and reduce sail accordingly, and in a real blow would set just the storm sail. Most schooners carried a bowsprit, though a few left it off for safety's sake. This remained the most common configuration for working vessels, and was popular not just with fishermen but also pirates, privateers, and slave-ship captains.

These were not trivial vessels. They averaged around 120 feet but could be bigger, and were capable of carrying 175 tons of cargo; their masts would reach 120 feet and in ideal conditions carried nine thousand square feet of canvas. But they were not brutes; elegance was bred into their bones. Shipwright drawings of the *Bluenose* show her lean and sleek, a 143 feet and a few inches overall, but only fifty at the keel; she was tapered dramatically at the stern to a narrow afterdeck, just wide enough for the wheel and the mainsheet and a streamlined rudder below.[76]

* * *

Pace Anaximenes's aphorism quoted at the start of this essay, boatyards needed wood, and lots of it. They would keep sheds of both green and seasoned lumber, birch and beech, spruce and hemlock and pine, red and white oak, maple, tamarack, and a pile of Oregon pine and American white pine for spars and booms. A smaller shed contained "knees," with hackmatack, or juniper, the most prized. A knee was the junction between trunk and roots, immensely strong natural right angles, destined to be the braces on which deck beams were supported.

The construction process outlined below is adapted from an earlier book of mine, *Witch in the Wind*, a life of the most famous schooner of them all, the *Bluenose*. First step was to lay down the lines in a shed large enough to take the finished vessel. The yard would work from a small softwood model of what was to be, whittled to size and shape by the man who conceived her. These were called "half models," for an obvious reason; they modelled only one half of the hull-to-be, a fore-to-aft slice down the middle. The model would then be taken apart to measure the size and shape of each frame and beam; the nature of the timber and the number of board feet would then be extrapolated from the model. Then softwood templates were produced for each framing member. In the nature of a boat's hull, with its double-ended taper fore and aft and its curved ribs, each template was different. Then the foreman would go to the sheds, mark and pull out what was needed.

Next was to lay out the keel blocks along the "ways" where the vessel was to grow; these were massive timber props on which the equally massive keel would rest. The keel itself was almost certainly American white oak; red oak was too porous for the task.

Meanwhile, the crew had been assembled. Some were general labourers, but most were practitioners of specialist trades, sometimes very narrowly focused. There were men whose sole job it was to drill holes in the massive timbers for bolting; they would work for a penny a hole, and some days could make three dollars (three hundred holes through fourteen-inch timbers in a working day, a hole every two minutes, using hand-turned auger bits). These were very strong men. There were caulkers and painters, riggers, mast-and-spar men; the rudder or rudder set guys were a different trade from the rudder port guys. There were men for the planking, sawpit men, bandsaw and steambox men, framers, treenail ("trunnel") setters, sailmakers, blacksmiths, joiners, block-and-tackle makers, cordage men for the rope and rigging, specialists in anchors or "bowers."

A keel for a 120-foot boat is a substantial thing, usually three layers of twelve-by-twelve-inch white oak, bolted together every two and a half feet. A keel for such a boat would be around fifty feet long, pieced together from shorter lengths and then joined with lap joints and bolted. The hole-driller lines up the bolt holes, driving his auger through almost a yard of hard oak while keeping his holes completely plumb.

With the keel in place, the foreman would mark the location of the stem and stern-post and the various frames or ribs, which were already being constructed in other parts of the yard. In a large vessel, they were built of several lengths, sawed or adzed into the necessary shapes and joined together with dowels and trunnels. The ribs, the framing skeleton, were substantial enough themselves. Each frame was made double, twin ribs of nine-inch timber bolted side by side to make a single rib eighteen inches thick, their depth tapered from ten inches at base to about eight at the top. Each frame has a different bevel, transferred from the model-derived templates and then run through the massive bandsaws in the yard. They were made of a combination of woods: pine and spruce, birch, some hardwood maple. Each frame was pieced together from half a dozen smaller timbers, butted with lap joints and fastened with screw bolts.

There would be sixty or so sets of ribs, set on twenty-one-inch centres, raised and set in place with blocks and poles. Each was held in place with stays, lined up properly, and "ribboned out fair with battens and scarfed in," meaning the whole was wrapped in a "scarf" of timber. But before that began, the stem and stern-posts were raised and fitted to the keel by aprons and other pieces of solid timber designed to hold everything together as strongly as possible, then bolted through.

The skeleton of the vessel erected, she was said to be "in frame."

To lock the frames to the keel was like constructing a gigantic vise. The feet of the frames that lay on the keel were overlaid with a timber almost as massive as the keel itself. This was a heavy beam of spruce called the keelson, which lay on top of the frames, which now had become the filling in a huge wood sandwich: keel on the bottom, frame filling, keelson on top. Sometimes there were also side keelsons called, rather prosaically, assistant keelsons, and to the side of those might be assistant assistant keelsons, cut from spruce, a long-fibred wood that bends relatively easily.

Holes were bored through the keelson and its assistants, through the frames and, finally, through the keel itself and out the bottom. Then massive steel bolts more than six feet long were punched down through the holes, heavy nuts were fitted at each end, and everything tightened down, bearing the keelson down onto the frames and the whole thing onto the keel, clamping the frames in an iron grip. The process made a skeleton that was incredibly strong.

The planking and ceiling were next. The ceiling is not what landsmen think, something overhead, or the underside of the deck. The ceiling in a vessel is the interior planking, attached directly to the frames.

The planking was usually birch and oak below the waterline, and Douglas fir for the top five "strakes" of freeboard. This inside and outside planking gives the vessel a double skin, and since each skin is two and a half inches thick, it adds a bracing of heavy timber fully five inches through, "making a fabric that knitted together keel, keelsons, frames, bow-stem and sternpost to form a ship's body of terrific strength and rigidity."[77] These planks were neither bolted nor nailed, but fastened with trunnels. A hole is bored through the plank, through the frame, and clear through the ceiling plank opposite the frame, and then a trunnel is bashed in with a maul. These trunnels are hackmatack or juniper dowels just slightly thicker than the hole and are driven in until they stick out on the other side. They are then cut off flush, the ends split with a blunt iron chisel, and oak wedges driven in. Nothing on earth could move those trunnels when they were set. A hundred-foot wooden schooner would use about 15,000 trunnels. There were workers whose entire workaday life was to set trunnels.

When she was "ceiled up" to the height of the deck, the shelf and clamp timbers were bolted on. These timbers would carry the heavy deck beams, and needed to be sturdy, consisting of two layers of six-by-six timber fastened with trunnels through to the outside. They were cambered and scarfed together to form a horizontal strake running the whole length of the ship, about six inches wide. The deck beams were then laid on the shelf, and heavy knees, essentially huge shelf brackets, were fitted for extra support. A deck of clear pine planks, three inches thick and four and three quarters wide, was laid on top of the deck beams, tightly butted together with a V groove cut into the seams for the caulkers to work with. Openings were cut out for housings, the deck-house, companionways, hatch coamings, stanchions, and, of course, masts. The rudder was then fitted to the stern-post. The rudder-post was a substantial piece of timber, twelve inches on a side, made of birch. The rudder itself was made of multiple pieces of pine laminated and rabbeted together.

The planks were still rough after fitting. They had come from the sawmills with only a single pass through a plane, so there was still rough wood to cut and smooth. This was among the most skilled of the shipwright's tasks. The men used an adze and a spokeshave, a sort of oversize drawknife, to make them true, and finished the job with a plane and multiple grades of sandpaper. A skilled man with a clumsy-looking but razor-sharp adze could finish the wood to a degree that would satisfy anyone but a cabinetmaker, and the plane would only be used to remove imperfections invisible to the outsider.

As soon as the planking and decking was finished, the caulkers moved in. This was dirty work, and tough. Wielding a sixteen-inch caulking hammer for ten hours at a stretch called for stamina and strength, and caulkers were usually paid a premium. They used hammers with a groove in the blade end, which muted the noise and lessened the number of workers who went deaf, a hazard of their trade. A first layer of oakum was driven far into the seams with what they called a "horse iron." Then a second layer was driven in over that, a process called, for no apparent reason, beetling. The two layers of oakum were then covered with putty, and the whole with pitch. When the caulkers were done, water was pumped into the hull and wherever a leak was noticed it was chalk-marked for attention and recaulked.

The railings were installed next, birch and oak timbers roughly shaped at the mill but smoothed to a satin finish on-site. All the necessary blacksmith work was done, such as channel plates, stay-bolts, and more, and the vessel was then ready for paint: a prime coat, more sanding, then the blue-black finish coat, and the gilded trimwork.

The vessel was ready for launching.

"Fitting out the sticks," the booms, the spars, and the masts, was done onshore while the shipwrights were busy elsewhere. The mainmast was a ninety-foot behemoth of timber, a square more than two feet on a side, transformed into a perfectly tapered cylinder, all done by eye and by adze, spokeshave and plane. The mainmast, foremast, topmasts, booms, gaffs, and bowsprit were all installed after launch, by the riggers. A few coins were placed under each mast for luck, they were carefully lifted into place and the stays installed and tightened to secure them.

Then to the rigging, which ties all the moving parts together.

There are two kinds of rigging. Standing rigging, which holds fast or "stays" the masts and transmits the power of the sails to the hull, is permanent. It includes the heavy shrouds which attach to the rails of the ship and stop the masts from falling sideways. The shrouds are fitted with horizontal ropes, called ratlines, which provide a ladder for the crew to go aloft. Running rigging is the complex system of adjustable chains, wires, and ropes (halyards, from the term *haul yards*) by which the sails are set and trimmed to the wind. On square-rigged vessels the sails hang from horizontal spars called yards; and on every mast the entire edifice of canvas is rotated by hauling on long ropes called braces. Except for topsail schooners, which have a small square-rigged topsail, schooners have no yards, only gaffs and booms, each secured with its own running rigging. A fully rigged schooner had about thirty halyards with sheets and downhauls secured to belaying pins.

All this complex and intricate apparatus of masts and booms, gaffs and sprits, halyards and sheets, was there just to carry and manage the sails, for the sails are the engines of sailing ships, their purpose to drive the vessel forward. The sails themselves were made of canvas (from the word Greek word *cannabis*, for early canvas was made of hemp) or flax. Sailors liked or were annoyed at flax, often at the same time. It was strong and pliable when wet, but it had a tendency to stretch and lose strength in time, and thus had to be replaced more often than canvas, which was strong but not at all soft, and "a bitch in hard weather, especially ice," as former *Bluenose* crew member Matt Mitchell once put it.

Most boatbuilding towns had sail lofts on the waterfront. Boston's sailmakers were famous, especially the Boston Duck Manufactory in Frog

Lane, with its 180-foot spinning shed. The McManus family, from which the boat designer Tom McManus came, were also Boston sailmakers, and their sail loft became the hangout for skippers between voyages, yachting people who felt the romance of the merchant marine, and tradespeople looking for work. Champion Sailmakers of New York produced the canvas for many a famous ship, especially for the *Thomas L Lawson*, the only seven-masted schooner ever built; the dry weight of the *Lawson* sails was eighteen tons. At the turn of the century in Lunenburg, Nova Scotia, Michelle Stevens was the fourth generation of her family to own a sail loft. Her great-grandfather was a builder of whalers on Tancook Island and the family has been in the business ever since.

In case outsiders didn't value them enough, sailmakers had their own ditty:

> *From Hemp and Flax may Canvas Sails*
> *And Ropes be drawn, that seldom fails,*
> *In stormy Winds, to act their Part,*
> *If twisted well by human Art.*
>
> —Ebenezer Cooke, *Sotweed Redivivus,*
> *or the Planters Looking-Glass*, 1730

Hardly a great poem, or even half-decent doggerel, but it makes the point.

A bolt of canvas, as supplied to the sailmakers, was thirty-nine yards long and, usually, two feet wide, the width traditionally dictated by the capacity of the hand looms that made the canvas in the first place. The desired width was often a matter of some argument. Samuel Pepys, the great diarist, once recounted a "high dispute" he had with two gentlemen, Sir William Penn and Sir William Batten, on how broad the canvas should be and how close together the seams. As a later (anonymous) commentator put it, "The latter gentlemen insisted that the individual cloths should be narrow, this giving the sail many seams and making it less liable to stretch. Pepys opposed the view, and here he was wrong. The two Sir Williams were trying to minimize the fault in flax sails that to the end of their days was to detract from the performance of working craft."[78] Sail canvas came in eight grades, the lowest number denoting the sturdier cloth, used for mainsails, the highest number reserved for lighter material used on royals and kites and topmast sails. The tools of the trade were a sailmaker's palm (an oversized thimble), a fid to stretch the grommets before inserting reinforcements, beeswax, thread, and a sailmaker's needles. Sails were constructed to size, seamed with a double seam, and the sail's leech (outer edge) shaped with gores (triangular pieces) to give it the required belly (ability to billow). A single large square-rigged mainsail could weigh a ton.[79]

A rope, self-evidently, is several plies of yarn or fibres braided or twisted together to form something larger and stronger than the individual threads. Also self-evidently, you can pull with a rope but not push with it, unless you wind it first into a tight ball. (The phrase "pushing rope" was a colloquial expression meaning to attempt sex with a less-than-erect penis.) Traditional ropes were made of hemp, manila hemp, linen, cotton, coir, jute, or sisal. Rope making is not a new technology: two-ply rope fragments were found in the caves at Lascaux, 15,000 or so years old. Leonardo da Vinci sketched out a rope-making machine, but it was never built: ropes from the medieval period until the nineteenth century were constructed in so-called ropewalks, long buildings in which strands of fibres were laid out to be twisted into rope—the "cable length" of the finished rope was dictated by the length of the ropewalk, usually about a hundred yards.

Long ropes were important for the sheets and halyards of sailing ships. Shorter lengths would require splicing, but any splice narrow enough to pass easily through pulleys would be too weak for the purpose; the tougher short splice, on the other hand, doubled the diameter of the rope, making it impractical for rigging.

To be useful, sails need ropes and ropes need pulleys, almost always a set of pulleys to make best use of the curious effect called "mechanical advantage." With a single pulley, the rope goes up, through the pulley, and down again. You haul downward and the weight you lift goes up. One thousand newtons upward resistance, one thousand newtons downward pull, as much work in as out, the law of the conservation of energy. If, however, the rope goes through a set of four pulleys, two up and two down, it will take only 250 newtons of force to lift a weight whose resistance is a thousand newtons. How is this possible? Mechanical advantage is a measurement of how much a simple machine multiplies a force: the bigger the mechanical advantage, the less force you need, but the greater the distance you have to use that force. The weight rises one metre, but now you have to pull the loose end of the rope four times as far (four metres). "That means each section of rope is supporting a quarter of the total 1000 newtons and to raise the weight into the air, you have to pull with only a quarter of the force—250 newtons. To make the weight rise 1 meter, you have to shorten each section of the rope by one meter, so you have to pull the loose end of the rope by four meters . . . a pulley with four wheels and the rope wrapped around like this gives a mechanical advantage of four, which is twice as good as a pulley with two ropes and wheels."[80]

In shipbuilding, a set of multiple pulleys is called a block and tackle. The pulleys themselves are the block, the rope the tackle. Just as with sail lofts, each seafaring town had a block shop somewhere close by. One of the most famous was Lunenburg's A. Dauphinee and Sons, self-described as "manufacturer of wooden commercial tackle blocks, wooden yacht blocks, Lignum Vitae deadeyes, parrels, ash belaying pins, tinned & not tinned fish gaffs, bailers, wooden ice mallets, hook sets, brass and (hand) trawl fids, maple fids, lignum vitae trawl rollers & miscellaneous wood hardware tholepins, bullseyes, misc. galvanized hardware." Dauphinee's tackle blocks were, in the words of the writer Silver Donald Cameron, the Rolls-Royces of the blocks business: "Regular works of art, turned and shaped out of mahogany, ash, or lignum vitae, according to the order, glowing and glistening in the sunlight with the deep rich grains of the wood under many coats of varnish . . . Blocks, single blocks, doubles, triples; blocks with beckets and twisted shackles; blocks with ring-bolts and screw eyes; turning blocks, cheek blocks, snatch blocks. Rows upon rows of them, hanging above the heavy, glue-lumpy [benches], or lining the window sill and gleaming in the sunlight."

* * *

Here's a passage from the maiden voyage of the schooner *Bluenose*, also adapted from *Witch in the Wind*:

> By the time they passed the point the foresail and jumbo were up with the mainsail sheeted home, then as they hit the crosswise groundswell beyond the headland she headed down the wind, and immediately the tone of the rigging, the sounds of the creaking blocks, the straining cords and squeaking sailcloth, rose a note or two. As the deck moved on the breathing swells, the skipper's hand on the wheel would have felt the schooner's living essence, a subtle vibration transmitted up from the water to the keel and the rudder and the deck itself and down from the thrumming of the rigging, "feeling the wheel's kick and the wind's song," as the poet John Masefield put it. Course east-north-east, all hands on

deck to raise the foretop, maintop, and jib, then after half an hour
the lead went over and the report came back: speed twelve knots,
sir, no bottom at forty fathoms . . .[81]

The boat was "in trim" as the saying went.

"Trim" was the tuning of a seagoing vessel. All ocean-going sailing
captains wanted their vessels well-trimmed, well-rigged, well-sailed. They
couldn't do much about the hull, for the hull was a given, but they could
trim the boat to maximum advantage. One clipper skipper found his vessel
sailed best a little nose-down, and he had on deck a massive crate filled
with the heaviest machinery he could scrounge from the knacker's yard.
When the conditions shifted, the crew would haul the damn thing fore or
aft on command, all to gain half a knot in speed. The vessel's trim was
further adjusted by shifting ballast and cargo. The rigging and sails were
one intricate machine: a web of mast, gaff, boom, bowsprit, canvas, and
rigging that was infinitely adjustable, and the wind and the weather were
infinitely variable, and keeping the two systems in harmony, to harness
the powerful bowing of the wind, required deep technical skill and a feel
for the tuning of the whole. This was a great skipper's skill, the feeling
he had for his boat and how she behaved, in weather where there was
no time for reflection, only reaction. Everyone who watched these men
acknowledged the speed of their reactions to minute changes in weather
and sea; they called it intuition, but it was sensitivity in the service of deep
knowledge and a quick intelligence. The crew were the gears of a skipper's
mechanical system, the capricious perpetual motion machine of the wind
his motive power, and how he used the two fixed his reputation in the
taverns and meeting houses when they finally got ashore.

This intuitive knowledge could go deeper still. In naval battles in
the days of sail, a captain could tell at once how other vessels were

being handled, and how skilled their skippers or responsive their crew. A studding sail not set right, a reef not shaken out, too little canvas for the wind (or too much), sailing a point or two off the wind, and the opposition could be judged from far off, dismissed or considered a threat. In the battles between England and France in the Napoleonic period, skippers could come to action (or avoid it) just by watching how the enemy sailed, and could judge from many miles away (even if the opposition was still "hull down") if they could catch the weather gauge and therefore gain an advantage in battle, or decide to "crack on" as much sail as possible in retreat. Topmast-men went up the ratlines when they were needed, storm or no, a heavy blow or calm. Sterling Hayden, who had been one of them, wrote in his memoir:

> The [vessel] soars now above a hill of a sea. It ceases to rise, pauses and hangs, then drops down into the trough, smashing a hole in the sea only to be quickly flung skyward again. "Oh now here comes a good one, boys, hang on you sonsabitches, for Jaysus sake hang on." Up aloft you hang on. Beyond the breakwater the wild Atlantic growls. Plumes of spray bounce on lighthouse windows. Your mainmasthead is six feet higher than where Jack Hackett lives, thirty feet away. His voice is high and loud. "Oh dyin' Jaysus boy, if she catches one o' them seas just right she'll pitch us clear to New-found-land!" Up here you feel the motion more. You feel her reach out over a sea and hang; then down she goes with a sickening rush, and the second after the crash your mast goes bucking forward with a sideways motion. You wonder how wood can take it.

If a schooner fell over under the long blast of a gale, or if a great sea broke over the bows and came curling down the decks and pouring over the lee rail and the vessel lurched and hung trembling on her beam ends, it was massively hazardous. Especially if a skipper had carried his mainsail too long, for when the men start to reef or roll her up, she can ship a great sea and wash men over the side. In high seas, the great boom was especially difficult to handle, and drownings from the boom footropes were lamentably common. The bowsprit, often called the widow-maker, for good reason, was one of the greatest culprits. The men would need to edge out over the front of the vessel, a dozen feet or more, in heavy seas, often buried to their armpits in water, the gale raging and the canvas heaving like a maddened beast, heavy and stiff with ice; they'd need to punch it down and furl it, doing all this while clinging with one arm, feet balanced on slender rope lines slung below the bowsprit itself, the lines themselves slick with ice and prone to snap in the cold.

* * *

If the fishing schooners were hazardous, the clipper ships were even more so, made worse by the way they were sailed.

"To sailors, three things made a ship a clipper," wrote the Australian adventurer and sailor Alan Villiers. "She must be sharp-lined, built for speed. She must be tall-sparred and carry the utmost spread of canvas. And she must *use* that sail, day and night, fair weather and foul." And use them they did, carrying not just full masts of square sails but skysails and moonrakers above that, studding sails on booms extending from both hull and yards, and in weather when other ships would shorten sail, take them in a reef or two or three, the clippers cracked on, often heeling so much that their lee rails were buried in green water. The clippers were "unbelievably, mind-numbingly fast," as the sailor Frank Melling once put it. And they weren't just fast over an hour or two, or on an exceptional day: "They managed [these] ludicrously high average speeds over tens of thousands of miles."

The American clipper *Flying Cloud*, built by Donald McKay, sailed from New York to San Francisco around the Horn (there was no Panama Canal, then), covering 16,000 miles in eighty-nine days, a record that stood for 135 years. The *Cutty Sark*, one of the few clippers to survive (she is dry-docked at Greenwich, on the Thames) recorded a single day's sailing of 418 miles; once she covered 3,978 miles in eleven days. Another of McKay's clippers, the *Sovereign of the Seas*, once managed twenty-two knots "making her easting" in the southern ocean, far faster than steamships of the time. She cut the sailing time from Canton to New York from 160 days to under a hundred.[82]

But it came at a horrendous cost. The skippers took reckless risks, and often got things wrong, carrying so much sail that the masts cracked and spars were lost, or the vessel heeled over too far and foundered. Of the ninety or so clippers built in the 1850s, more than half were lost at sea; if you run down the list of clippers built and sailed, you will see that the vast majority foundered or were wrecked, and none lasted more than twenty years. Only two clippers survive, the tea clipper *Cutty Sark* and the passenger vessel *City of Adelaide* (which did sink several times, once at wharfside, but was salvaged.) The original Baltimore clippers, descendants of fishing schooners and ancestors of the tea clippers, were so "sharp"—a V-shaped cross section below the waterline—that they were unstable even in good weather, and several capsized at anchor with all sails furled.

What drove this fetish for speed? Commerce, the need for profit. And war.

During the War of 1812 regular schooners were too slow and small to evade blockading British fleets. Baltimore clippers, purpose-built for speed, did the job just fine. They were larger, and faster, better armed and, as a consequence, many were given letters of marque as privateers. The four-masted clipper *Chasseur* captured at least six British ships and burned five of them; clipper privateers captured more British vessels than the still-amateur American navy during the war.

But trade was the real driver, especially burgeoning tea and spice trade with China, and the need to be first to market in Europe and America. For this, larger vessels were needed. Tea was a high-value cargo but low in mass and volume, which minimized the need for cargo space, and thus further encouraged speed. In 1845, American shipyards began building the first so-called extreme clippers, with a bow further lengthened above the water and a further sharpening forward (the *Rainbow*, at 757 tons, was the first).

Competition was fierce, pumped up by equally competitive newspapers, which vied to be the first with the news of the first vessel returning from China in the tea season, and ran tables showing times out, times in port, and times home, and adulatory profiles of their masters. When the extreme clipper *Challenger* set off from Shanghai for New York late in 1855 the papers reported, all agog, that she ignominiously ran aground before leaving the Huanpu river for the East China Sea, "but floated free without injury." That, however, paled before the reports that her cargo was valued at $2 million, "the most valuable cargo of tea and silk ever to be laden in one bottom at that port."[83]

The epitome of this competition was the Great Tea Race of 1866 between the Chinese port of Fuzhou and London, which caused a sensation in nautical circles in Britain and a great froth of prose among journals such as the *Glasgow Herald* and the *Leeds Mercury*. The star was the clipper *Ariel*, that "perfect beauty" described in the opening passages of this essay, and her master, John Keay. The other contenders were the clippers *Fiery Cross*, *Serica*, and *Taeping*. The incentive was considerable:

the demand for premium tea was such that the first vessel home could charge a premium of 10 per cent or more; a vessel that cost £12,000 to build might bring in a cargo worth £3,000 on just one voyage.[84] As Mike Dash put it in the *Smithsonian*, "Keay . . . had good reason to feel pleased with himself. He had secured the first cargo of tea to come to market at the great Chinese port of Foochow (modern Fuzhou)—560 tons of first and second pickings, freighted at the high price of £7 a ton: the very finest leaves available. The cargo had been floated out to him in lighters, packed in more than 12,000 hand-made tea chests, and stowed below decks in the record time of just four days. Now Ariel was weighing anchor at 5 p.m. on the evening of May 28—the first tea clipper to sail for London that season."

But Keay had unluckily hired an underpowered tug to get him across the bar of the Min River, and he was stranded overnight to wait out an ebb tide. *Fiery Cross*, under her master Dick Robinson, reached the exit to the China Sea two days ahead of Keay and the *Taeping*, with *Serica* yet another day behind. Still, by the time they rounded the Cape of Good Hope and reached Saint Helena the *Taeping* held only a slim lead over *Fiery Cross*, the other two a day behind. All four vessels passed the Azores close together, and were still close after ninety-seven days at sea, when "the two leaders [*Ariel* and *Taeping*] ran up the Channel in sight of each other, both logging fourteen knots for most of the day as they made for Deal and the Tea Race's unofficial finish. At eight on the morning of September 6, *Ariel* was spotted signalling her number by watchers on the shore, and not ten minutes later *Taeping* hove into view to claim second place . . . Ariel's winning time being seven thousandths of one percent faster than her rival's."

* * *

The race was a triumph, and a commercial success. But just eight years later, the miraculous *Ariel* vanished without trace in mid-passage. No one knows why. But like other clippers of her type, her "excessively fine form above the waterline" resulted in a relative lack of buoyancy, and she was probably pooped by a following sea. As Dash put it, "it was generally assumed that a following sea had struck from behind and washed her helmsman overboard. With no hand on the wheel, the clipper would have swung broadside to the following wave and been struck with such ferocity she would have sunk almost instantly."

The clippers vanished as the age of sail did. As Frank Melling put it, "like many of humankind's inventions at the extreme end of their development cycle, clippers had a very short life. They were very good at sailing fast before the wind, carrying high value cargoes, but that was all. Steamers, and a shift in global trade patterns, killed them." Steamers were often slower, but they were not limited by the vagaries of the wind. They were powered by coal, and coal was not yet the despised thing it has become. Steamers could be bigger, much bigger. Steel was stronger than the best wood. It was their time.

PART 4

Deep in the Forest

The Forest Family

WHAT WAS THE UR-FOREST, the forest primeval, the forest at the Beginning?

Was there ever such a thing? Or is the notion just a romantic fantasy?

Forests evolve, they change, they die. And then they come back, although seldom as they were, instead colonizing new places in new guises. Most of the world's woodlands were buried in the immense ice sheets of the most recent glacial episode and had to colonize anew. When the trees did return, they weren't always welcome. Our ancestors had become accustomed to hunting the prodigious herds of ruminants that came with the post-glacial grasslands; the forests decimated the herds and made nomadic life incrementally more difficult. No wonder the woods were filled with demons.

Even so, there are candidates for the ur-forest, if you define the Beginning as "before memory," and even more if you define that Beginning as "before us." Tropical rainforests, formerly known as jungles, are the poster children of the world's forests, the charismatic sisters of the forest family, and a few of them are outlined below. But emotionally appealing as they are, they're far from the only forests on the planet. The family is quite large and diverse, and by some measures tropical rainforests are not even the most important. The world's environmental poobahs, embodied as the United Nations Environment Programme World Conservation Monitoring Centre, have identified twenty-six "major" global forest types, which is comprehensive but way too fine-grained for everyday use. They include, for example, "disturbed natural forest" (#8) as a forest type, as well as "exotic species plantations" (#10) and "sclerophyllous dry forest," which seems to mean leathery-leaved forests comfortable with drought (#24). For practical purposes, these twenty-six are commonly reduced to six broader categories, but even these six include parkland and plantations, so we are reduced to four: temperate needleleaf, mixed temperate, tropical moist, and tropical dry.

Many useful categories are left out in these definitions: subarctic boreal forests, temperate rainforests, thorn forests, sequoia and redwood forests, mangroves, wax palm forests of Colombia, southern beech forests of Chile and New Zealand, open lichen woodlands, and others.[85] Some of these are included in the not-at-all-encyclopedic list that follows. The really important ones are there, but so are a few notable but more local forest types. And no reference is made in this taxonomy to the age of forests, perhaps because that is a shifting target; it ultimately doesn't matter if a forest is 15,000 or sixty million years old so long as it is robust now, and allowed to do its share of eco-services for planetary health. Even so, "primary growth" or virgin forests are important, and not just emotionally: they show we haven't despoiled everything, or managed it into unrecognizability. When looked at properly, the protection of primary forest can be a recognition of human fallibility. And responsibility.

(I) TROPICAL RAINFOREST

"Tropical moist," as UNEP rather blandly calls them.

On its leisurely way down the Congo River to the provincial capital, Mossaka, my pirogue had come through the great forests north of Ouesso, among the least tenanted, least explored forests in Africa, where the Central African Republic, Cameroon, and the two Congos come together. Even now, thirty years after my last journey, there is hardly anyone there except bands of nomadic pygmies and fishermen, and they stay close to the lemony rivers, the Ubangi, Sangha, and others that are the veins of the Congo Basin, the only paths through the largest tropical forest on earth outside the Amazon.

From the pirogue I could see nothing but trees, but away from the water it was busier. What few lowland gorillas remained were in there somewhere, although the only ones I ever saw were way over in Uganda, in the Bwindi Impenetrable Forest, and those were mountain gorillas. There were families of chimps in the forest, too, and monkeys of different stripes. All sorts of other creatures, forest elephant and buffalo, wild pig, bongo, the potto and galago, the African crested porcupine. Bulbuls, herons, cormorants, the cormorant-like anhingas or snakebirds, toucans, souminga sunbirds. The mysterious okapi, which looks like a zebra but is really a sort of giraffe. Pythons thick as thighs, cobras, mambas, vipers, and—worse—the water naja, very venomous. I knew they were there, but didn't see them. Unlike in the popular imagination, the creatures that live in rainforests are generally wary or shy, bent neither on socializing nor predation. There were just glimpses. In the steamy heat of a mid-morning, the pirogue rounded a bend of the Congo and a flock of grey and scarlet parrots beat overhead. Then some kind of fisher plunged into the water, a bundle of black feathers, muscle, talons, and fury. The forest came down to the river's edge, a tangled mass, impenetrable to the eye and the foot. But even that was misleading. Away from the rivers, where light was allowed to penetrate and therefore lush low-lying vegetation could thrive, the canopy closed overhead, and the hiking became easy, or at least easier. However, I didn't go far, no more than a kilometre. I was on a schedule and *really* didn't want to get lost. I went just far enough to see how, at intervals, massive trees, limbas, okoumes, sapelles forty to sixty metres high, pierced the sky, pushing through the surrounding canopy. Later, as we moved downriver, we passed hundreds of creeks and inlets, islands of weed and great mats of water hyacinths drifting slowly by, the eddy of the muddy Congo as it lapped against the boat.

Six months later, and a thousand kilometres to the northwest, I found myself in another such forest: Korup National Forest, which lies on the border between Cameroon and Nigeria. I crossed into Korup on a suspension bridge over the Mana River, a rickety thing almost a hundred metres long that swayed at every step. (I was told Prince Charles had officiated at the inauguration of Korup as a national park a few years earlier. I hope he had plenty of help crossing the bridge, although perhaps future kings are not prone to nerves.) The bridge was better than the first time I had come here, before this was a national park; it then consisted of three ropes, a slender and slippery one for the feet, one on each side as handholds. My guide of the time, a Bamiléké from Yaoundé called Abel, said the bridge was "very secure," but he panicked halfway across, which wasn't reassuring. It was okay to fall into the Mana, Abel had asserted. Nothing bad lived in that stream. Nothing except hookworm, leeches, and a particularly virulent black fly that causes liparia disease, whatever that is. Oh, and maybe a few slender-snouted crocodiles. And sharp black rocks. Lots of those.

Most of Korup is primary rainforest, even deeper, older, and more lush than the forests I had passed by in my excursion down the Congo, although much more accessible, being an easy drive from Douala, the largest city in Cameroon. It was steamy hot, approaching thirty-five degrees Celsius, and everything dripped with moisture. There were butterflies overhead as large as kites, dipping and swooping in cobalt, turquoise, scarlet, and garish green. Red-headed skimmers patrolled the streams, greedy beaks open. Now there are boardwalks and manicured trails through the forest but even then the forest floor itself was relatively clear and easily traversable, if thick with undergrowth and mid-story vines and canopy, loud with the buzzing, hissing, and crackling of fecund life that crept and crawled and stung.

Korup is what botanists call "rich in paleoendemics," by which they mean trees and shrubs that evolved in Paleolithic times or much earlier; so far, upward of 1,100 species of tree, shrub, herb, and liana have been catalogued, and no one thinks the number exhaustive. Just as along the Congo, some of the trees are immense. They tower overhead, creeping with parasite vines and lianas, stretching through the tangle of the underlayer. This may be part of the oldest continuous forest on earth, having missed at least the last two ice ages and survived the dryness of the Pleistocene as part of the Guinea Congolian Forest Refugium, so-called. It has existed here, in much the same form, for at least sixty-five million years and probably much longer. There were dinosaurs abroad when these trees (or their forebears) were shrublings. This is older than old-growth forest. This is primary or climax forest. It has never been cut or "managed" or otherwise disturbed by humans. Poor soil, for one thing, and too wet. Korup can get up to a hundred centimetres of rain in August alone, and more than six hundred centimetres in a year and all that moisture leaches the soil of nutrients. The canopy overhead is so dense that botanists have estimated it can take ten minutes for a raindrop to make it to the forest floor. More recently, Korup's reputation as the oldest continuous forest has been disputed. As suggested in the essay "Before Forests," the discovery of a primitive tree called the "idiot fruit" (*idiospermum australiense*) in the Daintree Rainforest in Queensland, Australia, has forced botanists to re-evaluate the age of that relic forest. The idiot fruit in its way predates modern trees altogether. Whether or not Daintree itself dates back 110 million years, the ancestors of this particular plant do.

The African rainforests are immense, covering some two million square kilometres, but they are not alone, nor are they the largest. Every equatorial landmass has tropical rainforests, some of them modest in size (the Sinharaja forest in Sri Lanka is only twenty kilometres across; and the Knysna montane tropical forest, the only such pocket left in southern Africa, is just three thousand square kilometres) and some of them huge. The Bosawas Biosphere Reserve in northern Nicaragua is close to 20,000 square kilometres. Among the best-known such forests are the Papua New Guinea rainforest, Sapo national forest in Liberia, the Ecuadorian rainforest, the southeast Asia rainforests ranging from India to Malaysia, the Monteverde rainforest in Costa Rica (and its associated Santa Elena Cloud Forest Reserve), the Montecristo rainforest in El Salvador, and Mount Kinabalu rainforest on the coast of Sabah, in Malaysian Borneo.

Obviously, the greatest of all is the Amazon Basin rainforest, in area more than half earth's surviving tropical forests, more than five and a half million square kilometres, sprawling over nine nations (Brazil has 65 per cent, the rest shared by Bolivia, Peru, Ecuador, Colombia, Venezuela, Guyana, Surinam, and French Guiana). All this is recent as geological timespans go. Amazonia proper seems to have appeared in the Eocene era, somewhere between fifty-six million and thirty-three million years ago, and then it wasn't always as great as it is now; pollen studies suggest that before the most recent glaciation period, the forest was limited to small *refugia* separated by temperate forests and even grassland. And in any case, more evidence is accumulating that Amazonia was under cultivation relatively recently, and had been so for millennia. It only seems eternal, integral to planetary identity, but it really is not. It is really rather new.

Rainforests have attracted their own narrow-cast, and quite recent, legends. Somehow, in the folklore of the West, these immense forests in Africa, Amazonia, and tropical south Asia, mutated in the colonial period from "unexplored" into "jungle." In the Age of Exploration, they changed from blanks on the map into exotica, home of the primitive, and then into exoticism, with its overlay of sexual decay and decadence, attracting explorers, adventurers, mystics and cranks, exploiters and prospectors, and romantics like the English adventurer Mary Kingsley, who once ascended Mount Cameroon in a day, Victorian petticoats notwithstanding, and who made expeditions into the forests and then up the Ogooué River, "dancing," as she put it, "many a wild dance with the wild river."

Because these forests remained unknown and unexplored (the locals didn't count), outsiders could impose on them whatever emotion they needed, and many *needed* to believe in their impenetrability and mysteriousness and otherness. Some were looking for riches in the deep forests, some went for escape, some as a challenge, or an adventure, or as prospectors, or were seeking the lost civilizations of Ur, or maybe Sheba, or simply to seek solitude and solace in a place that was hidden and perilous.

Joseph Conrad, whose *Heart of Darkness* has in African eyes much to answer for, employing as he did the fecund tropical forests as a metaphor for decay and corruption, expressed this view exactly: "ascending the [Congo] river is like travelling towards the early beginnings of the world, when vegetation covered the earth and the great trees were king. A road of empty water, grand silence, impenetrable forest. The air is hot, humid, heavy, languid ..." Conrad was followed by many others. Tarzan, of course. We met Tarzan and his cantankerous apes in the introduction. Edgar Rice Burroughs, who never went to Africa, was eloquent about the highways that the overstory afforded the ape man and his simian cousins. Rider Haggard's *She* (indeed, *She-who-must-be-obeyed*) ruled a "lost" city in the deep jungle, an example followed to good effect by Michael Crichton in *Congo*, who called *his* lost city Zinj. Legends of such lost cities, crumbling stones under the jungle canopy, pyramids overgrown with lianas, are commonplace in the legends.

A pristine example of this romantic notion is the so-called Ciudad Blanca, White City, also known as the Kao Kamasa in the local Pech language of Honduras, City of the Monkey God, and lately as the City of Jaguars (after the statue of a "were-jaguar," whatever that is, was apparently unearthed in the jungle). This lost city is to be found, according to many accounts, in the dense rainforest of eastern Honduras, in the Mosquitia region of the euphonically named Gracias a Dios department. A clue to the cluelessness of many accounts is the indigenous notion that the city is not so much lost as hidden, a refuge for alienated indigenous gods, which is why explorers have been unable to locate it.

As lost cities go, the Monkey God has a venerable provenance and just enough tantalizing fact to compound the obsession. Hernan Cortés began it all, five years after he conquered the Aztecs. He led an expedition to regain control over one of his rebellious lieutenants, and left a notation in his campaign diaries about a mythical city called Hueitapalan, loosely translated as Old Land of Red Earth. A hard-headed soldier, Cortés disbelieved the whole thing, but twenty years later the Bishop of Honduras embellished the story, recounting in an imaginative letter to the Spanish king how he had looked east from a mountaintop and had seen a shining city in the distance. Its rulers, he said, ate their meals from plates of pure gold; he had it on good authority from the locals.

Since then, the city (which had morphed into a White City from a Red one) has accreted legends and tall tales. It was the birthplace of Quetzalcoatl. Golden idols popped up everywhere, and elaborately carved white stones. Charles Lindbergh swore he saw it from the air in 1927. An eccentric explorer called Theodore Morde said he found it, although he wouldn't tell anyone exactly where. Since he was run over by a car in London shortly afterwards, those prone to conspiracies suspected "the US government or other forces were trying to silence him," for what reason is unclear.[86]

These fevered visions are mostly gone now. The "exotic jungle" has once again mutated in Western consciousness. The word itself, *jungle*, has fallen into pursed-lip academic disfavour. Gone are the mysteries, or at least those mysteries. No more unknown and magical creatures, no lost cities. The forest isn't impenetrable at all, but a source of food and building materials and trade goods and medicines and precious biodiversity. Rainforests are now seen as a purely good thing, home to indigenous cultures living in nature without despoiling it, an ongoing lesson for more rapacious cultures in how to care for the planet, should we care to learn it. Far from being mysterious and dangerous, rainforests are actually fragile and spiritual places to be cherished, or so activists will tell you.

That's the new legend. Better than the old one, but still a legend.

It is true that rainforests are biodiverse, home to almost three-quarters of the world's species, animals and plants both, on only 6 per cent of the land area. The numbers can be numbing: two-thirds of all flowering plants make their home in rainforests, and a single hectare can contain 42,000 different species of insects, up to 480 species of trees species, and 1,500 species of higher plants. Surveys suggest that Amazonia contains somewhere around 390 billion trees in 16,000 species, with many left uncounted and unidentified. Estimates of the full range of species, animal and plant, range from three million to more than fifty million.

Some governments have gotten the message. Far from fretting about lost White Cities, the Honduran government has set aside the rainforests of Mosquitia for preservation under the Río Plátano Biosphere Reserve, which itself is part of the so-called Great Lungs of Central America, and is encouraging a tourist industry, so far without much tourist infrastructure.

Prospectors in the rainforests are now mostly from pharmaceutical companies looking for the next big cure to emerge from all that furious fecundity. The cliché is now that tropical rainforests are the world's largest pharmacy, because a quarter of natural medicines have been found in them. Tropical plants and insects have been perfecting chemical defences over millions of years, the argument goes, and some of these have clear medical benefits. With many millions of plants, insects, and microorganisms still uncatalogued, there will likely be many more. Endlessly suspicious of Big Pharma, rainforest alliance NGOs are already at work protecting the "intellectual property" of the indigenous peoples that live there, looking to see that profit goes where profit should.

(II) THE BOREAL FOREST, A.K.A. TAIGA

Some years ago, we drove to Sioux Lookout, which was then not quite at the northern end of Ontario's all-season roads but as near as makes no difference. There was a tidy little municipal airport at Sioux Lookout. We wanted to get to Pickle Crow and Central Patricia, off to the northeast, and at that time there were no roads there. We rented a plane at Sioux Lookout, together with its pilot, we being no aviators. The plane was amphibious, able to take off and land on water or land as circumstances dictated. Thirty minutes out, our pilot, a not-yet-grizzled veteran who had been a dentist in Thunder Bay before he opted for the unstructured life of a bush pilot, asked if we would mind setting down on a small unnamed lake where he had dropped a sport fisherman some days earlier. He wanted to see if the guy was all right, there being no other way to reach him. The fisherman was on his own, a rich fellow from somewhere in upstate New York, wanting to get away from it all, which he had. He was in all likelihood the only human being in three hundred square kilometres. There were Ojibwa (Anishinaabe) bands to the north and west, around Cat Lake, and more at Pickle Lake, but this was an area where few First Nations people lived. The pilot's request wasn't really a request, because there was no plausible reason to say no, and he would likely have ignored us if we had. Bush pilot etiquette depends on keeping in touch whenever possible, and no doesn't carry much freight in their vocabulary.

In any case, we set down without difficulty and taxied to the shore where the fisherman had been deposited. There was no sign of anyone. There was no sign of anything. No camp, no tent, no fireplace, no gear at all. Just trees. Sioux Lookout was already north of the meandering boundary of the deciduous forest belt and the great boreal forest to its north. But this was not yet tundra. There were trees aplenty. Lush, too, this being the height of the short summer. I recognized balsam poplar, white birch, groves of trembling aspen and conifers, most of which I couldn't identify. But there were white and black spruce, Jack pine and tamarack, or larches. Probably cottonwoods, too.

After a few minutes the man himself emerged from the bush, doffed his hat at us in salute, and then waved us off with the universal shooing motion, indicating he needed nothing and was just fine, thank you. He had another week to go on his in-and-out contract and was clearly happy to be left alone.

We climbed into the air, heading northeast, and the little lake dwindled. After that, there was nothing to be seen but lakes and more lakes, forest and more forest. No roads, no communities, no development. There are about a quarter million lakes in Ontario, and many of them seemed to be hereabouts, some big enough for airports ("waterdromes" in the local parlance) and many comparative puddles. But even the lakes just punctuated the endless narrative of the forest, and forest is what there was above all.

Even this was but a small part of the Canadian boreal forest, which stretches thousands of kilometres to the north and west and east, swinging in an immense arc from the Mackenzie River delta and the Alaska border, past northeast British Columbia, across northern Alberta and Saskatchewan, through Manitoba, Ontario, and Quebec before fetching up on the shores of the Labrador Sea, almost a third of the Canadian landmass. The boreal forest is the largest undisturbed forest in existence, nearly two million square kilometres of it in Canada alone, most of it not yet touched by development. And even that is only a part of the worldwide boreal forest, at seventeen million square kilometres, the planet's single greatest biome, greater by far than tropical rainforests. To Canada's west is Alaska, whose boreal forest extends from the Kenai peninsula to Fairbanks, and north to the foothills and the Brooks Range, east to the Porcupine River on the Canadian border, and west down the Kuskokwim river valley. To the east, the boreal forest continues through Iceland, Sweden, Norway, Finland, Russia, Kazakhstan, Mongolia, Japan. In Russia, it is known as taiga, somewhere around twelve million square kilometres of scrub spruce, poplar, and aspen, shallow lakes, bogs, fens, patchy permafrost, thousands of kilometres of tangled undergrowth and swamp, much more impenetrable and inhospitable than the jungles of legend (where, as we have seen, the closed canopy of the forest giants generally keeps the forest floor open). So big, and important, is the taiga that it locks away vast quantities of carbon, and when the trees are in their maximum growth stage, during spring and summer, worldwide levels of carbon dioxide fall and oxygen levels rise.[87] To its north is tundra, where no trees grow; to its south are the great temperate deciduous forests of the northern hemisphere.

The taiga is new, as forests go, the very opposite of "ur." It overlays scoured basins from which the glaciers only departed twelve millennia or so ago. It remains a patchwork of what the botanists call "successional and subclimax" forests, vulnerable to climate change and thawing permafrost. It lies generally between the summer and winter positions of the arctic air mass. It has, obviously enough, severe winters, six months or more during which time the temperature never climbs above freezing, but can have very hot, if short, summers. Notoriously, Verkhoyansk in northeastern Siberia's Sakha Republic, on the banks of the Yana River, has recorded temperatures in Fahrenheit of both ninety below and ninety above zero.

At high latitudes, where the boreal forest thins towards tundra, is the species-poor, sparse growth of the so-called lichen woodlands, sometimes known as open taiga or forest tundra. This zone stretches from Newfoundland in the east to Alaska and the Yukon. Lichen woodlands are of scant importance globally, and are notable only because the pale colour of the lichens reduces the greenhouse effect and shrinks the already short frost-free growing season. They are also poor at retaining and storing carbon.

It is an ecologist's cliché: if the tropical rainforests were to disappear, human life would be imperilled. If the taiga were to die, so would we.

(III) TEMPERATE RAINFORESTS

The so-called Big Tree of British Columbia is a little decrepit, which isn't so surprising when you figure that it is rather more than a thousand years old, and maybe double that. Maybe *geriatric* is a kinder word than *decrepit*. Old, anyway. Branches all ahoo, untidy, some of them broken, roots gnarly and scarred, greenery sparser than it used to be. But there it is, still standing, good for another few hundred years or so, loggers and climate change willing. Big Tree is at the heart of the province's Ancient Forest Provincial Park (also known as Chun T'oh Whudujut Provincial Park and Protected Area) and at five metres in diameter is the largest of the western red cedars in the park. There are others nearly as large: the so-called Radies Tree, named after the graduate student who found it, is almost as big, and is bizarrely propped up by its own mini-forest of exposed roots. An antique forest, to be sure: no earthquakes, and no fires, have disturbed its slumber for at least a millennium, perhaps much longer.

Big Tree is easy to get to, an advantage for those who find pushing through dense undergrowth less than exhilarating. The Ancient Forest is relatively small as wilderness parks go, just shy of 12,000 hectares, with a network of cedar boardwalks that wander through the tangled rainforest, lush and moist, smothered in mosses and lichens and fungi, as fecund as its tropical cousins. The park's literature asserts that Ancient Forest is the only inland temperate rainforest in the world, which it is, almost. Inland, in any case: the Pacific coast, where most of world's other temperate rainforests reside, is about eight hundred kilometres distant. Not all is lush rainforest: the park's fifteen-kilometre Driscoll Trail takes hikers into hemlock and spruce territory, and into a subalpine fir zone. There are grizzlies and black bears up there, too, and wolverines, so caution is warranted.[88]

Ancient Forest may be small, but the Pacific Coastal Temperate Rainforest is not. It stretches from Prince William Sound in Alaska though British Columbia, Washington, and Oregon, down into Northern California, taking in Great Bear rainforest (6.4 million hectares), Haida Gwaii, the Central and Southern Cascades Forests, the Klamatch-Siskiyou forest, Clayoquot Sound (itself part of Pacific Rim National Park Reserve and Strathcona Provincial park), and the Northern California Coastal Forest. There are parts of it on Vancouver Island itself. Not far from the village of Port Renfrew, for example, is an old-growth grove of hemlocks, firs, and red cedars, including an unidentified evergreen that has earned the nickname of Canada's gnarliest tree. The grove itself has been given the name Avatar Grove, in the hope that naming it after the movie would serve as an amulet against logging.

The northerly forest species are mostly conifers, Sitka spruce, and hemlock. On the central coast the trees include redwoods, Douglas firs, western red cedar, and pine. Maples and alders are common at lower altitudes. Dense growths of mosses cover the boles, and the undergrowth is lush and perpetually green.

These forests are not called rainforests for nothing. In some areas annual rainfall can be more than three hundred centimetres, along with moderate temperatures, seldom falling below ten degrees Celsius, even in winter.

The giant sequoias of California, commonly called coastal redwoods or, further inland, Sierra redwoods, fall loosely into the rainforest ecosystem or, at least, overlap with it. It is commonly known that these are the biggest trees on earth, reaching more than ninety metres in height and nine metres in diameter, and among the oldest, easily reaching back 1,800 years. Before loggers got to them in the 1850s, they filled an area of 850,000 hectares, now much reduced. Those trees that are left are protected within Giant Sequoia National Monument and Sequoia

National Forest and by a scattering of state reserves in California and southwest Oregon. Alarmingly, a report from the U.S. National Park Service issued in draft form in June 2021 declared that up to one-tenth of all sequoias were destroyed in a single fire, the Castle fire of 2020, even though the sequoias were thought to be fire-immune (or at least highly resistant). The trunk of one of the giants was still burning in May 2021, months after the fire was reported out. On the other hand (there always seems to be an other hand in these matters) the staff at California's Big Basin Redwoods State Park found that the forest was recovering nicely a year after the devastating 2020 CSU Complex fire, a fire that completely destroyed the park infrastructure and dozens of vehicles.

Outside British Columbia, the crown jewel of temperate rainforests (to use the U.S. Forest Service's own description), is Alaska's Tongass National Forest, a massive and hard to reach 68,000 square kilometres of almost entirely pristine forest, including massive groves of old-growth western red cedar and Alaska cedar, Sitka spruce, and hemlock. It is isolated enough to be home to many scarce animals and plants, and more brown bears than you can shake a salmon at. Tour guides will take you to see easily found otters, beaver, schools of wild salmon, and, in the fjords, orcas. Tongass is more than a forest. It contains thousands of small islands, streams, and brooks, fjords, lush valleys flanked by mountains. You can also think of it as the poster child for the U.S. Forest Service's Roadless Rule, which protects millions of hectares from human predation. And you can think of it as endangered, since Alaska's governor, with accomplices in the Trump administration in 2020, contemplated opening the forest to logging, mining, and hydroelectric dams, or what the state numbingly calls "active resource management.[89] These outrages were scrubbed by Biden in 2021, but whether the future is really secure depends on how presidential politics will play out.

Temperate rainforests are found in many other places, notably the Valdivian rainforest of southwestern South America (Chile, extending into Argentina), as well as Japan, parts of the Ozarks, New Zealand, and elsewhere. In Tasmania, the Tarkine forest, home to the extraordinary Huon pines, is the largest temperate rainforest in the southern hemisphere, and its trees some of the oldest (a few were saplings before Julius Caesar was born). Huon pines grow very slowly, maybe a millimetre a year, and they don't reach sexual maturity until they are somewhere between six hundred and eight hundred years old. As in many such forests, the miners and loggers are nibbling away in the Tarkine too, and the forest is a mere remnant of what it used to be.

Japan's Yakushima forest, beloved of folklorists, has cedars even older, at least 2,000 years and possibly much more. *New York Times* correspondent Hanya Yanagihara published an elegant description in 2018:

> The east side [of Yakushima Island] is semitropical: the road is edged with giant bromeliads and chusan palm and camellia bushes whose fallen petals paint the tarmac with fuchsia. There are dragonfruit trees, with their cacti-like, three-planed leaves and spiny pink fruits, and trees bearing two different kinds of oranges—the sour-sweet ponkan and the thick-skinned, meatier tankan—that, along with flying fish, are the island's culinary specialty. But just ten kilometers south is the 400-hectare Shiratani Unsuikyo Ravine. Here, atop the 800-meter mountain, the air is damp and chilly, and smells sharp and piney and sweet, and in place of palms and succulents are trees, so many that from the air, the area appears as a dense block of dark green, like an occluded tourmaline. The trees are, most of them, Cryptomeria japonica, a cedar-like species endemic to Japan known as sugi. What makes

this forest exceptional, though, is that many of its trees are yaku sugi, which means they are at least 1,000 years old, and some are jomon sugi, which means they are thought to be at least 2,200 years old.[90]

New Zealand's North Island has Waipoua Forest, the largest remaining stands of kauri trees, a species unique to the island, some of them immense: Te Matua Ngahere, more than fifty metres tall and sixteen metres in girth, is thought to be somewhere between two and three thoussand years old. Kauri trees are protected from logging, but there are, rarely, pieces of kauri wood that turn up in exotic wood warehouses; these are from trees that were buried in floods and covered with peat bogs, and only recently excavated. Lucky woodworkers might get a small piece more than 40,000 years old.

(IV) DECIDUOUS HARDWOODS

Henry Longfellow, in the prelude to his famous tearjerker *Evangeline*, had this to say of the place from which his melancholy heroine was expelled:

> *This is the forest primeval. The murmuring pines and the hemlocks,*
> *Bearded with moss, and in garments green, indistinct in the twilight,*
> *Stand like Druids of eld, with voices sad and prophetic,*
> *Stand like harpers hoar, with beards that rest on their bosoms.*

Longfellow was writing as a poet should, for his grist was gloom. His story was both a romance and a tragedy and tragedies were the province of the Druids of the Elder Days. But as a silviculturist, he missed his mark.

Acadie, where Evangeline grew up, did have its share of murmuring pines and hemlocks, and some of them would have been bearded with moss, but they would have been a small part of the glorious deciduous forest that covered most of northeastern North America at the time of the scattering of the Acadians: a temperate jumble of broadleaf hardwoods (oaks and beech and maple and birch) along with hemlock and tamarack and pines. Forest yes. Primeval? Not really. Primary forest, possibly, before the loggers came.

The dominant species were, and still are, sugar maple and American beech. Yellow birch and ash are scattered throughout, as are white and red oaks and poplar, elms, a few of which are left. Eastern hemlock and white pine are common, and so are red and white spruce, with sarsaparilla and wintergreen less so. A smaller subset would be the deciduous forests on the northern shores of Lakes Ontario and Erie, and to the west, of Lake Huron. Species there include the tulip tree, the cucumber tree, the black gum, blue ash, and walnut, magnolia, sycamore, and silver maple. To the south, the northern hardwoods shade into oak-hickory forests of the lower U.S. latitudes. The understory is mostly regenerating trees, plus shrubs such as striped maple, mountain maple, beaked hazelnut, fly-honeysuckle, hobblebush, and alternate-leaved dogwood. Typical ferns include hay-scented fern, New York fern, northern beech fern, evergreen wood fern, and Christmas fern.

The sugar maples, the beeches, and the poplars are the trees that give the forest its extravagantly vivid colours in the fall; the maples ranging from pinkish through brilliant reds to scarlet, the beeches golden yellows and then lustrous browns. These colours are not accreted so much as revealed. As the trees slow down their photosynthesis to enter dormancy for the winter, the chlorophyll, the green pigment, is lost, and the other colours, hitherto hidden, are revealed. This is the Little Death of winter.

The leaves are stripped of their green coating, and fall into senescence and then death. Until the trees shake themselves awake again in the spring.

We once owned a small piece of this paradise, in the Ontario midlands a few hundred kilometres north of Lake Ontario and just south of the wilderness park called Algonquin. Our piece was less than fifty hectares, just a freckle on the landscape. On its southern boundary, some feckless previous landowner had planted a few hectares of Scotch pine, in the forlorn hope that they would grow straight enough to be cut and sold for Christmas trees, but they were out of their climate comfort zone, and the venture failed. He then sold the land to a fellow who used the old barn on the property to dismantle stolen cars, and who had scant interest in forests of any kind, except for concealment. We bought it from him. He was in jail and didn't need the land anymore.

Beyond the crooked Scotch pines was an open field on a steep hill, and from the top we could turn and look back, to the south, a very long vista, wave after wave of rolling hills covered in the fall in reds and scarlet and brilliant yellows against the deep greens of the conifers, stretching down to the lake country around Peterborough, before petering out in farmland and villages, all the way down to the Lake Ontario. To the north of the field (which itself contained isolated maples in extravagant fall colours), stretching to our northern boundary and beyond for eight hundred kilometres and more, maybe a thousand, was a dense forest of sugar maples and oaks, white birch, and ash. Most of these were fifteen or twenty-five metres tall, and slender; this was no virgin forest, having been logged and cleared for farmland in the late nineteenth century, and the regrown trees were not much more than a hundred years old. In this, our little stand was typical enough. Here, as elsewhere, not many old-growth northern hardwoods are left. The land was cleared either for timber harvesting or for farming, and then left to regrow when farming moved west. While the trees were young, they were vigorous. The canopy twenty five meters overhead was dense enough to keep the forest floor clear, and for a year or two a band of timber wolves took up residence not far away, preying on the hapless white-tailed deer in the deep winter snows. On the edge of our property, in a ravine, was a small stand of massive first-growth hemlocks, and on the eastern boundary a row of old-growth beech along a fence line, left alone to prosper. Longfellow would have been well pleased.

Every eco-region in both hemispheres, outside deserts and the tropics, has pockets of such deciduous forest. There are thought to be almost eight million square kilometres worldwide. A few grow in the southern hemisphere, in parts of South America, in Africa, and even Australia. But the largest by far are in the northern hemisphere, stretching across North America, Europe, parts of Russia, and into China, both Koreas, and Japan. In North America these forests are variously called the Great Lakes–St. Lawrence forest, the Acadian forest, the northern deciduous forest, or the northern hardwood forest. In Canada, northern hardwoods, often mixed with boreal species, stretch from southeastern Manitoba to the Gaspé Peninsula in the St. Lawrence Delta. In the U.S., they are native to New England, New York, and Pennsylvania, and west to Minnesota. The New England Acadian forest covers most of northern New England, New Brunswick, Prince Edward Island, and Nova Scotia. In Russia, they are generally just called "the forest." This forest is much smaller than the taiga, but big enough, because Russia itself is big enough. It is found in a wedge from the Baltic republics to the Urals, and then beyond as far as Novosibirsk in central Siberia, before dipping to the Mongolian border. Endemic are pines and hemlock, maples, beech and oak, and birch, endless stands of yellow and paper birch.

Much more than the taiga, these forests are central to Russia's understanding of its landscape and its people. Many a Russian poet has matched Longfellow, both in his melancholy and his sentimentality, on the endless woods. Many of the Russian stories revolve around the Volga, the longest river in Europe, which ambles first through the southern taiga and then these immense deciduous forests, the home of so much gloomy history. Trotsky, from his lonely Mexican exile, wrote eloquently of "a people that geography had condemned to a life of savage individualism, condemned and thinly scattered in this inhospitable place, who found their community on the great rivers." Russia, he believed, was the loneliest country on earth; small hamlets huddled in an immense forest wilderness that the folk legends filled with demons and wild wolves. Chance meetings on the river were the occasion of orgies of good fellowship. Trotsky always believed that Russia's "natural communalism," such as he thought it was, was born on the Volga's banks. That may be, for most of Russian history these forests held more than half the population, and other writers found different instincts there: the peasant working with an axe must coax a living with infinite slow labour from the grudging soil. The forest teaches caution. Behind every tree may lie danger. It also teaches slyness, for one might hide in its depths. The forest is a refuge and a trap.

Near the shores of the Volga, this famous forest now looks forlorn, consisting mostly of stunted spruce, alder, a few birch. Most of the hardwoods have disappeared into the sawmills of Tver, and there are few oaks left.[91]

Longfellow lived near the coast of Maine, at a time when pristine wilderness really did still exist in the Americas, just as it did before the European invaders arrived with their axes and draught animals and a desire to do what their ancestors had already done to much of Europe: clearing it for farmland, leaving only managed forests, suitable for wildlife and hunting, less than 1 per cent of the original. The northern hardwoods still cover huge swathes of countryside, but less than they used to, for logging and farming have taken their toll. Just as on our own property, 90 per cent of North American hardwoods have been logged at least once, recently enough that forests defined as "first growth" hardly exist any longer.

Now that the farmers have (mostly) moved on for less hilly, more easily tillable and pesticide-receptive lands further west, and now that fall foliage tours are drawing revenue almost as steadily as logging (and with a wider distribution), efforts are under way to restore at least part of this forest. With some, partial, success.

In Europe, as indicated, deciduous forests have been exploited since prehistoric times for wood-pasture (that is, grazing), agroforestry and timber, as well as for hunting, and only a single per cent of the original remains. Studies on the few relic patches that remains suggest restoration is slow and halting, and limited due to past disturbances and management practices. In fact, hardly anyone cared enough to try to fix what had been wrought despite the occasional banning of practices such as wood-pasture. In North America, again as suggested, logging and farming cut out most of the existing forest. As cities grew and farms diminished, parts of the forest were left on their own to regrow. Test plots, such as at the Hubbard Brook Experimental Forest, within the White Mountain National Forest in New Hampshire, showed the limits of this approach. The forests are too fragmented, with most patches isolated by urban sprawl and highways, to be able to regenerate easily. When they do, the quality of the forest is poor, the soil too depleted, the diversity of species too small, the habitat too sparse.

Generally, passive restoration can work in "partially logged or disturbed forests (e.g., stochastic events such as a wind storm, or the ice storm in Canada in 1998) . . . The soils in these forests have kept most of their original nutrient and hydrological properties and remain favourable for natural regeneration. Passive regeneration can be advantageous in stands small in size and ideally surrounded by original native forests. Their capacity to reach the status of old growth forest may still be slow."[92]

Otherwise, foresters suggest, the only remedy might be "adaptive regeneration," which essentially means active management—control of invasive species, multiple seedings, fire management.[93] Then, the studies show, regeneration is possible. Restoration improves ecosystem functions, reintroduces lost species, and increases biodiversity.

And gives us back something that has been lost. That's no small benefit.

(V) TROPICAL MANGROVES

Across the Manda Channel from the sleepy Kenyan village of Lamu (no vehicles allowed, taxis are free-range donkeys) is Manda Island and the ruined Swahili town of Takwa, abandoned sometime in the seventeenth century and now just broken coral-brick walls, a pretty little mosque, and an enigmatic tomb. The ruins are in poor shape and getting worse: elephants and the roots of baobabs are not doing the remains any good.

I crossed to Takwa on a dhow manned by four Swahili teenagers. We wound in past the coral brickworks and in among the natural channels of the mangroves. While I poked about the ruins (keeping a wary eye out for a bull elephant said to be in musth) one of the lads stayed in the mangroves, dipping for tropical fish, which he stored in plastic bags. Later, he would take them on an eight-hour bus ride to Mombasa and sell them to a broker for the export market. It was how he made his living.

Such forests are found in the warm water of tropical oceans worldwide, on the American east coast from Florida to Argentina, on both coasts of Africa, and in many parts of Asia. Mangroves in Indonesia alone cover about three million hectares (30,000 square kilometres), along the country's 95,000-kilometre coastline. Brazil is second with somewhere around 13,898 square kilometres, though the number is uncertain and may be exaggerated. By far the largest single mangrove forest is the Sundarbans forest in the Bay of Bengal, on the estuaries of the Ganges, Brahmaputra, and Meghna rivers, which covers an estimated 10,000 square kilometres. By way of comparison, the second largest is Bahia, in northeastern Brazil, at 2,100 square kilometres. Other significant mangroves are Pichavaram in Tamil Nadu, India; Cedar Key in Florida; Godavari-Krishna Mangrove in Andhra Pradesh, India; the Gulf of Panama; the Indus river Delta in the Arabian Sea; the Belizean coastal mangroves; and the Manabin in Ecuador.

Mangroves are unlovely things, scrawny and very dense, with thick and impenetrable roots that are both deep in the tidal sands and above the water, rather resembling twisted stilts. They thrive in muddy and salty conditions that would be fatal to most other plants; to do this they have evolved a unique filtration system that keeps out most of the salt, and a complex root system that manages to keep the plants upright in the shifting tides and currents.[94]

Unlovely, but useful. They protect the coastline, and the people around Manda are fiercely protective in turn, having successfully fought off multiple attempts at "development," which mostly seemed to involve swimming pools and fancy bars for outsiders. Mangroves everywhere are nature's best buffer against erosion, acting as natural engineers. Their root systems trap massive amounts of sediment and, where they are dense enough and the groves large enough, have been known to create whole new islands. They offer a significant protection against typhoons and storm surges, and protect seagrasses and coral reefs by isolating harmful sediments. Rich breeding grounds for species above and below the tide line, they shelter fish, shrimp, molluscs, sea turtles, and dozens of nesting and migratory birds.[95] More than 200 million coastal people are dependent to some degree on the ecosystem services that mangroves provide. They can also sequester more carbon than other trees of their size. Area for area, they hold four times as much carbon as tropical rainforests.

Mangroves are also (or were also) critically endangered. Globally, mangrove forests cover 15.2 million hectares, but 3.6 million hectares have been destroyed since the 1980s, and until recently were still diminishing by one or 2 per cent annually. Culprits vary. In Indonesia, Thailand, and, to a degree, Mexico, mangroves have been cut to make way for coastal shrimp farms. In common with other forms of open-pen fish farming, the detritus from the farms poisons the environment. When the shrimpers move on, the mangroves seldom recover. Mangroves in the Caribbean are being cut for different reasons, mostly by charcoal manufacturers, there being little other natural energy on the islands. A 2007 paper in *Science* warned that we were facing "a world without mangroves." More recently, as Gabriel Popkin reported in *The Washington Post* in mid-2020, there has been some rare good news: "[Satellite pictures show that] mangrove loss has fallen dramatically in the past two decades, with human-caused mangrove destruction declining even faster than loss from natural causes."

Even so, climate change is still a threat. Mangroves are vulnerable to sea-level rise. While they can and do thrive with their feet in the water, it cannot be too deep, and its levels cannot change too quickly. A study in *Science* in June 2020 suggested that mangroves could adapt if the annual sea-level rise were limited to 6 to 7 millimetres a year. The "global mean rate of SLR is now 3.4 mm and is projected to exceed the threshold and reach 10 mm by 2100 under business-as-usual scenarios."

(VI) ACACIA FORESTS (AKA WATTLES)

Anyone who has been to the great plains of Africa (or, indeed, anyone who has seen any one of a thousand documentaries on African lions, wildebeest migrations, giraffe foraging, elephant wandering, and more) is familiar with the acacia tree. Like flat umbrellas in profile, they grow maybe ten metres tall, with sharp thorns and a mild toxin to discourage foraging, mostly successfully. They can even "warn" other acacias downwind of predation by emitting an ethylene compound that will in turn encourage downwind trees to increase their tannin production to make themselves unpalatable (giraffes will often eat their way upwind, one tree at a time, to prevent alarming neighbouring trees). In Australia, the only other place where they are endemic, acacias (known locally as wattles) are the second most common forest type, after the eucalyptus (or bluegum) forests; wattle groves cover almost a million square kilometres, not quite 10 per cent of the country's forested area.

The acacia was first identified by Linnaeus, the famously enduring taxonomist; he called the "type species" *A. nilotica*, after the place he first came across it. So far about 160 acacia lineages have been identified, all of them loosely associated with the pea family. In the early 2000s the various Australian acacias were found to be unrelated (or "not closely related") to the African varieties, and a grumpy academic dispute erupted as to what to call them. The name *racosperma* was proposed, and widely ridiculed by the Australians. In the end, the name acacia was kept, and the trees were divided into four lineages: two Australian (*Acaciella* and *Mariosousa*), and two African (*Vachelllia* and *Senegalia*). It is fair to say that this rancorous discussion caused barely a ripple outside its specialty. More than a thousand subspecies of acacias have been identified, though to be sure hardly anyone but severe taxonomists cares. When I was growing up in South Africa, we mostly just called them *doringbome*, or thorn trees.

Whatever they are called, acacias are critical to the semi-arid landscapes in which they are mostly found. Their mixed roots, a central stem going deep for groundwater and a wide root ball that serves to hold moisture and prevent erosion, are helpful in preventing desertification; at the same time, their leaves transpire very little water. They also help to stabilize rainfall and nourish soils. More interestingly, the trees go dormant and shed leaves in the rainy season, and then regrow them in the dry season. This curious cycle helps farmers because it doesn't compete with food crops for light, which means that the trees can be planted in fields, further conserving moisture, and it also means that seed pods and leaves are available as fodder when everything else is bare. They are mildly toxic, but only mildly: they are edible when needs must.

People of the forest

I ONCE HAD A RATHER embarrassing conversation about water with a Baka pygmy hunter in the tropical rainforest of Cameroon, the same person who had earlier shown me his spear and his bow, the tools of his craft. I knew that his people foraged for their foodstuffs, tubers like wild manioc, or hunted it with their poisoned arrows, but (bearing in mind those *E. coli*) where did they get drinking water? My informant at first looked incredulous, then started to laugh. Water? That was a knee-slapper! It rained every day! It fell on their heads every afternoon! Later, one of the band showed me a trick. He snapped a vine, a liana seemingly like all the others, and a litre or more of fresh perfumed water cascaded out, the forest equivalent of a roadside vending machine.

The World Wildlife Fund (WWF) has estimated that 300 million people worldwide live in forests, and 1.6 billion depend on forests for their subsistence or livelihood. These are mostly, but not always, tropical rainforests. There are forest dwellers in the deciduous forests, too, and even in the northern boreal forests, or taiga.

It's hard to know where these numbers come from. Various global estimates of forest dwellers range from one million to 250 million, to 500 million, to over one billion, depending on definitions and methodology.

A World Bank table breaks it down by region and the number of forest dwellers in it: thirty to sixty million in Central Africa, 140 million in Southeast Asia, 481–579 million in Asia Pacific, 805 million in tropical rainforests, forty million in Latin America and the Caribbean, thirty million in the Amazon basin, and sixty million in various boreal forests. But these overlap. The tropical rainforest number includes most of the others except the boreal forest.

In a general sense, the Food and Agriculture Organization points out, all people, including urban people, have *some* dependence on forests, at least for products such as construction wood and paper. How many of these actually rely on forests for their livelihoods? And how many of those actually live inside forests, either as hunter-gatherers or as cultivators, or live near forests, usually as farmers, but who use forest products every day, such as timber, medicines, bushfood, and fuel? Moreover, how many of the WWF's 300 million live near or in forests but are not directly dependent on them for sustenance? They may be involved in commercial logging, for example, thus generating income from forests rather than using them directly. Another World Bank research paper estimates that about 240 million people live in "predominantly forested ecosystems" and that roughly a quarter of the world's poor and 90 per cent of the poorest depend substantially on forests for their livelihoods.[96]

The WWF, hard-headed in some of its views but prone to sentimentality in others, is a proponent of a view widely shared among Western environmentalists that tropical rainforests are little more than "immense reservoirs of biodiversity—a wild and virgin milieu with only a few indigenous tribes who, before the arrival of the Europeans, were living happily and in equilibrium in an abundant, untouched paradise." This same sentiment was expressed in my introduction, but the above quote is from Alain Froment, a specialist in biological anthropology and human ecology at the Musée de l'Homme in Paris.[97] Froment led me to Julio Mercader, an anthropologist at George Washington University, who edited *Under the Canopy: The Archaeology of Tropical Rainforests*, and who has demonstrated that human interactions with, and modifications to, rainforests have been much more extensive, and much older, than conventional wisdom allowed. Humans have lived in and used rainforests for forty millennia, Mercader says, and have practised agriculture in them for at least three thousand years. Hunter-gatherers modify forests, too, sometimes directly through extensive foraging, and sometimes indirectly, by altering the mix of animals and plants that make up the forest itself.[98]

And this notion of a happy equilibrium between forest and people is grossly oversimplified. I have been prone to this myself. My notes on the regrettably few days I spent among the Baka pygmies of Gabon were not inaccurate, exactly, but lacked context, and made everything seem more comfortable than the more difficult reality would suggest.

I had asked one of my pygmy hosts, for example, how long her village had been where I had found it. She didn't really know, but said the community generally moved whenever someone died, or when foraging became difficult. How did they move? My notes say: "You just picked up the kids and the drums and the weapons and off you went. Where to build a new village? Wherever you liked. Who was to stop you? Find a likely clearing, drop your bundles, cut a few poles—home! The world was full of stuff. Food was everywhere . . . Hunting was not always successful, and there were accidents, but game was still plentiful. There was little to break, and therefore little to fix. Smoking meat and firewood gathering took some time, but not much. I tried to work out a typical day, a typical workload. Compared to Western farmers, I thought, these guys had it easy. Three, four hours a day and you were done. You had brought home the bacon and it was time to relax."

But this was naïve. It's no accident that population densities in hunter-gatherer lands are very low. Game is relatively abundant and hunting not arduous, but there is not enough edible greenery or tubers like manioc growing wild to sustain more than a sparse population, and consequently they must be constantly on the move as resources are depleted. Froment quotes another anthropologist, Serge Bahuchet, that "wise use [of edible vegetables] can feed small bands of mobile hunters-gatherers. But these groups must maintain a low fertility rate, usually with birth-spacing managed by a long breastfeeding period. If the size of the group increases, as happened recently for Pygmies as a result of health campaigns attempting to control transmissible diseases, collecting food becomes insufficient, and cultivation is the only choice."

Another problem is disease. A Western cliché is that early European explorers died in the tropics because they were unaccustomed to the many diseases found there, the implication being that the indigenous people had acquired immunity. Not so. Almost a quarter of the hunter-gatherer population suffers from infectious and debilitating diarrhea; some estimates suggest that the typical pygmy adult can suffer from as many as twenty parasitic diseases.[99] Even in my small sample, I saw boils, diseased teeth, and unhealed sores. Folk medicines weren't enough.

There are pygmies throughout the Central African rainforests, in Cameroon, both Congos, the Central African Republic, as well as Gabon, and perhaps 40,000 of them in Cameroon alone. They have intrigued outsiders for centuries, not just because they are so small (a substantial male reaches little more than a metre fifty), and not just because they were here first (all the Bantu tribes concede this), but because their culture is so particular, and because they adhere to it with a stubbornness that is a marvel. They adopted virtually nothing from the Bantu invaders, and when the Europeans came, the pygmies refused to have anything to do with their culture, either. Instead, they continued their in-turned, early Iron Age existence, rejecting not just technology (an achievement in itself) but the entire Western cosmology. For example, despite the pygmies having lived for centuries among the Bantu, a people and a culture as prone to violence and warfare as any other, none of the pygmy languages had a word for war, and violence was virtually unknown among them.

All this is changing, and quickly, since my last visit twenty years ago. Unlike many of the other isolated hunter-gatherers in the world's forests, the pygmies don't shun contact with outsiders. For the moment, their culture remains intact, but they are a gregarious people, and happy to socialize, and they are beginning to adopt outsider ways. They are trading more with the surrounding Bantu peoples than they used to. They are beginning to cultivate manioc, and not just forage for it. Missionaries have been moving among them, with some success. So have educators, some of them at odds with the missionaries. And medical people. As Froment put it, "the pace of change is accelerating. In a place called Le Bosquet, near Lomié, in south Cameroon, there is now a small town of 1,000 Baka Pygmies, with a church, a hospital, and a large private school. Many Pygmy groups now travel to Europe to perform music and dance, and bring back a lot of memories. Not far from Lomié, at Messea, a group of returnees decided to use the money they earned in Europe to build a dispensary, and to open it to Pygmies and Bantu."

Elsewhere, hunter-gatherers are smaller in numbers, more isolated, and more threatened. The World Bank study that was quoted earlier lists many hunter-gatherer people, like the Huli of Papua New Guinea, or the Yanomami on the Brazilian-Venezuelan border, as among the "very poor of the poor." Even more so are the various "uncontacted peoples," by which is meant tribes who are known but not visited, and who remain out of view of the societies that surround them. They would include the Toromona people living near the upper Madidi and Heath rivers in northwestern Bolivia, the Ayoreo and Pacahuaras people, also in Bolivia, the nearly seventy such isolated peoples in Brazil (including the Awa, the Kawahiva, and the Korubu), and the Sentinelese people on North Sentinel Island, one of the Andamans in the Bay of Bengal. Most of these groups are very small, numbering in the hundreds, not thousands. There may not be more than a hundred Sentinelese left. The Awa of Brazil are maybe 450, the Akuntsu just four by 2020.

What is to be their fate?

Many governments are wrestling with the problem of how to deal with fragile and isolated cultures. Recently, the phrase "uncontacted people" has fallen out of favour (who hasn't contacted who?) and has been largely replaced by "indigenous people in isolation" as better expressing some kind of cultural neutrality. Sometimes this self-isolation is voluntary, as it is among the Baka, but sometimes it is out of fear of conflict or exploitation, amply justified. And sometimes authorities keep them isolated, fearing the ravages of contagious diseases. The Bolivian government has set aside an "exclusive, reserved, and inviolable" section of the Madidi National Park for the exclusive use of the Toromona. Brazil tried for several decades to assimilate their reclusive cultures, but in 1987 set up the Department of Isolated Indians, and declared huge swathes of forest as "perpetually sealed off" (except, often, to loggers, land speculators, ranchers, and illegal poachers). By 2007, the last official survey I could find, there were sixty-seven such isolated groups in Brazil, up from forty in 2005. The National Geographic organization estimated the number was eighty-four by 2018.

The Sentinelese, who have always rejected attempts to contact them (sometimes with the lethal force of skilled hunters) are protected by the Indian Navy, which patrols the sea around their island and turns back any attempt by outsiders to interfere. The Andaman and Nicobar Islands

Protection of Aboriginal Tribes Act of 1956 still prohibits travel to the island and forbids any approach closer than five nautical miles because of the danger of contamination. The islanders have no natural immunity to outsider diseases. (Notoriously, in 2018 an American missionary, bent on bringing Jesus to what he apparently regarded as one of Satan's last strongholds, breached the perimeter and went ashore, having piously received all the immunizations he could think of. The islanders promptly killed him. The evangelical organization that sent him called him a martyr. The less forgiving called him an idiot.)

Elsewhere, too, contacting the uncontacted can have its hazards. In September 2020 a Brazilian expert on isolated Amazon tribes was shot in the heart and died in the far-western state of Rondonia, near the Bolivian border. Rieli Franciscato "cried out, pulled the arrow from his chest, ran fifty meters and collapsed, lifeless." This from a police officer who accompanied the expedition, in an audio recording posted on social media.

Some years ago I was talking to a Botswana government official in a café on the outskirts of Maun, near the Okavango delta. We were talking about the San, formerly misnamed as Bushmen, but the thoughts apply to hunter-gatherers everywhere. The official, Gosetsemang, had worked with the nomads years before, trying to settle them down. It wasn't easy. Their culture was fragile. Cutting into one part of it risked destroying the rest—it was all so interdependent. The problem, he said, is that nomads had little interest in time, the future, or the past. It was hard to explain to them how necessary it was for their children to adapt to new ways. They had never seen the need for adaptability. It wasn't that they were ignorant of the modern. They actively rejected it.

I remembered a phrase in a column by the American magazine editor Lewis Lapham. He had been talking about how their schools had failed modern Americans, leaving them without a sense of their own history, or of human history. "People unfamiliar with the world in time," he'd written, "find themselves marooned in the ceaselessly dissolving and therefore terrifying present."

I recounted this to Gosetsemang.

"No," he said, "it's not like that." He sat quietly for a long while, groping for meaning. "Elephants," he said finally, "are easy. You manage the population, and balance their needs against the needs of the human population, and out of that comes policy. But what is correct policy towards other cultures, fragile cultures, the nomads among us? They are not livestock to be managed. We are not their parents, their guardians, their custodians, or their keepers. Do we risk destroying them by forcing change on them? This is one of the great dilemmas of all Africa—how do we preserve the old cultures while accepting the new?"

"Perhaps," I said, "these are loaded terms. Instead of speaking of the loss of culture, or the destruction of nomadic bands, why not speak of the adaptability of culture, the readiness to accept new ways? If a San throws away his bow and arrow and drives a tractor instead, is he any less San?"

He looked wistful. "It's easy for you," he said. "It's not your culture at risk."

I remembered something a history teacher of mine had once said. Monica Wilson had argued that it was the readiness of cultures to borrow inventions and accept new ideas and techniques that built civilizations. Cross-fertilization worked in politics, just as it did in the arts. Peoples who failed to adapt to changing circumstances were doomed to extinction. The more efficient economy always drives out the less efficient. Hunter-gatherers become pastoralists; subsistence farmers become migrant labourers in an industrial economy. In this definition, the pygmies and the San and the many uncontacted, romanticized as people who have lived in harmony with the land for millennia, were doomed by their own inaction, as fish die when drought dries up the streams.

"I'm still thinking mostly of the children," Gosetsemang said again, after a long silence. "That's why we intervene."

"My point is that traditional cultures are doomed whether you intervene or not," I said.

"Then we may as well do it right," he said.[100]

Wood and its uses

The Staple of the Stuff is so exquisitely fine, that no silkworm is able to draw near anything so fine a Thread. So that one who walks about with the meanest stick, holds a piece of Nature's Handicraft, which far surpasses the most elaborate Woof or Needle Work in the World.

– Nehemiah Grew, plant botanist, physician, and pioneer of fingerprinting.

REW WAS ENRAPTURED ABOUT the structure of wood. He was seeing it close-up for the first time though a new invention, the microscope.[101] Inside the bark of the tree, and inside the phloem, and inside the cambium, is indeed the *Staple of the Stuff.* Wood, after all, is what trees are made of.

But there are woods, and woods, and then more woods: lumbermen conventionally divide the *Stuff* into three broad categories, softwood, hardwood, and engineered wood, the first two further subdivided into sapwood and heartwood.

But these divisions are not as simple as they sound. Hardwood isn't necessarily hard, nor softwood soft. Balsa, for example, a lightweight and fragile wood used for model airplanes, is defined as a hardwood, although it is softer than such softwoods as pine and spruce. On the other hand, yew is called soft, although it is harder than many hardwoods. This soft-hard business is just convention, and measures nothing in particular: the wood from conifers is called soft, and often is, and the wood from deciduous trees is called hard, and it usually is. The differences lie elsewhere. Softwoods are generally simple in structure, and more uniform throughout (technically, their wood cells are only of one kind, called tracheids). Hardwoods are more complex, not so surprising since they evolved later than conifers. They also contain cells called "vessels," which are like pores if seen in cross-section. These vessels can be in a tight band in the annual growth ring, or more diffuse, with smaller pores and a greater proportion of wood fibre (which gives the wood strength). They vary greatly in size. They can be microscopic in some species, or larger and easily seen in others.

Sapwood is thus called for obvious reasons: it is the transport mechanism for the sap, that is, for nutrients flowing up from root to trunk and branch.

Heartwood, for its part, is so called because of its position, not because of its importance to the tree. In fact, some trees can live on, albeit weakened, even if the heartwood has rotted away. We once saw this for ourselves. We had an old spruce on our property in Nova Scotia that one day took an alarming lean toward the house. We engaged a forester to take the thing down. When we looked at the stump later, it consisted of bark and a thin layer of sapwood; the rest was crumbling, a Mar-a-Lago for mice but not much use for holding up the tree. Yet the tree had been alive, if weakened, when it was toppled. Some species, such as chestnut or locust, grow heartwood very early in their lives, and so have only a thin layer of sapwood. Others take more time, like maple and ash, and thus have thick layers of sapwood.

In its makeup, wood is a compound of just two materials, cellulose and lignin (or, if you want to be picky, three substances: cellulose, hemicellulose, and lignin, but hemicellulose is just cellulose weak enough to have sand kicked in its face; it has an amorphous and seemingly random structure with little strength).

The best way to think about wood is as bundles of minute straws glued together, the straws being cellulose fibres and the glue lignin. Put another way, the lignin is the matrix in which the cellulose is bound. Stronger woods have more lignin, because more glue. Extra lignin makes a wood like padauk very strong; the grain of padauk is not very different from maple, but the wood is stronger and heavier because there is so much additional lignin. Sapwood, the living outer layer of the wood, has less lignin because it needs to transport moisture; heartwood ("retired" sapwood, the heart of a tree), is lignin-rich.

In addition, the thickness of the "straws" of cellulose can vary widely; there can be between two and four hundred fibres per centimetre of wood, depending on the species. Thicker straws make for stronger wood, and thick straws separate a strong wood like oak from a weak one like alder. The combination of cellulose and lignin gives wood its strength; the cellulose fibres are strong in tension (that is, they resist efforts to pull them apart lengthwise), and the lignin resists compression (being pushed together). In lignin-rich woods, a small piece no more than two inches in diameter and twelve or so inches long can support a weight of twenty tons without buckling.

These things are important for those who use wood in their work. It is useful to know how hard a wood is, not in the hardwood/softwood dichotomy sense, but as a measure of how easy it is to work with, and for what it can be used.

Until recently, density was often measured by the Janka hardness test, which tests a wood's resistance to denting and wear. (Gabriel Janka, its inventor, measured the force required to imbed a steel ball of 0.444 inches halfway into a sample of wood. Why that number and not an even half inch? Alas, Janka is no longer around to ask—he died in 1932. Possibly it was the size of the steel ball he happened to have on hand; none of the texts seem to know, or care.) The USDA Forest Products Lab lists sugar maple at 1450 on the Janka scale, Osage orange at 2040, Ipe at 3680, and lignum vitae at a massive 4500. The Janka measurement has now fallen out of favour, not surprising since proponents of the metric system were always impatient at the arcane process Janka had cooked up. Density is now more usually measured by kilograms per cubic metre (kgm^3). Examples are white oak at 770 kgm^3, ash 650, balsa 110, bluegum 1000, ebony 1100, and juniper 560.[102]

The density number is important not just because it measures hardness per se, a useful thing to know in itself, but because it predicts the difficulty in sawing, nailing, sanding, and carving a given piece of wood. How easily does the wood break? How much weight will it take? How much will it bend? Is it hard enough to blunt chisels and saw blades? Does it crack when dried? Lumbermen and woodworkers know these things by experience, and by feel. Even so, the texts and encyclopedias of wood will always list the specific gravity (or density) of the woods they cover, a clue to their best use. Poplar, which is not very dense, is good for plywood but not for fine furniture. Balsawood won't do for a settee, but is perfect for small models. Super-dense black ironwood is impossible for furniture but perfect for small turned objects. Obviously, there is no magically desirable density. The number should be high if you want to bridge a long gap with a wooden board, but it can be low if the piece is wanted for a decorative panel. A block for a sailing ship should be as dense as possible; a carver will look for a number that makes the wood more malleable. The makers of fine furniture want the sweet spot in the middle, hard enough to be durable, soft enough to work easily: walnut, oak, maple, and birch all fit the bill. Mahogany and cherry are also medium-dense hardwoods, wasteful for firewood but great for a chest of drawers, although not for its back, where the wood's beauty won't be seen. Engineers will have one set of desirable criteria, woodworkers another.

Those who work with wood can afford to be choosy: there are, at last count, 60,065 species of trees on earth. True, many of those are unsuitable: either rare, inaccessible, or endangered, or would make poor workpieces, either too hard or too soft, too rigid or too pliable, or merely boring. Even so, the wood encyclopedias list several hundred trees suitable for whatever it is you want wood to do. Magazines devoted to high-end furniture-making typically list about fifty, depending on where they are published and what the local supply is.

Best woods for chopsticks: chestnut chopsticks for wealth, black persimmon for longevity. Also cherry, sandalwood, or paulownia, sometimes called "the other balsa," lightweight but strong.

Best woods for music: drums are sometimes made from beech, which is said to yield a tone between those of maple and birch, otherwise the most popular woods for drums. Paulonia is good for electric-guitar bodies. Violins, as we shall see, use mostly maple and spruce but sometimes and in places ebony, rosewood and willow. Mahogany, maple and ash for guitars. Pianos use multiple woods for various parts; birch, maple, oak, mahogany, ebony, spruce, and rosewood are common. Orchestral woodwind instruments are hardly ever made from wood any more, but they used to be, often from African blackwood (*Dalbergia melanoxylon*) but also from the fruitwoods cherry and pear. The traditional Australian didgeridoo was made from a eucalyptus branch hollowed out by termites. Chakte Viga, a tropical hardwood from Mexico, is now scarce but was used for many instruments; wooddatabase. com says "it has great acoustic/tonal qualities, [and] it turns like a dream."

Best woods for the Bible: cedar and thuya for the Temple, shittim for the Tabernacle; acacia for the Ark. Shittim wood, from the shittah tree, was probably also an acacia variant. Aspen was supposedly used for the cross itself, but that was a later European fable, for aspens were scarce in the Middle East. The Romans typically used olive or acacia for their crucifixions. The Eastern Christian tradition says three woods were used, cedar, pine, and cypress. Dogwood is also a popular candidate. Alas, when Saint Helena, the mother of Constantine the Great, came across the True Cross in 326, she neglected to jot down the species. The redbud, a.k.a. the Judas tree, was the prop used by Judas to commit suicide; the tree produces prolific deep pink flowers in the spring, but whether that's why Judas chose to hang himself from one is of course unknown. The Crown of Thorns was supposedly made from the Rose of Jericho, a.k.a. the Resurrection tree; there is a pretty little legend in my own family that an ancestor who had helped pillage the Holy Land in Richard Lionheart's army brought back a seedling Rose of Jericho to plant in France, in the village of Saint Jean d'Angely, near Cognac. Unsurprisingly, no evidence for this afforestation exists, and indeed, such plants were hardly rare even then.

Best woods for water divining ("dousing"): hazel or willow. The Druids used yew to douse for lost property, but it was no good for water.

Best wood and trees for food: fruit and sap, mostly; the bark, leaves, pollen and flowers sometimes; roots and tubers occasionally; the actual wood not so much. All the fruit trees, obviously. Coffee trees. Tea trees. The cacao tree for chocolate. Apple and pear trees for cider and perry. Olives for their oil. Drinks and syrups: chestnut and butternut sap can be drunk unprocessed. The Russians have traditionally made a beer from birch, called *medovukha*, the sap fermented with a little honey added. Maple syrup: not just the sugar maple, but the black and silver maples, too. Sycamore makes a dark, intense syrup, not to everyone's taste. Nut trees include chestnuts, beechnuts (often bitter but sometimes mild and pleasant), walnuts, acorns, and pine nuts. Pine cones, or at least seeds of the female cones, can be shelled and roasted. Male cones are too strongly flavoured, but their pollen is edible. The inner bark of many trees is edible, birches, for example. American aboriginals dried and ground it for flour, or cut it into strips, like noodles. Beech bark can be pulverized and eaten, though no one would claim to actually like it. Maple bark can be eaten raw or cooked. Poplar and aspen inner bark, too, and willow. Slippery elm bark is gluey but edible. The inner black pine bark is rich in vitamins A and C. Some of the cedars have edible bark: Jacques Cartier was given bark from the eastern white cedar by his native guides, and he used it on their advice to cure scurvy. Occasionally leaves can be eaten. Linden leaves, when they are young in the spring, are good raw or lightly cooked. Fresh from the tree, beech leaves resemble a mild cabbage, though softer in texture. Steep them in gin and you get a pale yellow liqueur called beech leaf noyau. Sassafras leaves make good salads. Occasionally roots are edible: sassafras tea is well known, fragrant and pleasant to drink.[103]

Seepings from the sapodilla tree, called chicle sap, was used for centuries to make chewing gum; there are references to it in ancient Greek literature. Indigenous North Americans chewed the resin from spruce sap; the first commercial chewing gum, developed and sold in 1848 by one John. B. Curtis, was called the State of Maine Pure Spruce Gum.

Other woods are used indirectly. Oak barrels from Limousin and redwoods from California are used to mature wine. Slats of beech are used in fermentation tanks for Budweiser beer. Beech logs are burned to dry the malt in some German beers, and to smoke Westphalian hams and sausages.

There is a wood pathology called Lignophagia, or the abnormal desire to chew and eat wood. Children will occasionally do it, for reasons not well understood. In any case, it could cause problems: humans cannot digest cellulose or lignin. Eating tiny bits of wood can be manageable, but chunks too large for the pyloric sphincter are problematic.[104]

Best woods for charcoal (not just barbecuing, but for smelting, too): most woods will do, although the most common are alder, oak, and maple. Hickory makes famously great charcoal for cooking food, but doesn›t coppice very well, and if you are trying, say, to make horseshoes, its pleasant aroma doesn't signify. To quote a blacksmith: "I work through a lot of charcoal in my forge and I try to do single species burns just for experimentation. I've never tried soft wood on account of not having any, but of the hardwoods that I use they are mostly fairly equal. The only things that have stood out are that oak sparks a lot and generates the most clinker, sweet chestnut fragments easily and doesn't burn away completely (meaning you have to constantly rake out unburnt fuel). I'm using birch at the moment and that is great, beech was also great, mixed batch of alder and London plane [a version of sycamore] was pretty good too."[105]

Best woods for medicine: Most of these fall into the deep and rather opaque vat of folklore, and may or may not be regarded as credible by those who study these things. One real medication, though, is derived from the Pacific yew. The anti-cancer drug called Taxol (generic paclitaxel), is still the only drug to have needed an environmental impact statement, since the Pacific yew, found mostly in America, is scarce and large-scale harvesting would push it onto the endangered list; drug makers have urged the timber industry to stop logging practices destructive to yew trees, so far with moderate results. Taxol is currently on the World Health Organization's Model List of Essential Medicines as a cytotoxic drug that blocks cancer cell growth by stopping cell division; it is used to treat (not cure) breast cancer, ovarian cancer, pancreatic cancer, and AIDS-related Kaposi's sarcoma.

The leaves of the Moringa tree (sometimes called the drumstick tree or the horseradish tree) have been used for centuries for their anti-inflammatory and antifungal properties, and these days, too, as an antiviral medication and an antidepressant. Yew wood, slightly poisonous, was used to induce abortions. Ash wood was used for warts or rickets: rub your warts with a strip of bacon, and put the bacon into a cut in the ash bark (the warts will transfer to the tree). Balm of Gilead *(populus candicans)* was used to heal wounds and, taken internally, as an expectorant. Camphor oil, extracted from camphor trees by steam distillation, is (still) used topically for pain, irritation, and itchiness; classically it was used to ward off plague. The main ingredients of the proprietary Vicks VapoRub were camphor, menthol, thymol, and emollients; it was banned in the United States until its makers agreed to limit the camphor content to 11 per cent because of its toxicity. Cascara is used as a laxative. Cassia, sometimes known as the golden shower tree, is a mild laxative. Periwinkle is for the brain, bilberry for the intestines. The bark of the chinchona tree produces quinine, used to combat malaria, although it has been supplanted by the artificial compound called chloroquine. Clove oil was a traditional medicine for toothache. Curare is sometimes (but very carefully!) used as a muscle relaxant. Eucalyptus is both a germicide and an expectorant. Lignum vitae was used to treat venereal diseases; there was a brief trade in lignum vitae shavings in the bordellos of Europe before its evident lack of efficacy drove it from favour. A shrub that grows in deep forest glades is called *chaste aignel*, sometimes called *agnus castus*, and in English the "chaste tree." According to Bartholomaeus Anglicus, writing in 1556, it suppressed unseemly feminine lust: "When women are too anxious for the company of men, when they have too much ardour for making love, a fumigation is done from below and they are immediately healed."[106] The seeds of the strychnos nux-vomica tree, sometimes called the vomiting nut or the poison nut tree (not surprisingly, since it yields strychnine) is a homeopathic catchall remedy for diseases of the digestive tract, disorders of the heart, circulatory system malfunctions, diseases of the eye, and lung disease. The ground bark of the red African ironwood treats headaches, the star anise colic and constipation, and the wild black cherry bronchitis. In 2020, the American football star Tom Brady was touting an "immunity blend supplement" for the COVID-19 virus: larch extract mixed with elderberry.[107]

Best woods for biofuels: willow and poplar are fast-growing trees that can be densely planted. They can also be "coppiced," the trunk cut close to the ground every three to five years or so. This is called "short-rotation coppicing."

Best woods for paper: wood pulp comes softwoods like spruce, pine, fir, larch and hemlock, and hardwoods like eucalyptus, poplar, aspen, and birch.

Best woods for tool handles: hickory, very strong and flexible. Oak, high-density and durable. Ash. Sugar maple. Yellow birch. Hickory was also used for cartwheels. Greenheart is as strong as any wood, with exceptional rot resistance. Most woodworkers avoid it for their projects, however. "It is a pain to work with. It's hard to glue, hard to saw, and it's also hard to find."[108]

Best wood for clothing: Dutch clogs were made from alder, willow, or poplar. The tottery footwear of the classical geisha, called *geta*, was made from paulonia. In the Renaissance fashionable Venetian women wore *chopines*, which were similar in style and just as impractical, though generally made from cork. Bark cloth, once common in Asia, Africa, and the Pacific Rim, was made primarily from the paper mulberry or the breadfruit tree (also a mulberry) and sometimes in southern and eastern

Africa from the *mutuba*, or Natal fig. The cloth is made by beating water-soaked strips of the inner bark into sheets, which are then made into household items or clothing. Pulped beechwood is used to make modal, a rayon-like fabric.

Best woods for art: the pigment bistre is made from boiled beechwood soot. Beechwood tablets were commonly used for writing, before paper. (The English word *book* is derived from the Old Norse word for beech tree.) Sap green is made from buckthorn berries, and olive green from, well, olives. Grey is from wood ash. Larch, a.k.a. tamarack and hackmatack, was used to produce the nine-foot-tall Shigir Idol, the oldest wooden artifact carved by man known to exist, 11,500 years old, and uncovered on the eastern slopes of the Urals, now come to rest in the Sverdlovsk regional museum. The intricate patterns incised into its wood have so far defied interpretation, guesses ranging from a creation myth or a navigational aid to mythological creatures or even a "keep out" notice to rival tribes, threats being a venerable human device. The famous sculptures of the Luba tribes of west Africa were made from a variety of woods, with no species dominating but bubinga and iroko were common. The linenfold panelling in English Tudor houses was almost always oak, although walnut and lime were used in the decorative bits. The rood screens that separated the altar from the rest of the nave in medieval churches were sometimes oak but often limewood; the word *rood* means a figure crucified, and some English churches carried disturbingly grotesque depictions of the agony of the cross. The marvellous carved panels in the reception rooms at Bletchley Park were made of various fruitwoods and oak. The cosmologically complicated carved granary doors of the Dogon people of southern Mali were incised on planks of acacia, and more rarely, iroko. Wood used for marquetry was often the clean white of boxwood and the clean black of ebony, and woods that stained well, like sycamore. But the Japanese were more inventive. They used a wide variety of woods in their intricate marquetry designs, including dogwood, the spindle tree, the Japanese wax tree, and cherry; the katsura tree, sometimes known as the caramel tree for its beguiling odour, was used for its black wood, mulberry and the lacquer tree for yellow, the camphor tree for brown, the black walnut for purple, the Japanese cucumber tree for blue and Chinese cedar for red.

The Arts and Crafts movement, William Morris, then Greene and Greene and Stickley, used oak, usually stained a gorgeous reddish color, and walnut for the larger pieces, a lot of of pear and ebony for accents, more walnut for the plugs the style demanded.

Totem poles of the Pacific Northwest were almost always cedar, soft and easy to carve and rot resistant; mostly western red cedar, but sometimes yellow cedar; cedar trees were everywhere until loggers and shingle/shake makers turned up to hack them down. French *boiserie*, a more elaborate version of English wainscotting (which itself could be elaborate enough) used mostly native woods like lime and wild cherry for the panels (lime has nothing to do with the fruit; lime trees are plane trees by another name). As trade with the Orient and the Americas became more common, decorators for the wealthy turned to the more exotic woods appearing in entrepôts across Europe. From Asia came amboyna (burl from the padauk tree), violetwood (a.k.a. purpleheart) from South America, rosewood from Brazil, thuya from Morocco, satinwood from the West Indies and Sri Lanka (it is also called Ceylon satinwood), mahogany and tulipwood from Brazil. Limewood, because of its soft and even texture that made it ideal for intricate carvings and detail work, remained popular for altarpieces and screens; the most famous examples would include the massive altarpiece at the Saint Jakob Kirche, in the medieval Bavarian town of Rothenburg ob der Tauber, carved in 1499–1504 by the master craftsman Tilman Riemenschneider, and the High Altar of the Virgin Mary, carved by Jörg Zürn in 1613–1616, at Saint Nikolaus Münster in Uberlingen, on the shores of Lake Constance.[109]

What wood was used in the eight-foot-tall Face of Lucca statue of the crucifixion has never been recorded, but then it was supposed to have been carved by an angel when Nicodemus found himself unable to complete it, mere days after he helped lay Jesus in his tomb. Whatever it was, the famous statue was made from wood grown in the eighth or ninth century, so the angel took his own sweet time.

Best woods for
fine furniture

TAKE A MOMENT WITH MASTER cabinetmaker Leonard Michalik in a storehouse of wonders, a 30,000-square-foot warehouse containing ranks and stacks and piles of local and exotic woods from hither and all the yons, each piece legitimately harvested, but some now desperately endangered. Often, when craftsmen such as Len come here, they can be seen rummaging in the racks of wood, if rummaging is the right word for sorting samples perhaps three metres long and with substantial mass, shifting piles of oddly shaped and roughly sawn hardwood planks, searching for something unusual, or appropriate, or interesting, to turn into whatever piece of furniture has taken their fancy. In this case, rummaging wasn't required. Len had been alerted to the presence in the storeroom of a piece of exotica, a root burl from North Africa, shaped rather like a three-foot potato, as he put it, weighing in at several hundred pounds.

It was not as though Len was a stranger to the warehouse. Striking woods are integral to his cabinetmaking business, and the Matheson family, owners of East Coast Specialty Hardwoods, have known him for years, and such woods are even more integral to their business. The patriarch and founder, the late Bob Matheson, started the company with a single load of lumber, mostly oak and maple and domestics, including a single pallet of cherry, his personal favourite working wood, but they now carry a rotating inventory more than sixty species, some of them exceedingly rare. All the usual native woods are there, mostly hardwoods, and the exotics. Stacked and neatly labelled are samples of woods from a dozen countries: acacia from multiple places; from Brazil, boards of bloodwood, canarywood, jatoba, leopardwood, muiricatiara, pau amarello, and tulipwood; bubinga and zebrawood from Cameroon; balsa from Costa Rica; Mexican woods include chechen, bocote, chatekok, and cocobolo; from Nigeria and Gabon come ebony, iroko, mopane; from west Africa padauk and sapele ribbon stripe; from Malaysia Indian rosewood, from Bolivia jacaranda and pau ferro. There are racks of purpleheart from Guyana, granadillo from Central America, red palm from Indonesia, sapele and wenge and ipe from Congo, here still labeled Zaire; Spanish cedar from Peru; Swiss pear from Germany, teak samples from Myanmar; and mahogany from various parts of Central America. Some of the samples are small boards, others massive slabs, and a few just chunks, if that's a woodworker's term, burls and knots mostly, a lucky dip for woodturners.

That's what Len has come for. He's not a turner, but he wanted a burl anyway. Burls have other properties.

The day before I had spent a few hours browsing the "gallery," which is what *Fine Woodworking* magazine calls its showcase of pieces made and photographed by its readers, to see what woodworkers were up to and what they were making, and with what wood. This gallery is the cabinetmaker's version of the centrefold in less salubrious publications, a source of astonishment, envy, and, yes, lust. In my quick survey I saw a whimsical little display case with roots in Swedish design and the Arts and Crafts movement, made with eastern red cedar with curly maple veneer and African blackwood handles; a copy of a classic Victorian wooden cabinet secretary made entirely from Australian red cedar; a rocker made from black and claro walnut, its seat from hickory bark, among other pieces.

The thing that struck me (apart from the lamentable fact that I could never in a lifetime produce anything so fine, despite a good deal of persistent amateur effort) is that all the woods thus employed seemed, after the fact, inevitable, as though they had chosen themselves. Of course they hadn't. The finished pieces were the product of a woodworker's experienced eye, but they all *seemed* perfectly suited to the finished piece. Even where the wood's figure and grain were striking and unusual, the design seemed to require or accommodate them. Everything looked purposeful, which is what I suppose good design should do.

Sometimes the wood comes first, and the craftsman designs a piece to express it. Perhaps (an actual example) he has lucked into a piece of chatekok from Mexico, a fine-textured wood with creamy sapwood and heartwood in a rich red colour. The boards are 4/4 thick (in lumbermen's terms, 4/4 means one inch; 8/4 would be two inches) and a dozen feet long, rough-sawn with poorly squared ends. What to do? The solution was a hallway table, the tabletop made with two narrow bands of sapwood in a heartwood base, as though the paler wood was inlaid.

More often, the design comes first and the woods follow, chosen through a complicated process that includes memory, experience, desire, but also, naturally enough, availability and, yes, a modicum of wanting to show off a little (call it advertising).

Not uncommonly, a piece is born in serendipity. A dealer might call a woodworker with a simple message: "Hey Len, we've got a nice piece of [insert wood here], would you like some?" Len, with a new gleam in his eye, will succumb and drive home with the piece in his van, its destiny to follow.

In this case, Len needed material for a pair of end tables one of his clients had requested and designed. This giant gnarly potato was it, although by the time Len saw it, it was a giant potato no longer; it had been cut into chunks, maybe three feet long and a third that wide, somewhere around three and a half inches thick. As Len said, it was like taking a fat French fry out of a potato. Even in its rough-cut state, it was already showing the grain and figure that was its potential. It was a burl of thuya, grown in the forests on the northern slopes of the Atlas mountains, east of Essaouira, the Moroccan coastal town known since antiquity for its production of the brilliant pigment known as Tyrian purple, made from the mucus glands of the marine murex snail (just behind the anus, if you must know), and much in demand by Phoenician traders. Thuya, *tetraclinis articulata* is a variant of cedar, but there is only one species in the genus, and it is native only here (though a small population has been successfully transplanted to Malta). They are not particularly impressive trees, seldom more than sixteen inches in diameter and about fifty feet tall, and can take eighty years or more to reach maturity. The bark is just bark, unremarkable as most barks are. But once the bark is stripped off, Thuya's palette, when sanded smooth and polished, is honey and caramel, its figure intricate and elegant, with multiple swirls and curves and shadings, and pieces made from it seem to glow, as though lit from within.

Which may be why thuya wood was chosen for the dashboard and interior wood panels of the 1921 Rolls-Royce Silver Ghost, the car that first established itself as "the world's best car," at least according to company propaganda (a pristine example was recently sold at auction for better than $7 million U.S.). But thuya has an even longer and more prestigious provenance that that. It owes some of its fame to Solomon, who famously had commanded the King of Tyre to demand of the timbermen of Sidonia (Phoenicia) "that they hew me cedar trees out of

Lebanon . . . for thou knowest that there is not among us any that can skill to hew timber like unto the Sidonians." He also sent some of those same Sidonian axemen to North Africa, looking for something to nicely set off the already acquired Lebanon cedars installed in his new temple; there they discovered the thyine tree, as they called it, with its curiously figured and fragrant wood, and hewed down vast quantities of it to ship back home. Eight hundred years later it was still fashionable: Cicero, the Roman statesman and orator, recorded paying 300,000 denari for a dining table of thyine, also known to the Romans as *citron*. Solomon's carpenters used frame saws, derived from the Egyptians, and very similar, save for the hardness of the steel, to bow or frame saws still in use.

This particular thuya burl, it turned out, had embarked on a complicated journey to maritime Canada. It had somehow made its way to Libya, and then to the United States, but its new owner ran afoul of trade sanctions against whatever then passed for the Libyan government, and what he had bought was declared unsellable within the U.S. There was a lot of stuff other than the thuya, too. A container load. Bob Matheson picked up the whole shipment.

How do cabinetmakers choose the wood they do? The wood's workability is one thing, but there are other factors more important. How was the lumber milled? What is its true colour? Will it take stain well, if stain is wanted? What is its grain? Are there knots, burls, crotches, forks, and are those things suitable, even desirable, for the purpose, or just a nuisance? All these considerations intersect and overlap, and together they give wood its character, and are the reason no two pieces of wood are exactly the same.

Grain used in the technical sense is the direction, orientation, and regularity (or lack thereof) of the cellulose wood fibres. Grain can be straight, irregular, spiral, interlocked, or wavy, or a combination of all those things. How grain shows on a piece of lumber depends also on how the log is milled. The most common cut is called flat-sawn or plain-sawn, cut at a right angle to the vascular rays, which will yield a board where the growth rings appear as roughly parallel lines running the length of the board; this is the most economical method, and can yield wide boards with a straight grain or, sometimes, with a cathedral-ceiling appearance. Quarter-sawn or rift-sawn lumber has growth rings at sixty to ninety degrees to the face and thirty to sixty degrees to the face respectively. They make a more interesting grain pattern but yield only narrow boards, making them more expensive (a lot more waste).

The natural design or pattern found on a board is not its grain, though grain is an element. That pattern is called "figure."

Grain and figure are intertwined. Figure is the patterning of wood, a result of the fact that end grain and face grain reflect light differently, and the way a log is sawn (by varying the angle of the grain with its surface) can radically change its look. Figure in turn is influenced by many factors: "the presence, absence, abundance or conspicuousness of growth rings; the prominence and abundance of the vascular rays, the type of grain and its modification in the presence of knots, burls, crotches, buttresses and swollen butts, local variation in color due to the uneven deposition of coloring substances."[110]

Woodworkers have many curious names for the figure they see: crotch, ray fleck, spalting, stump or butt, bird's eye, blister or quilt, burl, curly, tiger, fiddleback, mottled, bee's wing, pommele, plum pudding, and ribbon-stripe among them. They are necessarily choosy, a basic part of their tradecraft, sometimes preferring highly figured woods (crotch mahogany, walnut) and sometimes looking for woods with little or no figure (quartersawn oak has very straight grain, lending itself well to certain designs). What does the piece you are making demand?

Texture is another factor to consider. It will affect the feel of the finished piece. Open-grained woods include oak, elm, hickory, and ash, medium-grained woods walnut, mahogany, and butternut, and closed-grain woods maple, birch, cherry, and pine. People who use lathes, woodturners, need closed-grain wood. Some furniture pieces demand muted colours in the wood; some period reproductions demand stronger colours.

You have grain, you have figure, you have texture, then you have burls, which are like warts on the trunk or branches or sometimes the roots. They're like excrescences, boils, tumours—they have been called all sorts of unattractive and unpleasant names, and they *are* deformities, although unlike tumours they seem to do the tree no harm. Still, they seem to grow when the tree is undergoing some stress, whether it be an injury, virus, or fungal infection, so in that way they are the consequence of harm, not its cause. They are unsightly on the living tree but also highly sought-after by woodworkers once they're cut; they yield a complicated, intricate, highly figured wood. They're hard to work with because their grain, such as it is, is twisted and knotted, making them very dense and hard, but also susceptible to chip or even shatter.

Thuya's burls are almost always underground, on the root system and not the trunk. Oddly, and fortunately, thuya roots are prone to "coppice" (put out new sprouts) underground; when these sprouts die, a beautiful burl reliably forms. These burls have a deeper colour, a more concentrated aroma, and a more complicated figure than the wood of the trunk, are highly sought-after by cabinetmakers, and can fetch very high prices.

The slice of thuya burl Len bought was unusual in another way. It was all end grain, through and through.

Back at his shop, Len prepared his French fry for use. He didn't need the usual preliminaries, the jointer, planer, and tablesaw, because the initial millwork had already been done. But he did need it absolutely flat.

So he ran it through a machine called a thickness sander, which moves the workpiece through a rotating drum of sandpaper. To make sure it made proper contact with the sander, he used a series of little wedges and blocks to elevate it where necessary. Then, one side flat, he flipped it over and did the other side, this time not needing the wedges. The pair of end tables he was making were square, seven and three-quarter inches on a side, and seventeen inches tall. He didn't have enough wood to make them out of solid thuya lumber, so he needed veneer. For this, he moved to the bandsaw. But because the wood was all end grain and could easily break, he first made a sandwich, gluing sheets of three-quarter-inch Baltic birch plywood to both sides. The thuya was in the middle, the filling between the birch. He repeated this glue-up sandwich for every slice he needed, eight of them for the sides, another two for the tops.

Standard hardwood veneers are one-eighth of an inch thick (three millimetres), although with sophisticated rotary slicing machines that can reduce all the way down to one-twenty-fourth of an inch (one millimetre). Len needed the veneer to be no thicker than one-eighth of an inch; he would then need to mitre the corners so the veneer seemed to wrap all the way around the piece as though it were a single sheet, the grain, what there was of it, and figure seeming to flow around all four corners. To get it right, he numbered the slices as they came off the saw. Then he needed another set of mitres, for the square top. He made the slices a hair thicker than needed, so he could run the pieces through the sander again, to eliminate any toothmarks from the bandsaw blade.

Even with the thuya glued to the plywood, using a bandsaw for this purpose demands meticulous measurement, a steady hand, and skill earned through hundreds of hours of work. It also, of course, demands a sturdy saw with a very sharp blade, and a "resaw fence" (the piece that holds the wood against the blade) as tall as the piece being milled. Thuya is more brittle and easily spoiled than many woods, so this was an intricate, painstaking, and hazardous task.

After that, the mitred corners and tops, done on the tablesaw. After that, glue-up. After that, ever finer sanding and scraping. After that, polishing. After that, delivery. After that, admiration. After that, aw shucks, it wasn't that hard.

Art made to look easy.

Prodigious wood

T O SAY THAT THE CHURCH of the Transfiguration on
Kizhi Island in Lake Onega, the Церковь Преображения
Господня in Russian, is made of wood is like saying the giant
redwoods of California are trees. Both statements are true, but rather
understate the case.

Even the site is striking. Onega is the second largest lake in Europe.
Kizhi itself is just one of a thousand tiny islands scattered across it, most
of them thickly wooded and uninhabited. Eighty kilometres or so to its
west is the town of Petrozavodsk, the capital of the Karelian republic,
and in summer there is a thrice daily *raketa*, hydrofoil, between the city
and Kizhi. But first you have to get to Petrozavodsk, which you can do
on a six-hour train ride from Saint Petersburg's Ladozhsky station. Kizhi,
at a latitude of sixty-two degrees north, is about the same latitude as
Anchorage, Alaska, and is also not that far from Arkhangelsk on the White
Sea. Arkhangelsk has an airport, but there is no point flying there, because
there are no roads from Arkhangelsk to anywhere, except a difficult drive
south to Moscow, 1,200 kilometres away. The border shared with Lapland
is 150 kilometres off to the northwest, but unreachable from here. There is
a village on Kizhi island, a hamlet really, called Velikaya Guba, a goodish

hike to the north, but you can't get anywhere from there, either. (On the other hand, one of the hamlet's houses is available as an Airbnb rental.) You can also come to Kizhi in winter (Kizhi is open year-round) if you don't mind temperatures that hover twenty or thirty degrees below zero and the occasional blizzard; there are rental snowmobiles and hovercraft that will get you there.

When you do debark from your summer *raketa*, you will follow the path up a gentle slope to the brilliant green meadow beyond. And there, across the lush grass is Kizhi *pogost* and its jewel, the octagonal Church of the Transfiguration, thirty-six metres tall, nineteen by thirty metres in its footprint, topped by no fewer than twenty-two onion-shaped domes, built on this spot in 1714 by unknown carpenters using locally hewn wood and erected with not a nail or piece of metal anywhere in the structure, the whole thing made of white pine logs pegged together with hardwood dowels—the treenails, or trunnels, of the shipbuilding trade. The only metal nails used were for the shingles, themselves hand-cut in an oakleaf shape from aspen, 180,000 nails for 60,000 shingles. Local legend has it that the main carpenter used only a single axe to build the whole thing and then, when it was done, he threw his axe into the lake declaring that "there will never be another one to match it," presumably meaning the building, not the axe. This is almost certainly fanciful, but the building is so extraordinary that you wish it could be true. UNESCO, in the text declaring Kizhi a World Heritage Site, mentioned the carpentry as a compelling reason: "Russian carpenters, whose fame goes back to the Middle Ages to Novgorod, had [here] carried the art of joinery to its apogee."

A *pogost* is an enclosure, usually with a church and a graveyard, and possibly a small settlement. Kizhi *pogost* has a second, smaller, church with nine domes called the Church of the Intercession, or in Russian the Церковь Покрова Пресвятой Богородицы, plus a bell tower added in 1862. There was a *pogost* here in the Middle Ages. Kizhi itself is mentioned several times in the Russian chronicles of the sixteenth century. The current churches were built when earlier versions were "taken by thunderbolts," as the church records say (destroyed by fire).

This little *pogost* has an interesting political side story. I first visited in the early 1970s, just ten years after it was cobbled together into a state museum, and that just a few years after Stalin had died. Stalin, notoriously, had no use for folklore or religion, and scant tolerance for nostalgia, unless it was for the muscular energetics of Peter the Great. He went heedlessly into the future, regardless of the cost in human lives. I found in my notes a speech he gave in the 1930s that gives the flavour of his impatience, full of Stalinist exclamation points: "It's sometimes asked whether it's possible to slow down a bit in tempo, to retard the movement [to socialism and modernity]. No, comrades, this is impossible! It's impossible to reduce the tempo! On the contrary, it's necessary to accelerate it! To slacken the tempo means to fall behind. And the backwards are always beaten. But we do not want to be beaten! No, we do not want this! The history of old Russia is the history of defeats due to backwardness!"

So when the decision was made to convert the little hamlet into a museum and to gather a dozen or more wood structures from around Karelia to be restored, it was regarded as a cautious step away from Stalinism and a way of recovering lost history, so recently trampled into the Stalinist muck. The museum has kept growing ever since, and now contains eighty-three different structures, most of them moved in from elsewhere, all in wood: houses, barns, windmills, bathhouses, and chapels, intended as a showcase of traditional village life.

* * *

Half a millennium before Kizhi's woodworkers first put froe and cant hook to timber, carpenters were fanning out into the Île-de-France looking for oak. They needed lots of oak trees, big ones, too, more than 13,000 trees from more than twenty hectares of forest, as it turned out. Each tree would yield just one massive beam, which would then be carted to Paris and put to use in the Gothic cathedral then abuilding on the Île de la Cité, a small island in the Seine, which would come to be called Notre-Dame de Paris. Once put together on the ground to see if the fit was good, the intricate structure would then be pulled apart, lifted into the sky by a system of pulleys and reassembled *en place*, above the stone walls recently erected and topped out in 1220. (Construction began in 1163, and it wasn't "finished" until 1345.)

To reach the heights demanded by the high vaulted ceiling and fifty-five-degree angle of the prevailing Gothic style, the carpenters had needed tall trees, which means they must have been mature when cut, which means that they had been seedlings as far back as the eighth or ninth century.

The intricate filigree of ancient oak that held up the cathedral's 210-ton lead roof would come to be called Notre-Dame's "forest." It was this forest that was destroyed in the fire of 2019.

The forest cannot be replaced. Not by trees from France, in any case. They don't grow oaks that large anymore, or not enough of them to matter. They would have to come from elsewhere, if there *was* an elsewhere. Or be manufactured. Or made from something other than wood. The debate was far from over when the pandemic hit the capital, and everything shut down until July 2020, when the president's office announced that the cathedral would be built without modern embellishments, to look just as it was before. This was not helpful: it would *look* the same, but would it be *made* the same?

Maybe, just maybe, the forest can be replaced in wood, albeit imported from Ghana.

When Ghana's Akosombo Dam was built in 1965, it created Lake Volta, the world's largest artificial reservoir. It flooded 8,502 square kilometres of what had been tropical hardwood forest (conservationists didn't have much of a voice in those days of decolonization and headlong development). The most common tree in the submerged forest is ikoko, a tough, dense, and very durable wood beloved of cabinetmakers and often used as a substitute for teak. Ikoko is hard, with a density of 660 kilograms per cubic metre, similar to oak. More interestingly, the trees have been submerged in anaerobic bog-like water and thus preserved from decay, and have begun to fossilize, making them stronger than before. Several companies have been licensed by the Ghanaian government to harvest some of these trees. One of them, Kete Krachi, was already exporting logs to Europe, South Africa, and the Middle East by 2018, and in late 2019 submitted a proposal to France's ministry of culture to supply the wood for Notre-Dame's rebuilding. Francis Kalitsi, chairman and co-founder of Kete Krachi, says that "underneath the lake, you have typical African hardwoods that are similar to oak trees— their density may range from 650 [to] 900 kilograms per cubic metre. They are structural timbers which could be useful in the reconstruction."

The ministry was noncommittal. Jérémie Patrier-Leitus, a ministry spokesman, said in late 2019 that "right now, we don't know if the frame will be rebuilt in wood. We are in the process of securing the monument, and then we will have to rebuild the vault and the spire. Reconstruction will start once the structure of the monument is stabilised and preserved. We will study the different generous offers once we have confirmed the material used to rebuild the frame."

Conservationists, perhaps making up for their absence when Lake Volta was created, have been weighing in. Some fear yet more destruction of ecosystems, now that the lake actually has one, and have generally been taking a leave-it-alone point of view. Others are more enthusiastic. The BBC quoted Andrew Waugh, director of London-based sustainable architecture practice Waugh Thistleton Architects, as saying that using Lake Volta wood "could be a genius solution . . . It would seem to be a great way of solving a problem and helping a poorer economy."

Oxford University's Cathy Oakes, a specialist in French and English medieval architecture and iconography, suggested that the Lake Volta wood could be similar to "bog oak," which was widely used in medieval constructions and furniture, although not in the original Notre-Dame. "Bog oak has similarly been exposed to water for a long period of time, so it's stronger and more durable." The shortage of oxygen, and the acidic conditions of peat bogs and riverbeds help to preserve tree trunks from decay. The wood then begins to fossilise, making it significantly stronger.[111]

* * *

On the far side of the world, about eighty-five kilometres south of the once imperial capital of Datong (now an unprepossessing coal-mining city of three million or so souls), in a small community with a pleasant view of Mount Hengshan, artisans and carpenters were doing work very similar to that of the builders of Notre-Dame, except a little earlier, in the middle of the eleventh century in this case, 1056 to be more precise, in the second year of the reign of Daozong of Liao, for the Chinese have always been scrupulous record-keepers. The carpenters fanned out into the wooded countryside of Yingxian county looking for red pine and cypress trees, which they logged and hauled off to the building site. They would need, in the end, 2,600 tons of logs cut into 15,400 architectural pieces, for this was not to be a trivial building. It came to be called the

Sakyamuni Pagoda, in the grounds of the Fogong Temple, and when completed it would be a complex octagon sixty-seven metres tall, with six layers of eaves (nine stories inside), each layer supported by an exterior and an interior ring of wooden columns, linked in an intricate tracery of bracings, cross beams, squared columns, and pillars all held together by mortise and tenon joinery with hardwood dowels wedged into place, and supported by fifty-four different designs of brackets, all of which make up a framework that is immensely strong. Which is just as well, for the pagoda has survived at least seven earthquakes, three of them strong ones, in its nine hundred years, as well as withstanding two hundred rounds of Japanese artillery in the Sino-Japanese war. Like many pagodas, it is topped with a metal finial, which has the added benefit of acting as a lightning rod ("demon-catcher," in the phrase of the time).

It is the largest extant all-wooden pagoda in China. It has become so famous that it's now called by the generic name *muta*, or Timber Pagoda.

As with Kizhi and Notre-Dame, the pagoda has spiritual significance, as do pagodas generally. That this one is said to have been built in 1050 is no accident. The decade of the 1050s marked the end of a Buddhist *kalpa* (epoch), which made the Sakyamuni Pagoda the "ultimate death shrine to the Buddha of the age."[112]

Pagodas, common in China, Japan, Korea, Vietnam, and other parts of Asia, grew out of the much older Indian tradition of *stupas*, which were smallish conical stone domes that venerated a Buddha, and usually contained relics, "holy artifacts of the Buddha's body," a macabre tradition similar in spirit to the Catholic Christian one of secreting splinters of the true cross or blood of the Virgin or thorns from the Crown. The first *stupa* appeared soon after the death of the Gautama Buddha in the fifth century BCE. The first Chinese version, or pagoda, was built, of wood, in 68 CE, in the White Horse Temple. Those that followed were taller and more elaborate than the typical *stupa*, continuing an architectural style that had long been dominant in China under the Han and Tang dynasties, with many levels and multiple layers of eaves. Crowning each pagoda was a cupola or steeple in the shape of a traditional *stupa*.

Pagodas weren't churches in any Western sense. They were associated with temples, and did serve as symbols of veneration, but many of them were solid, with no interior rooms or places to assemble, though they almost always had a staircase from whose pinnacle visitors could contemplate the earth and their humble place in it.

Pagodas varied between three and thirteen levels, always an odd number, and many contained multiple statues, carvings, and decorative elements—this was not an austere architecture. In the artless prose of the Fogong Temple's online presence, "each story [of the pagoda] holds Buddhist statues. The first story has the eleven-meter tall Sakyamuni statue, with a peaceful face and easy expression. Above the statue is a beautiful caisson [sometimes known as a spiderweb ceiling]. Interior walls have six paintings of Tathagata Buddha. On both sides of the doorway are Buddha's warrior attendants, heavenly kings, disciples, etc. with bright colors and vivid figures. The platform is square in the second story, and there are a Buddha, two Bodhisattvas and two more Bodhisattvas on the side. The third story is octagonal and holds the statues of the four Buddhas from the four directions. The fourth story has statues of Ananda, Kasyapa, Manjusri and Samantabhadra [Buddhas]. The fifth story holds Vairocana and the eight Bodhisattvas." (A Bodhisattva is a would-be Buddha.)

In one way, the Japanese did the temple a favour: their bombardment, while not fatal to the structure, did smash several of the statues, and found in various ruined abdomens was at least one holy relic, a Buddha tooth, and a trove of written documents. These included eight handwritten scrolls, thirty-five scrolls of block-printed scripture, one of them thirty-three metres long, and, more remarkably, a twelve-scroll text of Buddhist sutras printed by the newly invented technique of movable type, this example dating to 1003 and originating in Yanjing (now called Beijing). There were also many carved sutras, and finely coloured silk pictures.[113] Housed in the temple museum are a few celebrity endorsements of the pagoda, including encomiums from the emperor Zhu Di (1406) and a lyrical tablet titled *Amazing View Under Heaven*, written by emperor Wuzong after he fought off an invading Tartar army in 1508.

PART 5

The Violin

I know that the most joy in my life has come to me from my violin.

—Einstein

I love power as a musician loves his violin,
to draw out its sounds and chords and harmonies.

—Napoleon

The tone of the violin is the most ravishing for those who play it perfectly . . . sweeten
it as they wish and render it inimitable by certain tremblings which delight the mind.
—Marin Mersenne, French polymath,
father of acoustics, besotted with *vibrato*.

THE LONGBOW WAS WHAT it was, a brutally efficient instrument of war, and many a soldier died of it, usually badly, for the arrows were bonebreakers. The schooner was a high-bred filly, beautiful as well as capable, ever and always a witch in the wind. The violin is a more sophisticated creature entirely. Its woods are not like those of a bow, chosen for their memory, and whose flexibility is key. Nor like those of a vessel, where strength is master. The woods of a violin are chosen for resonance, for voice, for precision, where a few millimetres' difference in shape and density can help fill concert halls.

The violin's strings are not like those of a bow, designed for a simple death-dealing task. Nor are they like the sheets and halyards of a sailing vessel, a complex harmony, to be sure, but utilitarian in their purpose. The violin, with its strings and its bow, is a way of giving voice to wood, or of freeing wood's voice, to shape emotions, melancholy or thrilling, joyful or sorrowful, profound, obsessive, involving. In the best hands, it is capable of teasing out every emotion in the wide human catalogue.

A small thing, to hold such power.

How did it get that way? The stories differ, because actual facts are sometimes overtaken by legend.

In many of the histories, the violin arrived "complete and entire," in as-near-as-no-matters the form in which it is still found, almost comically quickly, in northern Italy in the early sixteenth century. In 1500, there were no violins, this story goes. By 1530, there they were. By 1550, they were no longer rare, and by the turn of the century they were everywhere.

In many of the histories, the violin was invented by a single prodigious genius, sometimes identified as Andrea Amati, although there are other claimants.

In many of the histories, the greatest violin-makers, perhaps of all time, were the masters Antonio Stradivari and Bartolomeo Giuseppe Guarneri, known as Guarneri del Gesù.

In many of the histories, composers and musicians quickly recognized the brilliance of the violin as a solo instrument, and within a few decades it spread from Milan and its hinterlands into the rest of Europe, especially France and Germany.

Scrupulous historians will grade the truth of those assertions one out of four. Maybe one and a half.

Whatever the stories, the violin didn't come out of nowhere. There were antecedents. What they were depends on how far back you go.

Stringed instruments seem to have come into human culture at about the same time as devices for killing, at least if you can believe the physical evidence. A 13,000-year-old painting found in the Trois Frères cave in France appears to depict a hunting bow used as a one-stringed lyre, along with fragments of such a bow found buried in the cave muck. Which came first, the bow or the lyre, the killer or the entertainer?

It seems evident, at least, that the musical hunting bow, if that's what it was, developed gradually into a multiplying array of musical instruments, first with one string, then with two or more, each time adding new tones and notes, thus creating the first harps and lyres.

The earliest surviving chordophones, as stringed instruments are classified, date back 4,500 years or so, although the actual date is elusive. They were found in the luxurious royal tombs of Ur, in southern Mesopotamia. In the cosmology of the time and the place, the afterlife was bleak: everyone, including kings, was consigned after death to a dreary place called Kur, where there was nothing to do for eternity except to eat and drink, which doesn't sound too bad except that the only edible substance was dust. The rich, however, had an out, as the rich so often do.

The rich could take with them as much food and as many luxury goods as they wished, and servants to please them, and they did. The burial chamber of the queen, whose name was Pu-abi, contained a hoard of fancy stuff, plus the bodies of personal attendants who had been obliged to perish with the royal person. Gold and lapis lazuli were commonplace, often in the shape of eight-pointed rosettes. So were lyres and harps, presumably to soothe the troubled breast of Herself. The so-called Great Lyre, also known as the bull-headed lyre for the head carved into its frame, was found nearby, in the king's grave. The head, face, and horns of the bull were gold foil wrapped over a wooden form (the wood long decayed). The hair and beard were lapis lazuli, as were the eyes, inlaid into shell. The front panel was shell inlaid into bitumen.[114] Some of the lyres were shown in tomb frescoes with bows, so they were not just plucked. A cylinder seal from the tombs, dated to 3100 BCE or earlier, depicts a woman playing a stick lute. Fortunately, we have photographs and models of all these, for the originals, having lasted more than 4,000 years, were destroyed when the Baghdad museum was looted after the American invasion of 2003.[115]

Harps and lyres are also common in burial chamber frescoes from the Egyptian Old Kingdom, as far back as 3000 BCE. They were still primitive, still resembling a hunter's bow, the harps without the "forepillar" of more modern instruments (the forepillar is the third leg of a harp's triangle, carrying no strings of its own but bracing the legs that do). In later centuries the Egyptians developed many variants of lyres, harps, and lutes, mostly plucked and not bowed.

There were many others in history: among them the cláirseach of the Picts, the crwth of Wales, the erhu, a two-stringed "spike fiddle" from

China, the hudok or gudok of the Slavs, the Mongolian morin khuur or horsehead fiddle, the medieval European hurdy-gurdy, the lute-like rabab of Afghanistan, the pear-shaped five-stringed rebec of medieval Europe, and the three-stringed Mesopotamian version.

Some of these had no resonators, or sound boxes. Some were just simple open-sided boxes, some were closed. Some had sound holes, some didn't. Others used gourds, where those were available. We have a five-stringed African lyre whose sound box is a gourd covered tightly with python skin on its open face, with a single round sound hole, the gourd itself bound with a woven skein of string over a monkey-skin cushion, an east African design likely unchanged for many centuries, possibly millennia. The purpose of all these hollow chambers is to amplify the vibration of the strings: the strings vibrate, so does the body of the instrument, and the air inside the sound box.

The number of strings varied, too. There was no fingering or stopping on these early instruments, so each string played just one note. The more notes required, the more strings needed. Five were common, eight not unknown. Early Indian lutes have been discovered with anywhere from seven to twenty-one strings. The ancient Sri Lankan ravanastron, on a semicircular gourd, with a long neck and two strings, is still in use. The classical Greek kithara was a six-string variant of lute; etymologically, the word is the origin of *guitar*.

The first known literary reference to a bowed instrument is much later, in the writings of the ninth-century Persian geographer Ibn Khurradadhbih, who called it a lra (or lura). At that time bowing was still confined to the Arabic and Byzantine empires, and made its way from Spain into Europe sometime in the eleventh century, mostly in the form of the rabab and the rebec, both of which had shallow bodies, the rabab with a skin belly and the rebec with wood, plus a fingerboard. In this sense, the rebec was a clear ancestor of the violin, though its club-like body looks clumsy to a modern eye.

The medieval vièle, like the rebec, is sometimes considered a violin precursor. It predates the violin by centuries (it was already fully formed by 1100) and it also survived alongside the violin, especially in the form of its stylistic apotheosis, the lira da braccio, and was used by many a renowned artist, including Leonardo da Vinci, Timoteo Viti, and Raphael. The best-known depiction of the vièle is on the Gate of Glory in Santiago de Compostela, carved by Master Matteo in 1188; twenty-four elders are shown playing a variety of stringed instruments, eight of them oval-shaped vièles looking very much like violins, except that their ribs, or sides, are concave, "hollowed out like a Roman roofing tile," as the musicologist Christian Rault puts it. Other medieval carvings outlined the vièle in detail, similar to a modern violin, but with a longer and deeper body and three to five strings, with a leaf-shaped pegbox with frontal tuning pegs. The biggest difference is that the vièle was carved from a single piece of wood (except for the belly, or top) while the violin is pieced together from multiple pieces prepared separately before assembly.

Near the end of the Middle Ages, a bowed stringed instrument called a fiddle appeared in Europe, smaller than the current versions, and higher in pitch. It still used frets, and was tuned in fourths, unlike the violin which was and is tuned in fifths.

And so on and so on. The cross-cultural fertilization of music-playing was just as vigorous as the trade in goods. "In such a context," Christian Rault points out, "it is not easy to locate any particular innovation, and trying to situate the birthplace of the violin seems as easy as pointing out the first flower at the very beginning of spring."[116]

The modern group of bowed instruments, the viol, viola, violin, cello (violoncello), and double bass (bass viol) thus have complex antecedents.

They all came to be called some variant of the name viola, from one of two "families," the viola da braccio (viola of the arm) and the viola da gamba (viola of the leg), depending on how they were played, a rough division that depended partly on the instrument's heft. The four-stringed viola and the six-stringed viol thrived in the sixteenth and seventeenth centuries, and coexisted with the violin in the Baroque period, and in that sense are not direct ancestors. The viol, which was played upright, had a c-shaped sound hole instead of the f-shaped hole of the violin, and had six, seven, or more strings tuned in fourths, a fretted fingerboard, and a relatively thick body. Various sizes were made, but the viola da gamba, which has a lower register similar to that of the cello, was particularly famous.[117] A few are still being made.

In 1511, a luthier called Andrea de Verona built a violin lookalike. It was made from just three pieces of wood, and not the dozens of the later Cremonese instruments, so was a transitional piece.

True violins were in use by 1530, of that much we can be sure: a cherub playing a violin can clearly be seen in a 1529 painting by the Italian artist and sculptor Gaudenzio Ferrari, a fresco called *Madonna of the Orange Trees*, in the church of San Cristoforo, in Vercelli, a town near Milan. The instrument is as chubby as the cherub himself, a little more bulbous than the modern violin, and its centre bout (its indented "waist") more pronounced, but it is still clearly a violin.

A few years later, Ferrari was at it again. On a fresco called *The Glory of Angels*, painted inside the cupola of the church of the Madonna di Miracoli in Saronno, in the province of Varese, three angels are seen playing three of the instruments of the violin family: the violin itself, the viola, and the cello. They are all familiar to a modern eye. They have no frets. They have pegboxes with side pegs, and f-holes. Like his earlier cherub, they are a little more rotund than the modern instruments, but not by much. The only real difference is that they have three strings, not four.

There are a few other glimpses in history. In 1523, the treasury of Savoy records an expense for the importation of musicians from Vercelli (where Ferrari painted his cherub) called in the invoice "trompettes et vyollons de Verceil." No pictures accompanied the payment, so we cannot be certain that those *vyollons* were actual violins, but it is probable.

In 1533, a musicologist called Giovanni Lanfranco published his *Scintille di musica*, which can be translated, loosely, as *Insights About Music*. Lanfranco, not to be confused with the Baroque painter by the same name, was concerned with the technicalities of tuning and other such matters, and never mentions violins by name. Still, he investigated the sounds made by the new "little bowed violas without frets," which surely sounds like a violin. A year later Pope Paul III, presiding over a peace conference after one of the many Franco-Spanish-Holy Roman Empire wars of the time, imported a troupe of *Violini Milanesi* to entertain the various parties, presumably to calm everyone down after a tense day of post-combat negotiating. (It seems the French won that skirmish, and gained custody of Savoy and Piedmont, if only for a while.) The Milanesi reported could be the city of Milan, or its hinterlands, which after all included Vercelli, Brescia, Salò, Turin, and Cremona. In the same year, 1534, Catherine de Médicis, then queen of France, ordered a large set of violins, violas, tenors, and cellos from an unknown artisan in Cremona. Eight of them had all the features of the modern violin. By 1561, when Mary Queen of Scots arrived in Edinburgh from France, she was met by "five or six hundred scoundrels of the town [who] serenaded her with wretched violins and small rebecs," although it is not known if those were *real* violins.[118] A lovely portrait from 1606 by Guido Reni shows Saint Cecilia, patron saint of music, delicately holding a violin, its bow positioned in a sign of the cross—in the third century, no less. Still, legend has it that Saint Cecilia could play any instrument she picked up, and was so exalted she could hear the music of the angels, so the anachronism is a nice piece of artistic licence.[119]

Two early violin masters, Andrea Amati and Gasparo di Bertolotti, were both from the Milanesi region, Amati from Cremona, and Bertolotti (known as Gasparo da Salò) from, obviously enough, Salò. Gasparo's grandfather, Santino, was a landowner whose gut strings for musical instruments were famous; his father, Francesco, was a violinist of note. The family workshop remained one of the most illustrious instrument-making operations in Europe for generations.

It is Amati who is often said to have been the "inventor" of the violin, but since he was born in 1511, he would have been still in his teens when Ferrari painted his cherub, rather young to have produced an instrument so complex. Gasparo, for his part, was born a full decade after the same painting. In any case, to make the transition from a solid to an assembled instrument is unlikely to have been the work of a single craftsman in a single place, an argument against the brilliant inventor theory of origins. As Sheila Nelson puts it in her review of violins and violas:

> No inventor can be named with certainty, and it seems very probable that an earlier generation of makers produced the first violins. Certainly, Giovanni Maria dalla Corna of Brescia, who made the beautiful lira da braccio now in the Ashmolean museum, possessed sufficient technical skill to have contributed to the rise of the violin family, and Zanetto Montichiaro (1488-1568) or Girolamo Virchi, the teacher of Gasparo da Salò, were Brescian makers who may have produced three-string violins, though we possess no direct evidence of them.[120]

Violins produced by the two masters, Amati and Gasparo, still exist. The oldest known violin is one built by Amati around 1565.

Amati, whose family could have migrated from Barcelona a few generations earlier, was originally a lute maker, but turned to the new thing called a violin in the mid-sixteenth century. Whatever his role in legend, his family became prominent luthiers in Cremona, especially his two sons, Antonio and Girolamo. The latter's son Nicolò, Andrea's grandson, was himself a master luthier. He was one of the first to ensure that a fourth string was added to the existing three, greatly extending the instrument's range and carrying power, and he had several notable apprentices, among them Antonio Stradivari, and Andrea Guarneri, whose grandson Bartolomeo Giuseppe Guarneri is known to posterity as Guarneri del Gesù because of his habit of including a "Christogram" (a badge whose design contains the initials of Jesus) somewhere on his instruments.

"Notable apprentices," indeed, although there remain skeptics, Stradivari and Guarneri del Gesù are now widely considered the finest violin makers of all, and their instruments are highly prized, and stratospherically priced. However, both made very different violins, with very different tonal qualities, and lived very different lives.

Stradivari was born around 1644 and lived to a little past ninety, and continued making violins until his final days, creating an estimated 1,100 instruments over the course of his life, an average of 14.5 per year, a production schedule never seriously rivalled. Of these, roughly six hundred violins, violas, cellos, mandolins, and guitars still survive. He was, apparently, an obsessive. His instruments are known, as the critics put it, "for the attention to detail in every aspect and their splendidly lustrous tone."

In contrast, Guarneri, who lived for just forty-six years, from 1698, had a much shorter career, and was largely overshadowed by the more successful and commercially savvy Stradivarian studio, to the extent that he had to take up innkeeping in his later years to keep his family fed. In addition, Stradivari could afford to scoop up the most beautiful wood available, leaving lesser cuts to his competitors. A 1931 biography of Guarneri gave him a rather more lurid life: he was said to have been jailed for killing a rival and even to have made violins in prison, none of which seems to have been true. (What is likely, however, is that at least some of the violins emanating from his studio were actually made by his German wife, Caterina Roda.) Guarneri probably made about three hundred violins, of which 140 survive today. His violins are rougher and wilder than the elegant instruments of Stradivari, but they have a deep and powerful tone that appeals to assertive musicians.

* * *

If indeed Andrea Amati, Stradivari, Guarneri del Gesù, and a few of their contemporaries are considered the finest violin makers of all . . . why? What was their secret, if indeed there is one? What makes their violins so special?

Here is the opening sentence from a *Guardian* piece published in 2018, written by the paper's science editor Ian Sample: "The violins made by the Italian masters Andrea Amati and Antonio Stradivari are celebrated as the finest ever made, but the secret behind their perfect sound has mystified experts for centuries."

Sample, of course, suggests an answer to the mystification. So have others over the years, although their solutions inevitably differ. Some attribute the perfect sound to the varnish, which is thought to have some secret ingredient that it transmits to the wood (and no, only the lunatic fringe has asserted this secret is human blood). Others have speculated that the solution lies in the wood, that the spruces and maples around the city of Cremona, where Stradivari worked, had some unique quality of hardness and purity. Ian Sample, in his *Guardian* piece, quoted scientists from the National Taiwan University, who found that the famous violins mimic aspects of the human voice:

> The early Italian instruments produced human-like 'formants,' the harmonic tones that correspond to resonances in the vocal tract. Specifically, the Amati violins produced formants similar to those from bass and baritone singers, while the Stradivari instruments had higher-frequency formants, closer to those of tenors and contraltos . . . Stradivari violins are often described as having brightness and brilliance, both qualities that could be rooted in the higher-frequency tones that make the instruments sound closer to female voices.

The chief scientist of that particular study, Hwan-Ching Tai, speculated that Amati and Stradivari had done this deliberately. "The early violin was not a solo instrument but an accompaniment to songs and dances," he said. "It is conceivable that Andrea Amati may have wanted to build a string instrument that could imitate human voices to blend into such music."

Many other questions have been raised about these famous violins, usually without suggesting answers. For example, Stradivari violins are supposed to sound quieter "under the ear of the violinist" but to project better into the concert hall, a clear violation of the inverse-square law of physics (whereby a specified physical quality is inversely proportional to the square of the distance from the source).

Strads are *supposed* to behave this way. But do they?

The varnish is *supposed* to be special. But is it?

And the wood? Was there indeed anything special about the trees from which they were made?

Earnest scientific inquiries have been brought to bear on each of these matters. On the varnish, a heavyweight team from various French and German institutes analyzed the varnish from five instruments in the custody of Paris's Musée de la musique, and found to their satisfaction that Stradivari used completely common and easily obtained materials that were already in broad use in decorative arts and paintings of the period. "Stradivari first applied a layer of an oil comparable to the oils used by painters of the same epoch, without fillers or pigments, to seal the wood," the lead scientist, Jean-Philippe Echard, wrote in his report. "We did not find a mineral-rich layer, as some earlier work suggests. The master violinmaker next applied a slightly tinted oil-resin layer. We have detected nothing that would have suggested the use of protein-containing materials, gums, or fossil resins." They did find traces of three pigments in the varnish—again, all widely in use at the time: red iron oxide, vermilion, and a "lake pigment" (pigments made from organic substances) made of cochineal, yielding a carmine colour.

There is another side to the varnish story. The brothers Hill, whose joint book is the preeminent biography of Stradivari, had some sniffy things to say about some of the varnishes more recently used ("recently" being relative: the book, *Antonio Stradivari, His Life and Work*, was published in 1909). "If players would be content with instruments treated with colourless varnish, the difficulty of producing fine tone would be very greatly diminished, as the addition of many and various injurious colouring substances, or the artificial staining of the wood (at sometimes accomplished by the use of acids) in order to please the eye, in the one case mars what would be a varnish favourable for tone, and in the other adversely affects the material from which the instrument is made. In fact, tone is, and has been, though often unintentionally, sacrificed by many through seeking to gratify the taste for mere outward appearance." So, at least in this view, varnish *can* change the tone.

As for the wood, one theory is that the homogenous density of the spruces and maples from Cremona and its district was somehow special, giving the instruments an edge in stiffness and sound-damping characteristics, which both help to produce superior notes. Another is that the wood was pre-treated with several types of minerals, unspecified, which gave it those same characteristics. No evidence has been found to support either of these contentions. Wood from many other places has been shown to have the same homogenous density, especially from mature trees grown at high altitudes. No unusual minerals have been found.

Perhaps fungi have a role to play? In a 2009 behind-the-curtain test, a British violinist, Matthew Trusler, tested his Strad against several violins made by the Swiss master Michael Rhonheimer, one of them made of wood treated by a "specially selected fungus." To no one's surprise, given the intensity of the pre-test publicity, the fungus won. No one ever revealed exactly what this fungus was, and the experiment receded unlamented into the past.[121]

What about the actual shape of the actual thing? There is really no way to judge, because the basic feminine-torso hourglass shape of the violin has hardly changed since the early days, and that shape was chosen for sound reasons, literally, to make it easy to play, to get the bow on all the strings. True, there are minute differences between instruments, which have been traced back to the originals made by the early Italian makers: in this tiny sense, there are four lineages of violins, that of Stradivari, that of Giovanni Paolo Maggini (1580–1630), that of the Amati family, and that of the Austrian Jacob Stainer (1619–1683), Bach's favourite luthier.

Modern makers all follow these basic patterns. Even an iconoclast like New York's Guy Rabut, who once made a Picasso-like "cubist" fiddle, has stuck to tradition with his fine violins.

Maybe the answer, if there is one, has to do with the strings as much as with the wood? Or with the strings *and* the wood—the way that the vibrations of the strings interact with the wood, and give it resonance? Otherwise, Stradivari and Guarneri aside for the moment, why do some violins produce a heartbreakingly beautiful sound, while other nearly identical instruments do not?

An amateur violin maker and medical doctor in Chicago, Cal Meineke, has focused on these vibrational modes in trying to understand why some of his attempts succeeded, whereas others failed. "Holding his ear close to the early instruments he made, Meineke noticed that the pitch differed almost everywhere he listened," reported Jim Collins in a long piece for *Chicago* magazine. "He wondered: if a violin's pitch changes from one end of the instrument to the other or from its top plate to its back, could the sound be a composite of all those competing pitches? 'It's not subjective,' he says. 'No matter your ear, an A is 440 cycles per second, and if you hear that along with a tone that's 448 cycles per second, that's going to be dissonance, and it's not going to sound good.' In a beautiful-sounding violin, Meineke realized, the strings excited the wood in such a way that the sound waves moved in unison and reinforced one another—resulting in harmonic undertones and overtones that gave power and colour and texture to the notes. The thought led him to question the accepted notion that a string of a certain length and mass under a certain tension always gives a certain pitch. 'I came to believe that might be true of an ideal string,' he says, 'but it's not true for a real string attached to a wooden box'."

Meineke speculated that small changes in the thickness of the top and back of the violin could help eliminate the dissonance he was able to hear, and over the years developed special tools to scrape away minute quantities of wood, mere fractions of millimetres, "tap-testing" as he went. When he was satisfied, he gave his violins to professional musicians for their opinion. One of them, Ken Meyer, who had served as a judge for the Violin Society of America, was dismissive of the look of the violin he tested ("I'd give it an F for varnish and finish work," he said), but acknowledged that it sounded "amazing." As Jim Collins put it, "a well-tuned instrument, [Meineke] believed, had to be built in layers, like a boat being built up from the keel. He understood the violin to be a closed box that needed to function as a whole. But he theorized that if either of the two main parts of the box—the top or the back—wasn't by itself in tune with the strings, no amount of adjusting could make the whole box sound clear."

What he found was that different woods and wood thickness inherently produced different pitches from the same string. Merely copying the thicknesses found in an earlier instrument wouldn't do the trick, unless the wood was identical, which was impossible. He became convinced that a maker had to tune each plate to the strings, then the plates together, then the instrument as a whole. "The only way to do it . . . was the way Stradivari probably did it: by listening as he was building and by knowing what he was listening for."[122]

* * *

For decades, there have been murmurings among concert audiences, who often weren't sure they could tell the difference between a famous violin and a newer, very much non-famous, one. Much of the disquiet was *sotto voce* and lacked confidence. How could a listener be sure that he had the competence to quarrel with the experts? Even if he knew which expert to quarrel with, since they were hardly unanimous. And perhaps what differences were audible were due to the musician, and not his instrument. Famous violins tended to be played by famous violinists, after all. The occasional acoustic analyses that were done were inconclusive. No distinct sonic characteristics could be determined.

Finally, in 2014, researchers held two sets of double-blind tests, in which neither musician nor listener knew what violin was being played at any one time. In some ways, the tests were the equivalent of the blind tasting of American versus French wines in 1976, rather snidely known as the Judgment of Paris, in which two Napa Valley wines scored better than the French greats, to the consternation (and pique) of Burgundy and Bordeaux. In this case the comparisons were run not by a British wine merchant, the perpetrator of the taste-off (who had nothing to lose and mischief to make), but by Claudia Fritz, a musical acoustician at Pierre and Marie Curie University in Paris, and Joseph Curtin, a leading violin maker in Ann Arbor, Michigan. As Adrian Cho reported in *Science* magazine, the first test took place in Vincennes, near Paris.[123] Three top-quality modern violins and three Stradivaris were involved, with orchestral accompaniment. "An elite violinist played the same musical excerpt—for example, five measures from Tchaikovsky's Violin Concerto Opus No. 35—on each of the nine possible pairings of violins. Then, a second violinist played a different excerpt on all the pairs, with the order scrambled. The violinists wore modified welding goggles, so they couldn't tell whether they were playing old or new instruments. As [they] played . . . fifty-five listeners rated which instrument in each pair projected better by making a mark on a continuous scale . . . The researchers then averaged all those evaluations, and found that listeners generally thought the new violins "projected" better than the old ones—although they left it up to listeners to decide what that meant." A similar test was held in New York City, this time without the orchestra, with a different set of violins, three new and three old. "Again, the eighty-two listeners in the test reported that the new violins projected better. This time, Fritz and colleagues asked subjects which of the two violins in a pairing they preferred. Listeners again chose the new violins over the old, they reported . . . in the Proceedings of the National Academy of Sciences. The New York City study also showed that listeners' preferences correlated with their assessment of projection, suggesting the loudness of an instrument may be a primary factor in the quality of its sound."[124]

Other tests, of course, followed. All had results that were similar, although not exactly so. The year following the test recounted above, the BBC recruited Isaac Stern, Pinchas Zukerman, and the violin dealer Charles Beare to try to distinguish between the Chaconne Stradivarius (Stradivari's name Latinized), a 1739 Guarneri del Gesú, an 1846 Vuillaume, and a 1976 British violin played behind a screen by a professional soloist. The two violinists were allowed to play all the instruments first. None of the listeners identified more than two of the four instruments. In some of the tests, the antique Italians fared better, in some worse.

The publicity that followed these tests was almost always gleeful. The tabloid newspapers, particularly, took pleasure in *doing it to the toffs*, squelching the whole notion of expertise as being essentially anti-democratic, the same populist reaction that accompanies every story that suggests that experts don't know what they are talking about.

"Projection," the quality that allows the instrument to be clearly heard in a large concert hall, was a constant in the results. Most of the test audiences identified it as a major attribute. Still, is "projection" the only measure of greatness? Is loud-at-the-back-of-the-hall always good? These tests leave that issue unresolved. And as Cho pointed out in his news brief for *Science*, the study leaves open the strong probability that famous antique violins do sound better than their modern counterparts when the listeners know they are hearing a legendary instrument. "If you know it's a Strad," Claudia Fritz points out, "you will hear it differently. You can't turn off that effect."

As for Stradivari's so-called secret, the whole notion is misguided, according to Christopher Germain, a violin maker from Philadelphia, and a Violin Society of America board member. "Stradivari's secret was that he was a genius and that he did a thousand things right, not one thing right. Saying his success came down to just one trick is like saying that if I had the same kind of paint as Michelangelo, I could have painted the Sistine Chapel." If Antonio Stradivari was a genius, isn't that enough?

* * *

None of this devalues the violins of Stradivari and Guarneri. Their value is not dependent on their being unique. It is dependent on their exquisite sound, but also their history, their provenance, their condition, and, yes, their resale price. Which is considerable, and which has shown no sign of diminishing despite the various tests, and despite the now-acknowledged fact that you can acquire a top-quality violin for half a hundred thousand, U.S. dollars and sometimes less than that.

In 2011, a 1721 Stradivari violin called the Lady Blunt Strad sold for $15.9 million. It had been owned by the Nippon Music Foundation, which bought it from collector Robert Lowe, who in turn had owned it for thirty years, having shelled out £84,000. It was sold at auction, the entire proceeds going to the victims of the 2011 Japanese earthquake and tsunami. Who owns the instrument now is not known. It is not played. In fact, it has been seldom played, which may be why it is in such pristine shape. Yehudi Menuhin played it in 1971 and it has been closeted ever since.

The violin's history is part of its attraction. Its first known owner was Jean Baptiste Vuillaume, an award-winning luthier, who "found" the violin in Spain in the 1860s. At least, he is called an award-winning luthier in his Wikipedia biography, and might indeed have been. But he was rather better known for fudging the provenance of many instruments that passed through his hands, and was once described as a "notorious faker of antique violins." Indeed, at the same time he owned the Lady Blunt he was promoting another claimant to be the "inventor" of the violin, one Gasparo Duiffopruggar, a Bavarian who settled in Lyon around 1550. (Don't bother with the spelling—he is variously recorded as Tieffenbrucker, Tiefenbrugger, Tiefenbrucker, Teufenbrugger, Tuiffenbrugger, Deuffenbrugger, Dieffopruchar, Dieffoprughar, Duyfautbrocard, Duiffopruggar, Duiffoprugcar, Dubrocard, Dieffoprukhar, Diafopruchar, Thiphobrucar, Fraburgadi, his first name rendered variously as Kaspar, Caspar or Gaspard.) His candidacy was taken seriously in some quarters, but it later turned out that most instruments attributed to him were nineteenth-century forgeries, emanating from Vuillaume's studio. He had apparently discovered the financial benefits of creative labelling.

Where Vuillaume "found" the Lady Blunt, he never said. He sold it to Lady Anne Blunt, the daughter of Ada Lovelace, the mathematician and writer who is credited in some circles with conceiving the idea for a computer. Blunt was also the granddaughter of the romantic poet Lord Byron. She owned the violin for thirty years, and possibly played it, although she spent most of her time, it seems, setting up and operating a renowned Arabian stud, having eschewed both poetry and music. Lady Blunt eventually sold the violin to someone described only as "an important collector," whose identity remains a mystery. He eventually sold it to Robert Lowe.

A violin with an even more colourful history, and an even more extravagant price, is the so-called Messiah Stradivarius, now under glass in the Ashmolean Museum at Oxford. It, too, passed through the dubious hands of Jean-Baptiste Vuillaume, which became a cause for entirely justified anxiety.

The early provenance of the Messiah is better known than that of the Lady Blunt. Stradivari made the instrument in 1716. The original label, inside the violin, read *Antonius Stradivarius Cremonensis, faciebat anno 1716*, along with the initials *A* and *S*, surrounded by a double circle. When Stradivari died, his son, Paolo, inherited ten unsold instruments from his workshop, and in 1775 he sold all of them, including the Messiah, to Count Ignazio Alessandro Cozio di Salabue, who was then only twenty but who had already acquired a significant collection. (Cozio was the first great connoisseur of violins: "His copious notes on nearly every instrument that passed through his hands contributed enormously to the body of knowledge surrounding Italian violinmaking.")[125] Cozio kept the violin, without ever playing it, until 1827, when he sold it to Luigi Tarisio, who was building up a business dealing mostly in violins; his name survives in Tarisio Auctions, a web-based auction house for stringed instruments.

Buy and sell Tarisio did, but he could never bring himself to part with the Messiah. The notes on the instrument on the modern Tarisio company web page tell the rest of the story: "Instead, he made it a favourite topic of conversation, and intrigued dealers on his visits to Paris with accounts of this marvellous Salabue violin, as it was then called, taking care, however, never to bring it with him. One day Tarisio was discoursing to Vuillaume on the merits of this unknown and marvellous instrument, when the violinist Delphin Alard (Vuillaume's son-in-law), who was present, exclaimed: 'Then your violin is like the Messiah: one always expects him but he never appears'."[126]

Tarisio died in 1854 and by the following year Vuillaume "was able to acquire it," as the modern Tarisio company's web page rather delicately puts it. Vuillaume stuck the thing in a glass case, and never allowed anyone to play it, or even examine it, although he did once allow it to be shown, at the 1872 Exhibition of Instruments in the South Kensington Museum, London. When he died, his two daughters inherited it, and then his son-in-law Alard.

Alard held the violin until his death in 1888, and his heirs sold it in 1890 to W. E. Hill & Sons, "on behalf of a Mr. R. Crawford of Edinburgh." The price was £2,600, until then the highest price ever paid for a violin. In 1939, the Hill company gave all its collection to Oxford's Ashmolean Museum, where it has remained on display and never been played. That's still one of the reasons the Messiah is so highly valued: it has never been played in performance and is the nearest thing to a hot-off-the-workbench mint-condition Stradivari that exists.

In 1999, a bombshell dropped onto this tidy story. The bombshell (actually a salvo of bombshells) was detonated by an America expert on historical musical instruments, Stewart Pollens, in a series of articles published in the *Journal of the Violin Society of America*. The Messiah wasn't a Stradivari violin at all, Pollens declared. Its provenance had worried him for some time, he said, mostly because it had passed through the hands (his phrase) of Jean-Baptiste Vuillaume. Pollens said he found little or no proof that Vuillaume had ever acquired a Stradivari, but ample evidence that he had manufactured the provenance subsequently.

It had started innocently enough. Pollens had been hired to catalogue the Ashmolean's collection and, as part of the process, he took high-resolution pictures of all instruments on display. It was when he came to handle the Messiah and inspect it closely that he began to have doubts. He went minutely over the various points of authenticity: provenance, craftsmanship, documentation, and dendrochronology (the age of the woods used). On provenance, the presence of Vuillaume was enough to give pause. Documentation, ditto. When he looked at the craft that went into making the violin, he found several problems with the f-holes, and also with the rib structure and the finishing. He asked a tree-ring expert, dendrochronologist Peter Klein at Hamburg University, to give his opinion. Klein never handled the Messiah himself, but was given a set of what Pollens described as high-precision photographs. Klein's conclusion: the tree used to make the instrument's top was felled after Stradivari's death in 1737. As Melik Kaylan put it in a piece for *Forbes* magazine in 2001, "the whole controversy was further poisoned by sporadic problems of access to the instrument itself." The Ashmolean had gotten the wind up, and was refusing any further inspections.

Slowly evidence, some of it technical and much of it arcane, began to accumulate that seemed to cast doubt on Pollens's conclusions. Jeffrey S. Loen, geoscientist turned acoustician, a former editor of the journal *CAS* (*Catgut Acoustical Society*) reported on meticulous thickness measurements of the woods on the Messiah compared to those of other known Stradivari instruments: "Thickness gradation maps of the Messiah violin show similar characteristics to those of the Betts (1704), Cremonese (1715), Tuscan-Medici (1716), and other Golden Age Stradivarius violins . . . These characteristics do not prove the Messiah's authenticity, although such a hypothesis seems permissive because of the similarity of these commonly hidden, highly personal traits." Malcolm Cleaveland, a geosciences professor who led the Ashmolean's attempt to question Pollens, concluded at the end of the process that "we can't confirm that this is a Stradivarius, but we can say that it's in the right time frame."

Is the controversy over? Kaylan quotes Robert Bein of the Chicago dealership Bein & Fushi: "I've held three or four hundred Strads in my hand. He [Pollens] had no such experience. I can tell you from my experience that the discrepancies he detects, in quality and craftsmanship, are well within the confines of what makes a Stradivarius good. Also, the arguments based on the dubious character of some of the owners . . . So, what's new? That's never been a way to establish or deny provenance."

The market values the Messiah at $20 million U.S.. The market has spoken. The Ashmolean is not selling.[127]

Since the Messiah is not for sale (nor, apparently, for playing) the highest price actually paid for a violin is not for a Strad but for one of the last built by Guarneri del Gesù, commonly called the Vieuxtemps Guarneri (a.k.a. the V. Guarneri), not because it is old, although it is, having been made in 1741, but because one of its owners was Henri Vieuxtemps, a Belgian composer and violinist. It last sold to "Anon." in 2013 for $16 million.

So far, too, there have been no imputations of mischief in its provenance, even though it, too, passed through the hands of M. Vuillaume. Oddly, for an instrument so revered, its first critic was severe. That was Count Cozio, who described it in 1804 as being "too high in the ribs and strong in the wood," with a "small tone," a judgment disputed 270 years later by Yehudi Menuhin, who preferred it to his own Stradivari, the one called the Soil. Menuhin once wrote in a letter that "the arching of this instrument is very Brescian. In fact, the form is practically identical to an instrument made by Gasparo da Salò."

One of the V. Guarneri's small oddities is that it was made with new wood, especially the spruce, according to dendrochronological data. Perhaps its tone changed as the wood matured. Indeed, all violins need time to mature. "The Hill book on the Guarneri family estimates the seasoning period required for Stainer's violins as from 10 to 15 years; Amati, Stradivari and Guarneri del Gesù each progressively longer, with largest models taking the longest, so that the most massive models of del Gesù and Bergonzi might take eighty years to reach their peak performing power. Amount and intensity of use must be an important and variable factor affecting this maturation, for the sound of an unplayed violin does not mature at all."[128]

Yes, violins need to be played regularly. Violinist Christoph Koncz, who has been allowed by the Mozart Museum to play Mozart's own personal violin, still in excellent condition, had this to say:

> As it was very rarely played, at first its wood was stiff and it lacked resonance and its sound had fallen asleep. I played it for hours and days at a time and each time I played it its sound opened up and the wood was in harmony again. The time it took to get it into shape each day became shorter the more often I played it.[129]

In the shorter term, violins seem to retain some kind of molecular memory, the method ill understood, if it exists at all. "Seems" because no scientific theory has emerged, yet players believe it is true, and claim they can detect it when it is there. Thus, a wooden musical instrument will "remember" someone who has played it a lot—even after the player dies, much can be learned about that person just from studying and playing the instrument. Musicians often say that their instruments seem like living things, trying to "help" when and where they can. Does the violin (and the cello) "remember" the music? It seems too fanciful, but many believe it nonetheless.[130]

* * *

Like the two Stradivaris tracked above, the V. Guarneri has a somewhat colourful provenance. Its first post-workshop owner is not known, but from sometime later in the century until 1804 it was owned by Giacomo Antonio Monzino, who worked in a musical instrument workshop founded by his father Antonio. It was never quite clear why Monzino wanted it. The Monzino family made guitars, not violins, and while Giacomo learned to play the violin before he learned the guitar, he mainly wrote music for the guitar, and played that instrument alone in his later years.

Monzino sold the Guarneri to an unknown buyer, and it was then bought by one Dr. Benziger, of whom nothing else is known. In 1858, it was acquired by none other than the seemingly inevitable Jean-Baptiste Vuillaume, who kept it for a mere two years before selling to the firm Hart & Son, who bought it on behalf of Vieuxtemps himself, who kept it for twenty-one years. Although he had a Stradivari violin, too, the Guarneri was the instrument he used throughout his playing career.

Vieuxtemps, born in the town of Verviers, then in the Netherlands but now part of Belgium, was a child prodigy and a great virtuoso. He gave his first public performance, a concerto by Pierre Rode, at the age of six. He was a prolific composer and indefatigable touring musician, but was forced to retire early after a stroke left him partially paralysed. His funeral in Verviers in 1881 drew thousands of mourners, coming to witness the burial of the "musician who had had a seismic effect on European musical life, first as a child prodigy, then as a composer, and finally as the reigning violin soloist of the period."[131] Rumour had it that Vieuxtemps had wanted the famous violin buried with him. If this was true, he clearly had a change of mind. Instead, it was carried behind the hearse, on a velvet cushion borne by the also-eminent violinist Eugène Ysaÿe.

Ysaÿe briefly took custody of the violin, but never owned it. A year later, in collaboration with one of Vieuxtemps's brothers, he sold it to the Duc de Camposelice, so-called, a prolific collector of celebrated musical instruments. "So-called" because he wasn't really a duke, merely a "handsome and charismatic Belgian violinist," Victor-Nicolas Reubsaet, who, luckily for him, had married Isabella Singer, the fabulously wealthy widow of Isaac Singer, tycoon of sewing machines. Reubsaet had claimed for years that a lapsed aristocratic title could be found in his family lineage, and with his wife's boundless money at his disposal, he actually discovered two titles, not just one. In 1879, he reinvented himself as Vicomte d'Estenburgh, and then, in 1881, as the Duc de Camposelice, a duke being nobler than a viscount by any measure. Money being no object, he also bought himself a Stradivari violin, now named the Camposelice Stradivarius. He at one point owned seven Stradivaris, and two more Guarneris.

Camposelice sold the V. Guarneri in 1891 to Maurice Sons, a Dutch and English violinist and pedagogue, head of London's Royal College of Music, and sometime concertmaster of the Scottish Orchestra. Few reviews of Sons's performances survive. He is perhaps most famous for being the subject of a splendid portrait by the Anglophile painter Lawrence Alma-Tadema, called, unimaginatively, *Portrait of Maurice Sons Playing the Violin in Alma-Tadema's Studio*. It is not clear which violin he is seen playing in the painting, but it was probably a good one, maybe even *the* good one. (In 2020, you could buy a shower curtain from pixel.com called *Portrait of Maurice Sons Playing the Violin in Alma-Tadema's Studio*. Good water-shedding capabilities, too. Price, $62.)

Sons sold the violin in 1927 to W. E. Hill & Sons, the London-based company specializing in stringed instruments, and it was then picked up by members of the Wurlitzer family, the famous piano makers who later became even more famous for musical devices such as band organs, orchestrions, player pianos, electric pianos, organs, and, of course, jukeboxes and vending machines. Dozens of famous violins passed through the family firm over time, including at least thirty Stradivaris. The Wurlitzers sold the V. Guarneri the same year they bought it, 1927, to the violinist Robert Bower. Bower bought several Strads from the Wurlitzers, too, including one dubbed the Virgin, so-called by the irrepressible Vuillaume, who had re-carved its tailpiece to resemble Joan of Arc, the Pucelle d'Orléans, the Virgin (Maid) of Orleans.

In 1942, the violin was sold again, this time to Isaac Wolfson, a Scottish businessman and philanthropist, who later put up the money for Wolfson College at Oxford, which had Isaiah Berlin as its first president. It's not known whether Wolfson took time off from tycooning and giving away money to actually play his new possession. He didn't own it for long, in any case, but soon sold it to the violinist Philip Newman, a close friend of Queen Elizabeth (the wife of George VI, not the most recent one). Newman's last public performance was in September 1966. He played Kreisler's *Recitative* and *Scherzo Caprice*, on, of course, the V. Guarneri. He died two months later, in Majorca, one year to the day after the death of Queen Elizabeth.

From 1966, the V. Guarneri was owned (and played) by a London merchant banker, Ian Stoutzker who, in his teens, was a pupil at the Royal College of Music. "Stoutzker treasured his Guarnerius dearly," the writer Norman Lebrecht recounted. "He once took me upstairs in his Belgravia mansion and showed me where he kept it, underneath his bed, ready to be played first thing in the morning or during a sleepless night." Stoutzker was a former chairman of the London Philharmonic Orchestra and a founder, with Yehudi Menuhin, of the Live Music Now charity.[132]

When Stoutzker decided to sell, it was picked up by the well-known auction house denizen Anonymous, who sold it in turn in 2013 for the price of $16 million U.S. to Another Anonymous, the current owner, who then selected the American violinist Anne Akiko Meyers to take and use the violin for her lifetime, truly a gift without price.

* * *

Curiously, in very few of the old-versus-new violin playoffs were the new violins and their makers actually identified. Even in the most prominent test, by Claudia Fritz and others, the modern violins went unnamed. As the authors of the study put it, "the new violins were each by a different maker and were between several days and several years old. They were chosen from a pool of violins assembled by the authors [of the subsequent report] who then selected the three that they felt had the most impressive playing qualities and contrasted with each other in terms of character of sound." So why not tell us who made them? Similarly with the BBC's Pinchas Zukerman/Isaac Stern test; all the antiques were identified, but the modern one was only identified as "a 1976 British violin."

It was generally recorded that the violins were used "providing they were anonymous." But why? Possibly because their makers were nervous about losing, but the real if faintly ridiculous reason seems to have been that the organizers were leery of the publicity that would result, giving a few luthiers an advantage denied their compatriots. Still, some information leaked out. In one of the tests, already mentioned for its curiosity about fungi and how it affected the wood, the British violinist Matthew Trusler matched his 1711 Stradivari to modern violins made in 2009 by the Swiss luthier Michael Rhomheimer.

Clearly, as the blind tests showed, contemporary luthiers produce instruments as good, or nearly as good, as the Italian masters. Violinist Christian Tetzlaff, for example, formerly played a well-known Stradivari violin, but changed to one made in 2002 by Stefan-Peter Greiner. In his view, the listener couldn't tell the difference, but as a musician he considered the new one "excellent for Bach, and better than a Stradivarius for the big Romantic and twentieth-century concertos."

Hundreds of luthiers are currently plying their trade. Exactly how many and where they are is unknown, or in any case is a moving target— there are two within a thirty-minute drive of where I live, and I live in the boondocks in a sparsely populated part of the world. Violin societies in various countries list their members, but not all luthiers want to join or are invited to join. Still, there are some who stand out, either because they have won competitions, or because a well-known musician has adopted their work, or because their instruments are particularly striking in design, artistry, and tone, or because they are self-promoters, and sometimes all of the above. Among them would surely be Greiner, now a director of W. E. Hill & Sons. He built his first violin, a creditable effort, when he was fourteen; his professed aim is to make violins that mimic, or at least come close to, the human voice in song, within the range from 2000 to 4000 Hz.

One of the most famous of the moderns is Britain's Roger Hargrave, long recognized as one the world's preeminent copyists (a positive term in this context), specializing in detailed reproductions of classical Italian violins. Much of the wood he uses is a century old, and some of it twice that. His work is renowned for its aesthetic beauty and exceptional tonal qualities. He won a gold medal at one of the most prestigious competitions, the International Triennale in Cremona.

The following far-from-complete list is comprised of violin makers whose work is widely recognized as outstanding.

Patrick Robin has a studio on the Loire that has become a haven for musicians. Robin studied with Roger Hargrave when the latter was working in Bremen. He was a graduate of England's prestigious Newark School of Violin Making (he won that institution's Royal Oakden cup for "outstanding achievements," unspecified). In 1991, at the inaugural International Violin Making Competition, he won two gold medals, one for violin and the other for cello. Joseph Curtin, of Ann Arbor, Michigan, is another. He has made violins for many prominent musicians, including Erick Friedman, Ilya Kaler, Cho-Liang Lin, Elmar Oliveira, Yehudi Menuhin, and Ruggiero Ricci. A violin he made with his then-partner, Greg Alf, was sold in 2013 for $132,000, a record price for a work by a living craftsman. Another award-winning partnership is that of the Berlin-based duo Mira Gruszow and Gideon Baumblatt, whose instruments "are planned by two brains and realized by four hands," Mira doing the sculpture of archings and scrolls, Gideon "the play of colours and effects in varnish and its antiquing process" (their own self-description). They won a rare double gold medal (for tone and for workmanship) at the 2018 Violin Society of America competition.

Alina Kostina, a Russian-born violin maker living in Eugene, Oregon, takes a self-deprecating tone in her personal publicity, but her violins are unusual, renowned for their dark, somewhat brooding, tone. "She grew to love the violin through her early childhood music studies. Although the Soviet Union produced many great violinists, it provided its children with appalling violins. For many years of her early life, Alina lived in the conviction that violins were made in Moscow Furniture Factory No. 2. Armed with a greenish-yellow fiddle and a color-matched bow, complete with double bass grade hair, six-year-old Alina went to work, bowing hard, hoping one day this repurposed furniture would blossom into a real Strad and the black hair on her bow would turn unicorn white. Needless to say, much rosin was applied in pursuit of the coveted white hair."

The Armenious brothers, Hratch and Artak, live and work in Willowdale, a Toronto suburb. Hratch has been turning out highly prized violins and cellos for forty-five years, his younger brother Artak for more than twenty. Restoration work on damaged instruments is a specialty. Armenious violins show up on most of the Best Of lists on several continents; they are beloved for their clear tones, rich timbre, and elegant craftsmanship.

Anton Domozhyrov is another Canadian, born in Russia and living in Winnipeg. "As the son of two classical musicians," he jokes, "I have been in love with the sound of the violin from before my birth." Early in his career, Domozhyrov recalls, he had access to instruments by many of the great masters including Stradivari, Guarneri, Bergonzi, and Rogeri, through his apprenticeship with Anatoly Kochergin, curator of the Russian National Collection. "This . . . consolidated my absolute belief that a physical knowledge of the wood in the maker's hand—its feel, response, flexibility is paramount in the creation of a beautiful sounding instrument. This in combination with an eye for line and color and meticulous attention to detail is what is required to build a truly great instrument."

Lisa Gass, a Californian, is really a bass maker and restorer (she has referred to violins as "those tiny things") but one of her violins got her on the Violin Society of America's list of fifty modern American violin makers. Ute Zahn, German-born, British educated (Newark School of Violin Making) and long-time Hong Kong resident (she had her own violin making and restoration workshop in the city, and freelanced as a cellist); she now lives in Minneapolis. Jedidjah de Vries, sometimes of Boston and sometime of Washington, DC, calls himself a toolmaker rather than a luthier, his intention to make the "best possible tool I can for the musician and the music . . . I have been playing the violin since I was a young child. And while I enjoy playing . . . I was captivated by the seemingly magical relationship between the music in my ears and the beautiful object in my hand. That magic is the result of the violin's ingenious design, its rich history, and the fine materials and craftsmanship that go into its creation."

Finally, Mario Miralles, a legendary, if rather reclusive, maker of string instruments of all kinds, who works in Altadena, California. He has no web page of his own, and shuns publicity. He was briefly and reluctantly in the spotlight when an international stolen instrument alert was issue after the theft of one of his cellos from a hotel room in San Diego in 2018. Laurie Niles, in her piece on violinist.com on fifty modern American makers, was struck by the violin he showed at a recital, a beautiful thing made from hard-to-carve bird's-eye maple. Salestina, a society founded by and for violinists, called him "a rare genius."

* * *

In the centuries since the masters of northern Italy, there have been a few small improvements to the classical form. The fingerboard, for instance, was lengthened to reach the middle of the body. This was done to allow the players to play more of the high end of the E string, to match evolving musical fashion. Then, to increase the volume and brightness of the tone, the bridge was raised, along with the position of the fingerboard, to increase string tension, and the increased tension meant the interior bass bar had to be reinforced and strengthened. The addition of the chinrest, which allowed all sorts of sophisticated playing scarcely possible before, came as late as the 1820s, invented by the composer Louis Spohr. These small changes distinguish what are now called Baroque and modern violins. Almost all Stradivari and Guarneri violins still in existence have been modified into modern violins.

Modern or antique, a violin starts with the wood.

You need high-quality wood with the proper density and tone, and it must be beautiful, with attractive figure and straight grain, since it is going to be seen by many people for a very long time. Some eminent luthiers use antique wood, sometimes more than a hundred years old, but that is not really necessary. As mentioned, Guarneri was occasionally known to use new wood for his instruments.

Different woods are used in various parts of the instrument, spruce, maple, ebony, boxwood, willow (sometimes), poplar, and rosewood. Long trial and error has suggested spruce for the top, also known as the top plate, the soundboard, the belly, or the table. Spruce is hard, but also resonant and lightweight. The bottom and the side plates, also known as the ribs, are most often made from maple, from any of a number of maple species, because maple has a beautiful figure when cut right (being efficient is not the only concern here; beauty is an important part of the whole, and built into the craft). Modern luthiers, like Miralles, have even attempted the hard-to-carve bird's-eye maple, and some of the most striking can have a sort of corduroy look, rather than the satiny finish that plainly figured maple yields. The neck of the violin is mostly made from the same maple as the back. By tradition, the fingerboard is made of ebony. Other "fittings," like tuning pegs, tailpiece, and chinrest, are made from ebony, rosewood, or boxwood. The "purfling" (more on that in a moment) can be made of any wood that makes a good contrast to the spruce top, sometimes even fibre, or very thick paper. The first known purfling, on a violin by Andrea Amati in 1564, was made from two outer strips of pearwood stained black, and an inner layer of poplar. The inner parts of the violin, the parts unseen after assembly such as the structural corner and end blocks, can be made from whatever is to hand, usually spruce or willow. The bass bar should be straight-grained spruce. The soundpost, which is also internal but can be peeked at through the f-shaped sound holes, is also spruce. The bridge is usually maple.

The toolkit of a luthier would surprise no fine woodworker: planes, chisels, gouges, knives, saws, scrapers, clamps, and, often, steam bending irons. Also, of course, sharpening tools and honing devices. All who work with wood know to keep their tools razor-sharp. A woodworker might be surprised to find no sandpaper in a violin maker's studio, and a couple of other tools, while not unknown to woodworkers, are more specialized. Thickness calipers are essential for luthiers, as we shall see. Small curved-bottom thumb planes are necessary, too. Peg-hole reamers and peg shavers are useful (although more conventional tools can be substituted), and so is a purfling groove cutter.

To begin, you need a pattern or template. Start with a famous violin you particularly admire. There is almost certainly a pattern available for that, often in a downloadable document or in a plastic cut-out. Or, of course, you could design your own, as the masters did. You will need to cut a wooden form conforming to the pattern, around fifteen to eighteen millimetres thick. This will be an inside form, cut to the exact outline of the inside of the finished piece. Wood for the four corner and two end blocks are then cut and temporarily glued to cutouts on the form, then gouged and filed to exactly fit the pattern.[133]

The first step to actual construction is to cut the ribs, the sides of the violin. These are slices of maple slightly taller than the finished height (about thirty to thirty-two millimetres), run through a thickness planer to be no more than one millimetre thick. They are bent to the shape of the form with its six blocks, using a steam heater, and glued to the blocks, held tight while drying with a series of small clamps and some counter-forms shaped to match the outside contours of the violin. The traditional glue is made from rabbit hide. When the glue is dry, the "linings" are glued to the inside of the new ribs. These are pieces of spruce, two millimetres by eight millimetres, used to reinforce the ribs and giver a better gluing surface for the top and bottom. Finally, the corners are trimmed with sharp chisels, and planed to be level.

Next, the crucial wood for belly (top) and bottom. As indicated, spruce for the top and maple for the bottom. This is a matter for the utmost care, because the character of the wood chosen will be evident for all to see.

You don't need antique wood, but you would likely prefer old-growth trees, or trees from higher altitudes, because their wood is harder, denser, and stronger. It also matters how the piece was cut from the parent log. It should have been quarter-sawn, not straight-sawn, to give more attractive patterns. Then you want to choose exactly where to cut the boards. Where the age rings are denser, the cut will be thicker. The resulting piece is then sliced into two matching trapezoids, which are then "book-matched" or butterflied back into one piece, and glued back together. The hardest wood, because of its density, will be in the middle of the finished violin, where the bridge is placed, under the strings. This bookmatching also makes the wood symmetrical, which makes the vibration qualities symmetrical, while also adding to the harmonious look of the finished piece. Making the two trapezoids fit exactly is difficult and painstaking, but crucial. Then the inside of both back and front are planed flat. The glued-up ribs are laid on the flat side, the outline traced with a pencil, and the piece then cut to size, either using a fret or coping saw.

When finished, the top and bottom must be arched, not flat. This is where luthiers part company with pure woodworkers and take on an extra complication, for the design and shape of the arching strongly influences the tone of the violin and thus the music it can make, and minute adjustments are constantly necessary during the building process. The arching is also structural. A luthier will aim for a catenary arch, which is more or less the shape a fine chain will make hanging freely from its ends. The arch helps distribute the pressure caused by the tension of the strings pressing downwards, the same principle as an arch in a bridge, which distributes the weight of the roadbed it bears to the buttresses on each side.

The arching is achieved by gouges, thumb planes, and scrapers, very delicate work, a millimeter at a time. The interior is done first, then the piece is flipped and the outside scraped thinner. The aim is to finish with a piece of wood no more than 4.5 millimetres thick at the centre, and 2.5 millimetres at the perimeter. But you can't just carve the thing thin and hope for the best. The final thickness influences the acoustic values of the finished violin, and (as per Cal Meineke, whose method was described earlier) involves frequent testing of the frequencies by tap-testing the wood or, in more recent times, using a resonance measurement device. The idea is to establish harmonies in the frequencies of either plate, and then both plates together. Wood is continually removed between each test, until the maker's ear is satisfied.

Two more things need to be done before the top and bottom can be attached to the ribs. First the f-holes need to cut out of the top, one on each side. They're called f-holes because they're shaped like the italic letter *f*; no one *really* knows why it is no longer the c-hole of the traditional viola, or some other shape like the fleeting fashion for the flame, the half-moon, the *S* and others. These holes are not just for decoration; they assist in transmitting the internal vibrations to the outside and therefore resonate the frequencies better. They also, of course, help with air circulation and prevent the violin from overheating.

Lastly the bass board, or bass bar, a rectangular piece of spruce, is glued to the inside of the top, underneath where the strings will be, or more precisely under where the lowest string will be. Its purpose is twofold: it acts as a strengthening beam, and helps to even out and clarify the low frequencies.[134] This is also one part of a violin that has changed substantially since Stradivari's time. George Grove, in *A Dictionary of Music and Musicians*, explains:

> [Giuseppe] Tartini states, in the year 1734, that the tension of
> the strings on a violin was equal to a weight of 63 lb (29 kg),

while nowadays it is calculated at more than 80 lb (36 kg) . . . This enormous increase in pressure requires for the belly a proportionate addition of bearing-power, and this could only be given by strengthening the bass bar, which has been done by giving it a slight additional depth at the centre, and adding considerably to its length. In consequence of this we hardly ever find in an old instrument the original bass bar of the maker, just as rarely as the original sound-post or bridge, all of which however can be made as well by any experienced living violin-maker as by the original Stradivari or Amati."

The bass bar, as any musician will attest, amplifies the lower frequencies.

The interior finished, for now, the form is removed and the back and front glued to the ribs, the back with a tight glue and the front with a slightly weaker glue to allow easier removal should it become necessary at some point. Then the groove for the purfling is incised and the wood removed with a pick. *Purfling* is a term used in inlay work. It means a shallow groove into which a contrasting material to the surrounding wood can then be pressed and glued, yielding a sometimes intricate pattern. For the violin, the purfling serves a purpose beyond the merely decorative: it helps protect the body from cracks resulting from accidental bumps. The rest of the pieces are then carved and fitted. The neck is a long piece of maple to which the fingerboard is glued; the fingerboard is ebony, slightly curved, and runs under the strings; the pegbox and the scroll are one piece, the pegbox cut square with holes cut into its sides for the tuning pegs, the scroll, which is purely decorative, is an extension of the pegbox; the pegs themselves from ebony, one to tune each string; the tailpiece is a flared shape onto which the ends of the strings are attached; the tailpiece itself is attached to the end button, a small circular knob made of ebony, by a loop of gut; the saddle is an ebony ridge over which the tailpiece loop passes to prevent the tailpiece contacting the top plate when it is vibrating; the bridge holds the strings off the body, allows them to vibrate freely and transmits string energy into the box of the violin, increasing the sound volume; the fine tuners, small screws fitted into the tailpiece used for minor adjustments; and the chinrest, whose function is obvious. Finally, the sound-post.

The sound-post is an oddity. It has been called the "soul of the violin," for no particularly good reason. It is a thin cylinder of spruce, about the diameter of a pencil, that is pushed after glue-up into the interior of the violin through the f-hole near the E string, the thinnest one, and friction fitted to sit vertically between the top and bottom plates. The fit must be exact, and it may take multiple tries to get it right; it must be perfectly perpendicular to the plates and positioned properly in relation to the bridge. But "properly" can mean different things to different luthiers. By tradition, it is placed about three millimetres behind the treble foot of the bridge, but the exact placement can vary slightly. If it shifts to the right, the violin would have an enhanced treble. If closer to the bridge, the sound will become clearer but less mellow. What the sound-post does is transmit the vibrations of the strings to the back plate, and thus helps balance the various frequencies. Clever luthiers can shift a violin's tone by minute adjustments to the sound-post.

It is not certain that the earliest violins had a sound-post at all. Christian Rault, in his discursive summary of violin history, doubts that they did:

We have to wait until the final decade [of the sixteenth century] to meet with certainty, for the first time, clear mention of the use of the sound-post. In London in 1596 William Shakespeare [had just finished] his Romeo and Juliet. Three protagonists of this famous drama are musicians called respectively Rebeck [rebec], Catling [the smallest string instrument] and . . . Soundpost. Around the same year . . . real instruments had been put in the hands of music-making angels, sculpted in wood in the burial chapel of Freiberg Cathedral. Five bowed instruments from the violin family (small discant, discant, tenor, and bass) had been built in workshops near Freiberg, most of them bearing a central sound-post of a rectangular section, situated between the two upper circles of the f-shaped sound holes.[135]

If the body of the violin is the resonator and controller, the sound is made by the bow and the strings. And stringing sounds easy, but it is not.

First of all, why four strings, like the viola, cello, and double bass? After all, it started out with three.

To some degree at least, the four strings represent "a good engineering compromise, based on ergonomic and acoustic constraints," as the musicologist Richard Cownie put it. "The violinist has four fingers available for use on the fingerboard. To keep the technical challenges manageable, you want to be able to play a scale without having to change to higher positions, so it makes sense for the interval between adjacent strings to be no more than a sixth. And if it were a sixth, for music in the Western tradition you'd have a dilemma about whether to make it a minor sixth or a major sixth, so making it a fifth is a good compromise . . . Then with strings separated in fifths, how many strings should there be? That's where acoustics come in—the lower pitches will be weak unless the instrument has a large soundbox, so if you make an acoustic bowed instrument with a low string pitched much below the G of the violin, you converge on the design of the viola—which is kinda ok, but not really as big as you'd like for the low C, giving rise to the viola's poor reputation compared to the violin and the much larger cello."[136] Unlike on the bass or the cello, the violinist's left hand can reach a scale of slightly more than two octaves without changing position.

Technically, the pitch of a string can be varied and controlled by how it is made, by changing its linear density, its mass per unit length, and how thick and heavy it is. The frequency is inversely proportional to the square root of the linear density. Also, if two strings are of equal length and under the same tension, the one with the higher mass produces the lower pitch. A string twice as long produces a tone of half the frequency. A looser string results in a lower pitch. All of which may or may not make you play better.

Once, and occasionally still, the strings were made of catgut, though it was never from cats. Catgut is from cattle, or sheep, or sometimes from horses and mules (you wouldn't get much yardage from Tabby). A cow intestine can produce catgut strings up to fifty metres long. In any case, the word derives not from *cat* but from *kytte*, a narrow form of medieval stringed instrument popular with itinerant minstrels because of its portability.

Gut was and is freely available except in vegetarian cultures. The usable parts of cattle intestine are from the submucosa, and from the external layers, which contain the collagen, which is what you want. "Collagen is found throughout the bodies of mammals, and some other vertebrates. Wherever structural strength and elasticity is required in soft tissue, you may find collagen there. Skin, for instance, needs to be both strong and elastic. The intestines also need strength and elasticity, for they need to stretch without bursting, and then to contract back to normal size after food passes. At slaughterhouses, gut-takers split the intestines in half lengthwise, and the halves are then soaked in a series of caustic solutions to dissolve away all the tissue except the collagen fibres. Once all these fibres are clean and pure, they are then stretched, twisted, and allowed to dry under tension."[137]

Gut core strings are still regarded as having the best tone, but they are finicky, reacting to changes in the weather and small pressure changes. From the sixteenth century the lowest, and thickest, strings were wrapped with silver wire to give them increased mass. Modern strings are made from a synthetic core, usually nylon, wrapped in metal, usually steel but sometimes aluminum or even gold. There are many variants, and many brands. Some luthiers make their living designing and fabricating strings. One of the fascinations and occasional frustrations of violins is that a string may sound amazing on one instrument but sour, dull, or too bright on another. "Some instruments will respond better to some strings than other. Strings vary in their sound, playability, volume and responsiveness. Each instrument is unique and each player is unique."[138]

Strings don't always last, and some players go through more strings than others. James Ehnes, the Canadian violinist: "I go through strings pretty quickly. Strings are kind of like tires. For regular use, they can last for a long, long time, depending on the type of thing you do—if you're a race car driver, you change them several times a race, right? I'm not saying I change them several times a concert, but . . . the type of playing I do is just really hard on them. The higher the performing instrument—and in this case, a Stradivarius—the harder it's going to be on the peripheral parts, because you notice the little details."

The strings make the sound, but the bow makes the strings make the sound.

A bow is basically a stick with a ribbon of parallel horse-tail hairs stretched between the ends. The part of the bow that tightens (or loosens) the hairs is called the frog.

A bow maker is called an *archetier*, from *archet*, French for *bow* (no great mystery there; *archery* has the same root). The best wood for bows has always been pernambuco, usually called Brazilwood, endemic to tropical Brazil. It was first exported to Germany for use in creating dyes, but archetiers discovered that its exceptional hardness made it ideal for musical bows. Alas, pernambuco trees are endangered, and cultivations are not fruitful (you get something like a handful of bows from one tree over a thirty-year period). Modern bows use a carbonate material, similar to that in tennis rackets.

Bow hair is a hank of horsehair, somewhere between 160 and 180 individual hairs for each bow, attached in a ribbon. Horsehair, curiously, has a few advantages not readily seen without magnification. One of them is a series of small bumps that help create the friction that produces the violin's characteristic subtle weeping tone. The most popular horsehair is white horsehair from Mongolia, for Mongolian horses were renowned for their long bushy tails. This is no doubt because the Mongolians were good marketers: horse breeding is still a significant industry there. [139]

Rosin, used to create friction and thus sound (the friction causing the string to vibrate), is applied to the bow hair before use. Rosin is hardened pine sap, sold in either yellow or black cakes, both of which produce a sticky white powder that adds to the friction between bow and strings. The darker rosin works best in cool climates, but may be too sticky when humid.

Can a bow make much difference? Listen to Yo-Yo Ma (a cellist, of course, not a violinist, but still): "[Benoît Rolland is] an artist-scientist who is an inventor, and I mean that very seriously. For my sixtieth birthday, my wife surprised me and commissioned a bow from him. You know, I'm not an equipment guy. I never like to think about bows or instruments or even strings and rosin. When I'm on tour, I can't count on anything. If I'm an equipment freak, I'll just be a miserable guy all the time because things are not exactly right. So when my wife first presented it to me, I thought: 'It's wonderful. How thoughtful. Whatever.' Then I started playing—and then I just never stopped. It did something extraordinary. I never knew that a bow can make such a difference."

* * *

So much for the thing itself, the box and bits. But where's the *music*?

All these many hours of painstaking construction, all these minute shavings, all these tiny adjustments, all this varnishing and polishing and tuning (and rosining), all of it is in the service of making emotional sound. Which is why a violin in a museum offends. Locking a violin in a glass case is like unstringing a longbow and hiding it in the attic, or de-masting a schooner and keeping it forever alongside a wharf where it will bob up and down on the tides, but that's not what it's *for*. The music, after all, is what the violin is for.

No one goes to a concert to hear an instrument, as James Ehnes puts it. They go to hear the music. But they don't just go for the music, either. They go for the music as interpreted by the player, levels on levels, layers on layers.

But what music? The violin came alive in Renaissance Europe, the timing unsurprising. The violin was different, and the Renaissance was a synonym for ferment, a product of multiple forces, acting sometimes in concert and sometimes in antagonism. A hundred years had passed since the Black Death devastated Europe, but that apocalyptic event destabilized everything, and nothing any longer was sure. All the certainties that made up the medieval world were called into question. The Church, formerly the guarantor of stability and traditional moral values, was leaking credibility and power. Any institution that had serial Médicis at its apex struggled to assert moral authority, and cynicism was rampant. Spain sent a pope into Italy for the first time. Empires were crumbling. The Holy Roman Empire, as Voltaire's sardonic formulation had it, was not very holy, not at all roman, and not much of an empire. Small princelings and dukes contended; small wars were two a penny. Kings captured territory wherever they could, and then other kings seized it back. The French, when they weren't warring with England, were warring instead with Spain. Or whatever passed for Italy. Or the German fiefdoms. The English saw no reason they shouldn't own France; the French, similarly, coveted Piedmont, Tuscany, Sicily, and more. Spain was seized by the notion of *limpieza del sangre*, the cleansing of blood, and had expelled the Jews and the Moors. The Jews fled to the north shores of the Mediterranean and the Muslims to the south, a diaspora that further fertilized the creative ferment that was already there, adding to the existing migrations caused by disease and war. The European pot was melting.

The scattering of Europe into small contending but wealthy states created small courts that competed for status; costly entertainments were devised for the princelings to dazzle and impress. Dancing was the *art du jour*, and the Italians clapped themselves on the back for inventing ballet. Lorenzo de' Medici, ruler of the Florentine "empire" and peerless patron of the arts, had a dancing master, William the Jew, or Guglielmo Ebreo da Pesaro, who was knighted by the Holy Roman Emperor and who presided over the entertainments at the courts of Naples, Milan, and Ferraro (he later converted to Catholicism and started calling himself Giovanni Ambrosio). His *Trattato dell' arte del ballare* defended dancing as the noblest of arts, and contains choreographies and music for thirty-six dances by William and his contemporaries. King Charles VIII of France, when he visited Italy in 1494, professed himself astonished and impressed by the wealth of dancing he encountered.

For dancing, violins were the instrument of choice. Viols and violas did well in the drawing room. They were fairly easy to learn to play, and had a soothing rather than expressive tone; violins, on the other hand, were considered unsuitable for virtuous people. They were the instruments of dancing masters and professional fiddlers; celebratory dances demanded something louder, vital, expressive, and violins, with their emotional vibrato and virtuoso capacities, were perfect for the role. They were loud, too, almost brash. Their carrying power kept them out of salons, at least at first, but they were ideal for the ballroom, and later for concerto soloists.

In the early days of violins, which means in the closing decades of the Renaissance, musicians loved them for their ability to "sing like the human voice," as the early composers insisted they could, but they weren't revered, or at first taken very seriously. They were played, mostly, in what we would now call bands rather than orchestras. In 1581, violinists in the employ of the French court were still classed as members of the *ecurie* (stable), and were thus servants, entering the dancehall though a rear door. These violin bands played popular and dance music. They would typically have been a five-part ensemble, with two violins, a viola or two, and maybe a "bass violin," really a large cello tuned a step lower. Few musicians could read music (music printing was still very expensive), so most improvised on already well-known melodies; very little music for violins was actually written down before 1600. Giovanni Paolo Cima, a contemporary of Monteverdi and Frescobaldi who died in 1630, was one of the first to publish violin music, usually trio sonatas with two treble instruments and a *basso continuo* of double bass and maybe organ. Cima's Sonata for Violin and Cello is the first known work specifically written for violin. In France, Louis XIII became infatuated with the new sound and put together an ensemble (not yet an orchestra) in 1626 called *les 24 violons du roi*. In Italy the composer Arcangelo Corelli, "a rock-star violinist," as *The Economist* has called him, also published many sonatas, and as an instrumentalist was widely copied for his technique and his style. "To his contemporaries, he was a giant. Roger North, an English writer, thought that 'if musick can be immortall, Corelli's consorts will be so.'"[140]

As Christian Rault says, "the musical seeds of the Renaissance finally blossom during the seventeenth century in a flowering of many extraordinary composers and musicians throughout Europe. With the development of the orchestra and the arrival of new musical forms, such as the concerto, instrumental requirements had radically changed. Now soloists were looking for a really powerful and clear monodic voice, with equal volume on a very extended compass," and the violin suited perfectly. Monteverdi wrote parts for violins in his opera *Orfeo*, first performed in 1607. After that, all the great composers found room for violins, which had now decamped from the dance floor to more serious halls (and violinists were no longer just servants at court). Antonio Vivaldi, J. S. Bach, Giuseppe Tartini, and later, of course, Mozart, Beethoven, Schumann, Brahms, Grieg, and the rest of the pantheon, all recognized what the violin could do. "You can't play a sad song on a banjo," as Willy Nelson once sang. In the right hands, a violin, by contrast, can express any emotion in the human catalogue, and was encouraged to do so.

Sometimes music and musician, writer and player, are the same person. Niccolò Paganini is the paradigmatic example. Born in 1782, Paganini was a child prodigy who had a nervous breakdown at fifteen, took refuge in alcohol, gambling, and womanizing and was followed by lurid rumours, including that he had murdered one of his lovers and used her intestines as violin strings, thus imprisoning her soul in the instrument; female screams were said to be heard from his violin when he performed onstage. (He wasn't the only musician so suspected: Tartini, too, was accused of consorting with the Evil One, with whom he was said to be in "regular league"; he figured in Madame Blavatsky's short story "The Ensouled Violin"; and his Sonata du Diable was denounced as "the most weird melody ever heard or invented.")

Paganini is best known for his fiendishly difficult *24 Caprices for Solo Violin*. His "Caprice No. 24," it is said, has more technical wizardry in one piece than most other composers use in a whole career. He also popularized unusual string techniques such as bow bounces (spiccato) as well as left-hand pizzicato and harmonics. He also purposely mistuned strings to make certain pieces easier to play. It is said he could play as many as twelve notes per second; his joints were remarkably flexible, which allowed him fingering techniques impossible for those with tougher gristle. He became a massive celebrity. "A Paganini cult swept Europe, comparable to the Beatles cult during the 1960s but lasting a great deal longer. Paganini portraits flooded the shops of the towns he visited, cakes and sweetmeats, handkerchiefs, tie-pins, snuff boxes—anything that could be ornamented received a violin, bow or portrait of Paganini."[141] Paganini caught syphilis in 1822 and was treated with mercury, which didn't much help. He died, in the end, of larynx cancer and was refused burial in his local church cemetery.

Not long after the eminent violinist James Ehnes had re-recorded Paganini's devilish *24 Caprices*, I happened to sit with him at a small table in a cavernous banquet hall. The occasion was his induction into the Order of Canada, and he was there to receive the award from Governor General David Johnson, along with twenty or so other worthies (or, occasionally, not-so-worthies). While I was listening to the interminable speeches that accompany such events, I peeked at a critic's review: "Ehnes has recorded the *Caprices* before, in 1995, at the age of nineteen. Since then, his view of the music hasn't changed a great deal—the smoother, more subtly phrased chordal passages in No. 5 is a typical example of refinement of interpretation . . . There's the same daring, bold approach, relying on exceptional technique to deliver an inner vision of each piece . . . What has changed is that Ehnes's technique has got even better, the intonation more precise, the bow control more sensitive. And the new recording adds an extra degree of clarity so that the playing makes a more vivid impact. Even a solitary listener will feel the desire to applaud the *Presto* section of No. 11, with its jaunty rhythms and extraordinary leaps, or the quick *staccato* scales at the end of No. 21." Thus Duncan Druce in *Gramaphone*.

Truth to tell, Ehnes wasn't paying much attention to the speeches either, so it came as an unwelcome jolt when it was suggested from the head table that he might, well, play something for the august gathering? It was posed as a question, but it wasn't, really, because it left him no gracious way to refuse. Sure, he hadn't brought his violin to the event, but that should be no problem, he was told. An air force band had been playing at the back of the hall, and the ensemble's violinist, a young officer, was enlisted to offer her instrument to the maestro.

Ehnes tried not to look mortified, but it was clear that this was not what he had in mind for the evening. It was not *his* violin. He certainly hadn't tuned it. He hadn't inspected it, never mind tested it. He had no idea how it played. His own instrument, a 1715 Marsick Stradivarius on more or less permanent loan from the [David] Fulton Collection, is greatly coddled. Earlier he had spent ten minutes telling us how difficult it was to transport the thing from steamy Bangkok, where he had been playing, to wintry Manitoba, which was then home, and how the smallest change in temperature or humidity could affect how it performed. And now this . . . *thing* . . . which had clearly not been coddled at all.

I don't remember what he played. It wasn't Paganini. It was light, and melodic, and sure enough he brought it off with aplomb, and when he handed the instrument back to the young soldier she beamed at him, as though he had done her a huge favour, which, of course, he had.

PART 6

Hazards and Opportunities

Forests in danger

DEFORESTATION is accelerating, yes?

Yes.

Reforestation is gaining ground, yes?

Yes.

There are fewer trees now than formerly, yes?

Yes.

There are more trees than formerly on a different time scale, yes?

Yes.

The numbers sometimes seem ambiguous, but they are not.

Just so, early in 2021, in just a few weeks, I came across the following headlines: "Forests the size of France regrown since 2000" (*BBC*, March 2021); "Global forest losses accelerated despite the pandemic, threatening world's climate goals" (*Washington Post*, March 2021); "There is hope for South-East Asia's beleaguered tropical forests: they are being cut down less and conserved more" (*The Economist*, May 2021); "Is this the end of forests as we've known them?" (*The Guardian*, March 2021); "Invasive Insects and Diseases Are Killing Our Forests" (*Washington Post*, February 2021); "Why Dead Trees Are 'the Hottest Commodity on the Planet: Blame climate change, wildfires, hungry beetles . . . and Millennial home buyers" (*The*

Atlantic, April 2021); "'Mind-blowing': tenth of world's giant sequoias may have been destroyed by a single fire" (*The Guardian*, June 2021); "'It will be beautiful again': how California's redwood forest is recovering after last year's wildfires" (*The Guardian* again, also June 2021).

A few years ago I travelled with a film crew from the Yellow River Falls (still impressive in June's dry weather) toward China's northern frontier. On the way, we had passed a vast area of high hills deeply scored with erosional gullies, China's famous Loess Plateau. Like much of China, the hills were patterned with the parallel stripes of planting terraces. From the bottoms of the gorges to the tips of the hills, and for as far as the eye could see, which was a very long way, as the road traversed many high elevations, the countryside had been manicured for hundreds and even thousands of years by the busywork of millions of peasant farmers, until it sometimes appeared that hardly a centimetre of the Chinese countryside had escaped this mammoth labour. But on thousands of hillsides, the only plantings now were of trees. The peasants had been told they should no longer plant food crops. In an authoritarian country, that's how it works: they tell, you execute, sometimes grudgingly, mostly resignedly, but you do it.

China was once 22 per cent forest, a figure that had been more or less constant through Chinese history. But, beginning in the 1950s, tree cutting accelerated and new fields were constructed. By the year 2000, the percentage of the countryside covered by trees had been reduced to a paltry 6. That deforestation, it was now widely acknowledged, was a prime cause of southern flooding and of northern desertification, so the policy was reversed.

Desertification in China, as elsewhere, is subject to the self-reinforcing aspects of feedback loops. Cutting down trees elevates the local microclimate temperature, which calls for more water to irrigate thirstier crops, which depletes the water tables which in turn elevates the temperatures further. The whole process is plain to see in the dusty landscape north of Yulin, in Shaanxi province, where I spent a morning talking to a professor of forestry at the local community college, Dang Jian Qi. He wasn't technically a professor, but he had been planting trees, and managing plots of reforested land, for so long that the local government had sensibly signed him up to impart his knowledge to young students. We talked on a viewing platform hastily constructed for visiting bigwig Jiang Zemin, who was then in charge of China and wanted to see for himself what was what. The view was instructive. To the north and west, the reclaimed forest tailed off into sand. A few kilometres beyond that, the dunes of the Mu Us Desert began, then the Yin mountains, and the great Gobi beyond. The Great Wall once stood proudly nearby. This section has now crumbled into sand and has been overrun by dunes, so that only a few vestigial towers and one small rebuilt section remain. To the east and south the forest stretched to the horizon, neat rows of lindens and Jack pines, mostly, with test parcels of half a dozen conifer species. It looked like a success, and indeed it was. Several thousand hectares of land had been reclaimed from the desert and, as a bonus, 400 million tons of destructive yellow loess silt had been prevented from entering the Yellow River.

But it wasn't nearly enough, as the professor acknowledged. "When I was a boy," he said, "this was all verdant land, green as far as you could see. Now it is sand, and the sand is growing. We push it back here and there, but we need an effort such as it took to build the Wall itself to really succeed." Nevertheless, he said, the work was ongoing, and indeed our filming earlier that day had several times been interrupted by a low-flying military aircraft seconded to seed-laying duties, the plane crisscrossing the area just north of the Great Wall's ruins, putting down a dusty cloud of grass and tree seedlings. On every terraced hillside all through the northern provinces such seedlings had been planted. The intention, an official in Xi'An had said, was to double the amount of forest within a decade, from 6 per cent to 12 per cent.[142] (It actually reached 13.1 per cent.) All this was part of China's oddly named Three-North Shelterbelt Forest Program, sometimes known as the Great Green Wall, begun in 1978 and scheduled to be completed by 2050, by which time it will be around 4,500 kilometres long. You can't say the Chinese don't think big. By 2020, sixty-six billion trees had been planted in thirteen northern and western provinces. No one thinks it will stop there, or be enough. But at least they are trying.

So are others. A UN offshoot called Plant for the Planet (a successor to the Billion Tree Campagn) has planted, or caused to be planted, twelve billion trees in 193 countries. Canada has promised to plant two billion trees in the next decade. Boris Johnsn in 2020 said his government would plant three hundred square kilometres of trees every year across the UK.

Is that enough?

No, not really. Marc Benioff, the founder of the cloud-computing platform Salesforce, told the World Economic Forum in Davos in 2019 that his 1t.org initiative will plant between fifty and one hundred billion trees in the United States and one trillion globally by 2030.[143] What about that? Surely that would be enough?

Maybe. Possibly. If it ever gets done. And if we don't cut them all down before they mature.

And if we do it right. As a bulletin from the Royal Botanic Gardens at Kew, in England, put it: "Tree planting is . . . a solution to tackle climate change and protect biodiversity, but the wrong tree in the wrong place can do more harm than good."[144] Kate Hardwick, a Kew researcher, put it this way: "What we're trying to do is to encourage people, wherever possible, to try and recreate forests which are similar to the natural forests and which provide multiple benefits to people, the environment and to nature as well as capturing carbon."

What are the rules to follow? Protect existing forests first. Use natural forest regrowth where possible. Maximize biodiversity recovery. Select the appopriate tree species for planting. Select the right area for reforestation. Set aside enough land so that the new forests aren't disrupted by development.

Best estimate is that in prehistoric or even pre-human times, forests would have covered between two-thirds and four-fifths of non-arid land, colonized by trees after the last glacial period receded. This seems to have been true even at the start of human agriculture, somewhere shy of six thousand years ago. Pollen studies suggest that between 11,000 years ago and six thousand years ago, forest cover actually increased, from around 60 per cent to 80 per cent. But the beginning of "modern" farming practices had an early effect: the decline in forest cover started in the Bronze Age, and has been continued to the present. Probably 20 per cent of forest cover had already disappeared when the Iron Age began, about three thousand years go.[145] Europe lost more than half of its forests in this period. Later, the Romans were disastrous for Europe's forests. Their ravaging of nature in the service of commerce was unparalleled, and remained so until modern industrial economies adopted their ethos of plunder married to much-improved industrial engines of destruction. Under the Roman Empire, title to land was given to whoever deforested it; and when war came, which it did often enough, entire forests were destroyed to provide military and naval engines of war. Shipbuilding helped explore the world, but it was devastating for trees. Larches, firs, spruces, beeches, and elms all succumbed to the need for planking, masts, rudders and oars.

Even so, by the Middle Ages the northern forests of Europe still stretched across the continent "like domes of darkness," in author Robert Pogue Harrison's phrase.

Now? Forests currently cover about 30 per cent of the world's landmass.

A 2015 tree survey published in *Nature*, using satellite data plus density reports from researchers around the world, declared that the planet is home to somewhere around three trillion trees, far more than conventional wisdom maintained only a decade ago (previous estimates were that the total number was only 400 billion). In fact, tree cover increased globally over the past thirty-five years, partly due to reforestation (see that headline, noted above, that "An area of forest the size of France has regrown naturally across the world since 2000") but also due to farmland reverting to forest as cultivation moved elsewhere. The world lost 1.33 million square kilometers of forest, but gained 2.24 million, the gain driven by farmers leaving the land in Europe, North America, and parts of Asia, as well as by warming temperatures that allow trees to grow further north, China's Green Wall project, and other reforestation efforts.[146] More recently, cultivated land is being replaced by forests in many European countries and Japan, due partly to falling birth rates that have emptied large swathes of countryside. Fewer people, too, mean that the demand for food is falling. There are now thousands of "ghost villages" dotting the Spanish countryside, for example.

Many other studies have suggested that scores of countries, even those with stable populations, have reached "forest minimums," and their forest cover is increasing again.[147] One of those is the Acadian Forest of Atlantic Canada and New England, whose ground cover has changed substantially since colonization. As suggested earlier, the area once covered by Longfellow's "forest primeval" was reduced sharply by the middle of the nineteenth century as farming and settled communities took up 75 per cent of available arable land in New England. A century later, forest cover was once again up, this time to about 75 per cent, a consequence of New England farms shutting down. The forests that have regenerated are mixed:

northern hardwoods and spruce being the dominant types, and as indicated previously, fall foliage tours replacing agriculture as money spinners.

Again, this isn't good enough.

About five billion new trees now sprout or are planted annually, but humans are responsible for the loss of fifteen billion, giving a net decrease of ten billion a year. Or, as the World Wildlife Fund puts it, in one of those perpetually useless comparisons, the earth loses the equivalent of twenty-seven soccer fields every minute. The increase in total forest cover was not all good news, either. Sure, there was tree cover gain in temperate continental forests as well as boreal forests, but much of the "gain" is illusory: monoculture plantations are good for the timber industry, for palm oil harvesting and for pulpwood manufacture, but are horrid for biodiversity, for soil quality, and for carbon retention. Even China's tree planting doesn't result in useful mixed forests. Yes, they hold the desert back, but the regimented stands of Jack pines and lindens contribute little to the environment, and are inhospitable to wild creatures. As journalist Rhett Butler points out, "cutting down a 100-hectare tract of primary forest and replacing it with a 100-hectare palm plantation will show up in the data as no net change in forest cover: the 100-hectare loss is perfectly offset by the 100-hectare gain in tree cover. [However] . . . that activity would be counted as "deforestation" by the FAO." Worse, it is in the tropics, the most biodiverse primary forests on earth, that the losses are greatest. Unsurprisingly, Brazil is the worst culprit, losing almost 400,000 square kilometres of forest in the last few decades, as much as the next four combined (Canada, Russia, Argentina, and Paraguay).[148]

Another aspect is the relative youth of the forests and the trees. A study led by the U.S. Department of Energy's Pacific Northwest National Laboratory, with experts from Britain's University of Birmingham, analyzed forests over the last century and gave predictions for the coming decades. The study found that illegal logging and the impacts of climate change are altering the world's forests, making trees shorter and younger, greatly reducing the amount of planet-warming emissions they can suck up and store.[149] It is as bad or worse in Europe. Loss of forest biomass increased by 69 per cent from the period 2011–2015 to 2016–2018. Sweden and Finland were the biggest culprits.

Global forests are currently endangered in many ways, for many reasons. By ever-expanding human exploitation (even given falling populations), by simple human rapacity and the remorseless need of industry for ever more resources, by chemical and industrial pollution, through imported pathogens, through invasive insects and by climate change.

Forest trees, indeed, are among the most obvious casualties of global warming, trapped as they are in a climate regime they were not evolved to confront. Within the last two decades, massive tracts of wild northern hemisphere woods have begun to die. Pests that had been inhibited by severe winters in those forests now survive, killing as they move north. At the same time, species that had been exquisitely attuned to a certain temperature range and annual rainfall began to wither, and some of those, too, are dying. By one estimate, insects and diseases could destroy a quarter of all trees in somewhere around 7 per cent of American forests.[150] The forests are migrating north, and like refugees in the human world, their movement is neither orderly nor uniform, but chaotic and sometimes mortal.

Pockets of devastation can be found all over the globe. Conservation. org has catalogued some of the most endangered: the southern Asian Indo-Burma forest is down to 5 per cent of what it once was; Indonesian/Malaysian tropical forest, 7 per cent; the Philippines, 7 per cent; South American Atlantic forest, 8 per cent; coastal forests of east Africa, 10 per cent; Madagascar and the Indian Ocean islands, 10 per cent. Almost all of these losses are human-caused. Too many people, doing what people do.

"Forest dieback," which has to do with stands of forest dying without obvious cause, is almost always directed by climate change. The proximate cause may be something else: a beetle moving into a newly amenable climatic zone, prolonged drought, an imported virus, a new pathogen, or something simple like not enough frost. Sometimes overmanagement can do the trick, as it does with the dieback of Kauri forests in New Zealand. Kauri forests, and New Zealand beeches as well, require something odd to regenerate. They need gaps in the forest, caused by natural events like fires, landslides, or diseases to set new seedlings—"conifer gap-phase regeneration" in the jargon. Forest management that is too all-encompassing prevents these gaps happening.

The great conifer forests of the American northwest have a beetle problem, laying waste to vast quantities of otherwise healthy forest. Four known beetles are at work, their victims obvious from their names— mountain pine beetles, spruce beetles, Douglas-fir beetles, and western balsam bark beetles. All four beetles are looking for the cambium, the growing layer between the bark and the wood, cutting through the bark to do so, with ruinous results. The last of the four, the western balsam bark beetle, is the deadliest. The other three have one-year life cycles and can be fought, but the balsam fir beetles are persistent and can survive more moderate winters into the next growing season. Heavy frosts and snow cover used to limit their northern reach, but their range is marching steadily northward, a slow-moving invasion that is very difficult to combat.

Further south, in Tennessee and Georgia, there are spreading patches of dead hemlocks, killed by a creature called the woolly adelgid, an aphid-like creature whose eggs resemble balls of cotton. By the spring of 2020 the pest had reached the hemlock forests of southern Canada, and biologists were scrambling for a solution before it is too late, perhaps importing natural predators from Japan, where the creature originated, with all the risks such importation entails.

Other well-known imported pathogens/parasites are the *Cryphonectria parasitica*, which reduced the American chestnut from its position as the dominant tree species in the eastern forest ecosystem to little more than an early-succession-stage shrub, and the tiny bark beetle, a mere three millimetres across, that carried a fungus called *Ascomycota*, which killed off most American and European elm forests. There are more coming: ash forests in Europe and the UK are succumbing to another parasitic fungus, *Hymenoscyphus fraxineus*, which attacks mature trees from crown on down (it came from Asia, arrived in Britain in 2012, and by 2019 had killed millions of trees); a plague called *Xylella fastidiosa* is killing olive groves in Italy; it also attacks some oaks, cherries, and sycamores. *Guardian* columnist George Monbiot, from whose writings some of this is drawn, points to a 2019 paper in the journal *Current Biology* which estimates that another forty-seven deadly pathogens are crossing borders across Europe and elsewhere. There is no known cure for any of them; only quarantine and prevention can help, and international trade rules generally prohibit curbs on the live plant business.[151]

The great boreal forests of the northern hemisphere are particularly vulnerable to insect predation. Mid-latitude forests can, in theory, migrate northwards, but this is hardly possible for trees at the limit of trees, even if the limit itself shifts north. "Whether or not this carbon stock can be maintained is not a matter of forest management," reports AirClim, an air pollution and climate secretariat, "since half of the boreal forest belt consists of remote primary forests. Even though the timber frontier is constantly moving north, natural forest dynamics and the response to climate change will decide the fate of most of these forests for the foreseeable future."[152]

If forests can't migrate by themselves, should humans help? Or would assisted migration just be another way of ensuring unintended consequences? There are three ways to consider helping, according to a research paper from Canada's Natural Resources department: assisted population migration, a low-risk endeavour, meaning the human-assisted migration of individual trees within a species' already established range; a medium-risk activity called "assisted range expansion," helping forests expand just outside the borders of their current range; and a higher-risk activity called "assisted long-distance migration," meaning moving forests beyond areas accessible through natural expansion. The risks here would be that the new arrivals would turn into noxious invasive species, or, conversely, that they would fail to prosper.[153]

The environmentalist Richard Heinberg, a senior fellow at the Post Carbon Institute, has laid out the reasons for trying. Trees are important to terrestrial ecosystems and help humans survive; climate change is leading to shifts in rainfall and climate zones resulting in imminent threats to many important tree species. Trees can't migrate on their own very quickly, no more than a few kilometres per decade, but climate change is changing zones much more quickly than that. Assisted migration is feasible, needing only a rough idea of what climate will be like in thirty to sixty years.[154] In other words, forests are struggling and we need to help.

Assisted migration experiments are under way in many forested places, including western Canada and Alaska. In Claremont, Ontario, Natural Resources Canada and the Ontario Ministry of Natural Resources gathered six hardwood species from five hundred kilometers south (Pennsylvania), nine hundred kilometers south (Kentucky), and 1,400 kilometers south (Tennessee), using the local seed zone as a control. The conclusion: all three were plausible.

In New York State's Black Rock forest, scientists like Angelica Patterson are studying how trees adapt and move in response to increasing temperatures, with the aim of helping them do so. "When I first started learning about how plant communities change through time, I'd never associated trees with migration because they're sessile and don't move like four-legged creatures or fly like insects. So it's eye-opening to realise that tree communities shift their ranges to migrate to places where they can thrive," she told the *Guardian*.[155] The University of Minnesota's Center for Forest Ecology, under the direction of Lee Frelich, is running multiple experiments that simulate rising temperatures, using heat lamps and underground wiring, and plotting computer models to decipher where certain species might thrive. They are also planting trees from as far away as South Dakota that might take the place of stressed native species. "The forest can't perpetuate itself the way it once did. Forests are always evolving. It's just that with climate change, things are changing faster and in different ways. We're having to roll with that change a lot faster and be a much more active part of it." Thus Chris Swanston, a U.S. Forest Service ecologist and director of the Northern Institute of Applied Climate Science.[156]

The problems, of course, are obvious. Forests can migrate by themselves and we can help, but the enormous scale of the undertaking (shifting thousands of square kilometres of forest northwards, often from and into intimidatingly difficult terrain) is a massive undertaking. And do we really know what the climate will be like in sixty years? Do we really know what global warming, climate change, will bring about? Do we understand the havoc that will be wrought by changing patterns of fires, droughts, floods, and storms? The answer is no. Informed speculation is hardly possible at this point. We would be soothsaying, not theorizing. And yet it may still be worth doing.

Forests on fire

Siberia, one of the coldest places on Earth, is on fire.
The Amazon, one of the wettest places on Earth, is on fire.
Fires are burning across the planet, we need to act fast.

—Greenpeace, late 2019

A S USUAL WITH GREENPEACE, its heart was in the right place, sort of, but its facts were skewed and its assertions lacked nuance or context. "The situation with the forest fires in Siberia has long ceased to be a local problem and has turned into an ecological catastrophe on the scale of the entire country," the NGO declared. But Siberia isn't always cold. Anyone who has been to, say, Krasnoyarsk in August will know what sweltering means: windy and hot and very humid, with mosquitoes the size of Kamov helicopters, as the local saying goes.

Nor was Siberia on fire, let alone Russia. Siberia alone is one and a half times the size of Canada, and the smallish bits that were on fire (or were in 2019, and again in 2020 and once more in 2021) are remote and hard to get to. In fact, Russian authorities called them "control zones," which basically meant that the cost of reaching and extinguishing the fires would be more than the damage the fires would do if left to go out on their own, which they reliably did by fall. In all, the Siberian fires consumed about 170,000 square kilometres of the region's 13.1 million, around 1 per cent. Bad, but not catastrophic. It had been much worse in 2012.

As for the Amazon, it is called a rainforest for good reason, but most rainforests have dry seasons, and the Amazon is no exception. In the Amazon basin, 2019 was a bad year for forest fires, an increase of a whopping 75 per cent from 2018. In August alone, 30,091 fires were burning. Some of them were small, but still. It didn't help that the country's know-nothing leader, Jair Bolsonaro, blamed NGOs and firefighters for lighting fires, and the actor Leonardo DiCaprio for funding them. In any case, though the increase was massive from 2018, neither Greenpeace nor the other Amazon-watchers pointed out that 2018 was a very unusual year, and that 2019 was more or less average for its number of fires, and hardly the worst (that would be 2003).

Here's what we do know about 2019, and it's bad enough. The Siberian fires burned seventeen million hectares, and its smoke plume covered an area the size of the European Union. Indonesia counted 35,000 fires, large and small, many of them deliberately set to burn forest or peatland to plant more palm oil; smoky haze from the Indonesian fires spread as far as Malaysia, Singapore, and Thailand. Australia, with its hundred-degree-plus temperatures and wild winds, saw bushfires destroy more than eighteen million hectares and more than a thousand homes. California had another bad year, burning more than 10,000 hectares and leaving three million people without power, a lot better than the previous year, at least. As reported, Brazil recorded more than 30,000 fires (but see the disparities in numbers, below), hugely up from the previous year but average over the long haul. Lebanon, in a heat wave, lost 1,500 hectares of woodland to fires. In sub-Saharan Africa, thousands of fires were burning, but except for Angola, where the number was higher than normal, it was an average year. In Canada, by August, there had been 3,873 reported fires burning more than 1.8 million hectares, about the long-term average.

The 2020 numbers were similar, although considerably worse in California, with millions hectares and dozens of communities destroyed. In any case, the same dire warnings were being emitted by the usual suspects. By September it was looking bad, as bad as the previous year, but not yet awful. Bolsonaro was now blaming "Indians and other impoverished people" for setting the fires. On the evidence, they were being deliberately set by a wide variety of culprits, including criminal gangs flipping land for speculators, speculators clearing land for expanded soybean farms and cattle ranches, illegal deforestation, corrupt officials, and more. As a *Guardian* piece put it early in September, "during a two-hour monitoring flight through the skies around Novo Progresso, the *Guardian* saw giant columns of white and grey smoke rising from supposedly protected forests below. Elsewhere, illegal goldmines could be seen within the Baú indigenous territory—a chaotic tapestry of muddy pools and makeshift encampments where pristine forest once stood. Newly deforested areas of fallen and charred trees were visible within the Iriri forest reserve."[157] In the Pantanal, a tropical wetland shared by Brazil, Paraguay, and Bolivia, more fires were burning than since record-keeping began in 1998, but so far (late 2020) smaller.

In 2021 there were both ups and downs, but few fire records were set. The season coincided with a remarkable heat wave (Sicily reported a temperature of 48.8 Celsius, a European record), and the accompanying rhetoric about climate catastrophe notched ever upward. "A disaster without precedent," said Sardinia's governor (though it was later reported to be just "one of the largest fires for decades," so there were actual precedents). The same week, Greece's prime minister said his country was facing a "natural disaster of unprecedented proportions," as he watched the unedifying spectacle of tourists being rescued from resorts by passenger ferry. Still, it turned out to be just "the worst fire season . . . since 2007," so there was, again, that. In the summer, fires were burning in multiple countries: Algeria, where olive groves were destroyed and sixty-nine villagers killed; South Africa, where a wildfire destroyed historic buildings on the flanks of Table Mountain; Cyprus, which does seem to have suffered the worst fire season on record, razing dozens of communities and killing four people; India, where multiple fires burned but little damage was done to infrastructure; and Turkey, where more tourists took to the water after facing fires mishandled by the Erdogan government. As usual, there were bushfires in Australia, though in New South Wales it was the quietest season for decades; in Canada, where, notoriously, the town of Lytton first faced record high temperatures before burning to the ground, and of course the U.S. The number of fires was up in Canada, (126 per cent of "normal"), but in the U.S. the season's wildfires were moderate; in June, for example, the number and reach of the fires was the "11th least since 2000," according the to U.S. Forest Service, about the same as July. The Russian Siberian fires sent a plume of smoke across the North Pole, an unsettling precedent.

None of this is to say forest and bush fires aren't awful. But we need to keep our nerve.

The global numbers for wildfires are slippery, ambiguous, and often are comparing different things: not just apples to oranges, but apples to, maybe, kumquats, controlled small slash-and-burn field fires compared to wild kilometres-wide forest or bushfires. Many of the reports use language that is useless for comparative purposes: "vast swathes" of forest burned, and so on.

By way of illustration, the Sentinel-3 World Fire Atlas recorded 79,000 global fires in August 2019, of which 49 per cent were in Asia, 28 per cent in South America, 16 per cent in Africa, and the rest scattered across the globe (Australia was barely mentioned). On the other hand, data from NASA said that satellites typically detect 10,000 actively burning fires around the world, 70 per cent of which are in Africa, but it doesn't say over what period or in what season. In this reckoning, Brazil placed third in the number of fires, after Congo and Angola. Other numbers suggest that the global number of wildfires averages 72,400, destroying an average of 2.8 million hectares per year. Then Brazil was said to have reported 80,000 fires in a single year, according to the Brazilian space agency, INPE, which also listed 41,000 "fire spots," left undefined. *The New York Times* used a similar number, 40,341, calling them "fires identified by the agency INPE." Then the statistical analytics website called Statista listed 82,285 fires in 2019 from January to August, 40,000-odd being forest fires.

* * *

There is a larger-picture way of looking at fires and the purposes of forests.

As bits of the Amazon were burning in 2019, France's president, Emmanuel Macron, issued a series of alarmed tweets. "The Amazon rainforest—the lungs which produce 20 per cent of our planet's oxygen—is on fire," he wrote. The implication was clear: unless the fires were stopped, and the deforestation that accompanied them was reversed, life itself was in peril. Much of the media obediently followed, even usually careful outlets like *The New York Times*. The "paper of record" lamented that "the Amazon . . . could soon self-destruct. It would be a nightmare scenario that could see much of the world's largest rainforest erased from the earth . . . Some scientists who study the Amazon ecosystem call it imminent." Naturally, activists and celebrities were close behind. "The lungs of the earth are in flames," said the actor Leonardo DiCaprio. The soccer player Ronaldo tweeted to his 82 million followers, "the Amazon rainforest produces more than 20 per cent of the world's oxygen." The singer Madonna weighed in, too, with striking pictures of the forest in flames.

Nitpickers pointed out that the lungs reference is backwards. Lungs usually absorb oxygen and don't emit it, as trees do. The same nitpickers pointed out that the photos of fires that typically accompanied the assertions were (a) not from the Amazon forest itself and (b) from a different year. The nitpickers also noted that (c) the 20 per cent number was pure fiction, but their "corrections" were more or less lost in the haze.[158] Madonna's pictures were more than thirty years old; the photo Ronaldo shared was from southern Brazil, not the Amazon, and almost a dozen years old.

If the Amazonian rainforests don't produce 20 per cent of the world's oxygen, how much do they produce? Maybe 10 to 12 per cent? That's the estimate of Philippe Ciais, a researcher at the nine-lab French climate study Institut Pierre Simon Laplace. Others put it lower than that, at maybe 6 per cent. And even that is actual output, not net production. Most climate scientists now agree that the net effect is basically zero, since the oxygen produced by photosynthesis is balanced by its loss caused by the microbes that decompose dead matter.

Dan Nepstad, one of the lead authors of the most recent Intergovernmental Panel on Climate Change report, put the same thing another way: "The Amazon produces a lot of oxygen but it uses the same amount of oxygen through respiration, so it's a wash."[159] Most of the "replacement atmospheric oxygen" comes instead from the oceans, from photosynthesis produced by the unicellular creatures called phytoplanktons.

And by far the bulk of atmospheric oxygen comes from organic matter buried in the soil over billions of years. In fact, as Peter Brannen put it in an essay for *The Atlantic*, "Humans could burn every living thing on the planet and still not dent its oxygen supply . . . Contrary to almost every popular account, earth maintains an unusual surfeit of free oxygen—an incredibly reactive gas that does not want to be in the atmosphere—largely due not to living, breathing trees, but to the existence, underground, of fossil fuels."[160]

So oxygen supply is not a real climate concern. "It would take millions of years to change O_2, so we are not really concerned about asphyxiating in the next century," says realclimate.org. The real mystery, if there still is one, is about how and why the oxygen concentration in the air has been so stable in the half billion of so years since multicellular life appeared in the fossil record, "never high enough to explode (doubled atmospheric oxygen would lead to unstoppable continent-scaled forest fires), or low enough to wipe out the animals [that depend on it]," as James Lovelock wrote in his book, *The Revenge of Gaia*.

The other side of the lungs analogy is the forest's uptake of carbon dioxide. And this is more serious. Or is it?

CO_2 is the stuff that is warming the planet, and changing the climate.

Sure, there are many other things doing the same; methane emissions are another culprit, but on CO_2 there is something of a consensus. Carbon dioxide levels are too high, and must be brought down. The earth's rainforests (all of them, not just the Amazon) sequester somewhere between 5 and 15 per cent of the annual global CO_2 emissions, which amounts to somewhere around half of Europe's annual output, not an insubstantial number. As discussed, forest fires are bad not because they emit anything themselves, but because they increase deforestation, which is what does the damage. This is true even though the forest fires are not anywhere near the levels the scare stories would have you believe. It was climate reporter Eric Holthaus, for example, who went on Twitter to assert that the current fires (2019) "are without precedent in the past 20,000 years," an assertion for which there is scant evidence. Alarmingly, however, a 2021 research report found that the Amazon basin, for the first time, was emitting more carbon than it absorbed. Mostly, predictably enough, this showed primarily in the deforested areas of the basin.[161]

Still, even on CO_2 there are alternative views. The CO_2 levels on earth were regulated long before there was a rainforest, indeed, long before there were trees. The planet clearly does not *need* trees to maintain its equilibrium. The mechanism involved is called "silicate weathering." As rocks break down through natural mechanisms of water and wind, accelerated by the heat-cold cycle, and subsequently buried through subduction and other devices, carbon dioxide is removed from the atmosphere and buried in the form of oil, gas, coal, and carbonate rocks such as limestone. Over geological time scales, millions and even billions of years, the cycle was steady. Carbon sequestered, on one hand, and carbon released through vulcanism, on the other.

David Archer, in his review of James Lovelock's Gaia theories on realclimate.org, recognized that "Lovelock wrote very eloquently about the eerie stability of the earth system. The sun has been warming throughout its lifetime, and yet the climate of the earth has remained stable between the relatively narrow range of the boiling and freezing points of water. This observation was labeled the 'faint young sun' paradox by Carl Sagan, and now has at least a partial explanation in terms of the weathering of silicate rocks, the silicate weathering thermostat." In this view, life, including all plants and phytoplankton, does have an effect, but "the real heavy-hitting mechanisms for regulating CO_2 involve dissolution of rocks, chemical reactions that can be influenced by life but do not really require it."

Efforts are under way to expedite this slow weathering, in an attempt to scrub CO_2 from the atmosphere. Its proponents call it enhanced silicate weathering, and it involves deliberately introducing fast-weathering silicate materials onto coastal sediments, with the expectation of releasing alkalinity into the near-shore waters, thereby creating a coastal CO_2 sink. The advantages of this piece of geo-engineering is that it would not contribute to ocean acidification, does not interfere with land uses, and can be done with existing dredging technology. Its disadvantages are not known. It may work, if it can be done on a large enough scale. Or it may not. Or it may have unsuspected downsides. Small trials were under way in 2020.[162]

* * *

Fires start for many reasons, and in one of two ways: natural causes (mostly lightning, but also occasionally spontaneous combustion of dry sawdust or leaves), or human causes. Most forest fires are caused by human actions or inactions. Prominent among them is slash-and-burn agriculture, initiated generally by rural people with few fire-fighting resources. Careless campers cause fires, too, and so do even more careless smokers. Ill-tuned motors can spark and cause fire. And, of course, arson. In some cases, ageing infrastructure is to blame. Notoriously, the utility company Pacific Gas & Electric was bankrupted after being found responsible for California's Camp Fire in 2018, which destroyed the town of Paradise and killed eighty-six people. Increasing temperatures and dryness through climate change are a contributing factor, too, although it's hard to know whether such fires are any longer "natural" or, indirectly, human-caused.

Humans may cause more fires, but natural fires cause more damage. Obviously enough, this is because humans cause fires close to where other humans are found, which makes detection (and control) easier. Natural fires can burn for hours, even days, in sometimes remote areas, before being spotted.

Foresters divide wildfires into three kinds: crown fires, surface fires, and ground fires. Crown fires are the worst. They occur high in the canopy and require sophisticated equipment to combat. They can also spread swiftly, aggressively jumping from tree to tree, and can trap even wary firefighters. Surface fires are the easiest. They're generally not very tall, and can be swiftly extinguished. Ground fires are bad because they can be insidious; underground peat fires have even been known to smolder for months, sometimes through an entire winter, only to re-emerge in the spring.

Forest fires are not always bad for the forest. On the contrary. They can be beneficial.

As the U.S. Forest Service puts it, "wildfire is a part of nature. It plays a key role in shaping ecosystems by serving as an agent of renewal and change." Many forest-floor plants have adapted over the millennia to require regular burns in order to spread seeds, and thus survive. Fires have been known to kill insect pests and tree diseases, and leave behind, after regeneration, a healthier forest. They clear debris from the forest floor and allow sunlight to penetrate to new growth. Often, new grazing grounds are created for ruminants, shifting local ecological patterns in favour of more complexity. "As plants and vegetation die away, new life begins to heal and spring forth."[163]

"Healing" and "springing forth" sound fuzzy, but harder heads have made the same points. John Bailey, a professor at Oregon State University's forest engineering department, maintains that forest fires are a key to long-term forest management. "Burning is a natural ecosystem process and generally helps restore forest ecosystems. It's ironic that we spend so much money to stop fire, because we should learn to see fire as more of a partner and not always an enemy . . . Forest fires are an efficient, natural way for a forest to rid itself of dead or dying plant matter. And the decomposed organic matter enriches the soil with minerals that help new plants sprout up quickly." Provocatively, Bailey has suggested that Oregon needs more forest fires, not fewer. In an interview with *Science Daily*, he said that even the worst-case scenarios of climate change may not be that bad, "since forests have historically seen more fires than they experience today. And the huge cost of trying to prevent fires is unnecessary in many cases. Right now, we're spending billions of dollars to prevent something that is going to happen sooner or later, whether we try to stop it or not, and something that can assist us in sound land management. It may always make sense to put out some fires when they threaten communities, or in other select circumstances. But periodic fire has always been a part of our forests, and we need to accept it as such, sort of like how we plan for and accept a very wet winter that comes along now and then."[164]

Because such fires occurred frequently, the understory rarely had time to build up enough combustible material for the fires to reach the canopies of the mature trees, which is what causes the large, devastating fires we are seeing now. As a result, overstory trees might get wounded by the ground fires, but they would rarely get killed. And even on those rare occasions that they were damaged, they quickly recover, typically within three to five years.[165]

In the summer of 2020, Donald Trump was widely derided for saying that the California wildfires were merely a consequence of poor forest management, and suggested that proper "raking" would have prevented them. The thing is (raking aside), he was right: the fires are a consequence of poor management. For almost a hundred years, California's approach to fire has been quite the opposite of what was needed. Fire was regarded as something to be completely suppressed, not managed.

"The problem of fire in the nation's forests was reimagined as war, demanding militaristic solutions," wrote Philip Connors, a U.S. Forest Service fire lookout in New Mexico. "This wasn't just a metaphor. Several thousand soldiers had been called out to help fight the [epic] 1910 fires, and in subsequent decades the Forest Service would align itself ever more closely with military tactics. Smoke jumpers held the same pride of place as elite paratroopers; hotshots resembled on-the-ground infantry. The agency gladly made itself the second home of the U.S. military's castoff tankers, helicopters, and jeeps. The fallen firefighters of 1910 were cast as selfless martyrs in a great national struggle."

There is growing evidence that this was all misguided. Forests where natural small burns were permitted emerged healthier than before, the highly flammable tinder eliminated, the overstory trees remaining unscathed.

Alas, "the public had long since fallen for the bromides of Smokey Bear," as Connors put it.[166] With the consequences that are now plain to see.

Even fish, it seems, can sometimes benefit from forest fires. A U.S. Department of Agriculture research study found that while the immediate aftermath of fires creates difficult conditions through the removal of shade trees and increased sediment, in the longer term, fires actually helped. Rebecca Flitcroft concluded that "habitat quality for most life stages of spring Chinook salmon is compatible with wildfire . . . habitat for eggs and fry will likely decrease after a fire as a consequence of increased fine sediments and higher temperatures, whereas adult and juvenile habitats are likely to improve because wildfire kills trees, leading to the eventual addition of large wood to the stream. This introduces more habitat complexity, which is important in maintaining the resilience and productivity of aquatic habitats for salmon and other species."[167]

Fire can be a tool for conservation in another way, too, through controlled and prophylactic burns. Foresters call this technique backburning. A fire is set in the approach of an out–of-control wildfire; by deliberately burning up the flammable material, the wildfire will be starved of fuel and peter out. Even the World Wildlife Fund is cautiously positive, while acknowledging the risks. "Controlled burns are also used to prevent forest fires," as Lorin Hancock put it in a report called "Forest fires: the good and the bad:"

> Even before human involvement, natural, low-intensity wildfires occurred every few years to burn up fuel, plant debris, and dead trees, making way for young, healthy trees and vegetation to thrive. That new growth in turn supports forest wildlife. Forest managers are now replicating this natural strategy when appropriate, starting manageable, slow-burning fires to make room for new life that will help keep the forest healthy in the long term.[168]

If fires aren't always bad for the forest itself, they are generally bad for the humans and animals who live in or near them, and are definitely bad for the environment. Bad even for fish, despite the modest benefits for the Chinook salmon recounted above. Post-fire and the destruction of understory vegetation, the soil sheds water more easily, which then transports debris and sediment into lakes and larger rivers; post-fire, flash floods often deposit heavy metals from ash and soil into waterways. Air pollution is another obvious problem. Forest fire plumes can travel enormous distances on the prevailing winds and higher up into the jet stream. Smoke plumes can include generous amounts of carbon monoxide and sulphur particulates, both harmful to humans. And one of the reasons there is so much alarm about the Amazon fires is that deforestation through fires and other means pumps massive amounts of carbon dioxide into the atmosphere. The Amazon is not really the lungs of the planet, but it is a huge store of carbon dioxide. And more carbon dioxide in the air means more warming. With the consequences we have all come to know, to our peril.

Managing forests

PRISTINE PIECES OF MIXED Acadian forest remain in eastern North America, some of it in Nova Scotia, and a small piece of that is woodland that has been sustainably managed since the earliest European settler, Conrad Wentzell, first set axe to tree in these parts nearly 200 years ago. ("Sustainable" in this definition is that the biological diversity of the forest remains unchanged over generations, and the amount of marketable timber, as woodlot managers refer to it, is the same now as it was in the beginning.) True, the Mi'kmaq were here first, and they cared for, and were sustained by, this forest for hundreds of generations, but they didn't practise forestry management, exactly. It was more like housekeeping, or like tending a shrine. They called the forest Wapane'kati, land of the dawn, from which the sun was welcomed back daily on behalf of all people, to whom it gave life. But they didn't own it, or wish to change it, or try to manage it.

Jim Drescher, who made a brief appearance earlier "Life in the forest," is the current co-owner, forester, and sixth-generation-settler steward of part of this marvel, an eighty-hectare parcel of classic Acadian forest, hemlocks, tamarack, the various pines and oaks, red and sugar maples, ashes and elms and birch, and here and there pockets of cedar and beech.

To a gardener or a designer of urban parkland, his forest looks hopelessly jumbled, without order or symmetry or discipline; instead, just trees doing what trees have always done, competing for sunlight, nutrients, water, reaching for the canopy and sometimes beyond, pushing aside lesser trees or less vigorous species and then, when their time comes, dying. This is not old-growth forest, necessarily; most of the trees are still juveniles, not much more than a hundred or 125 years old, and have plenty of life left in them. Still, if you walk through the woods with Jim Drescher, perhaps on one of the twenty-two kilometres of trails he has picked out for the less than nimble, or simply by wandering through the forest itself, he will be careful to point out the hundreds of dead trees he has left standing, and others that he has girdled in order to kill them, because death is regenerative in a forest, and you must keep death a constant presence, for it gives life in turn. As Drescher says, "Almost half the animals in the Acadian forest live in or on dead wood. Reducing the volumes or changing the natural distribution of dead wood degrades the habitat for much of forest life." He has also marked trees for next season's logging, and for many of the marked trees he has a purpose in mind. Here a straight-grained spruce for a luthier in Ontario; there a maple for the same purpose because, why not? Maple has a beautiful grain. An oak might be marked for furniture, or for flooring; there is a woodworking shop on Windhorse Farm, which is what Jim and Margaret Drescher called the place when they bought it from the Wentzell family in 1990, managed by Justin Boudreau, who makes furniture both fine and rustic, and all sorts of beautiful objects.

When their time is come, Windhorse people will fell the marked trees, carefully, and have them skidded out under horsepower, doing the least possible damage to the surrounding woods. In a hundred years, if the Windhorse people have their way, the forest will look just like it does now. It will have changed, but stayed the same. They want it to change, because change is inevitable, and they want it to stay the same, because it has no need to be different. Besides, other creatures use the forest, not just humans. The whole place is impossibly old-fashioned, in the best possible way.

That is one version of forest management, sustainability. Another version can be found fifty kilometres or so to the south, inland from the former mill town of Liverpool. A different beast altogether, and a different sensibility: woodlands managed by corporate industry. This is not Acadian forest. It is not beautiful. No city people will come here on excursions, no Japanese tourists will sit under a spreading tree, reaching for the spiritual renewal they call forest bathing. This is second-growth, or third-growth, or fourth-growth spruce and balsam fir, mostly shallow-rooted ungainly things, growing on sour and rocky soil, fit mostly for pulpwood and papermaking, or for burning in the furnaces of the bioenergy industry. It is good for porcupines, and ticks—lots of ticks in the woods—but too sparse for much else.

The paper mill in Liverpool was half owned by Bowater Mersey, and half by *The Washington Post*, and was where the *Post* got its newsprint, in the days when the *Post* needed a lot of newsprint. The plant was sold not long ago to a conglomerate from Quebec called Resolute Forest Products, which grew out of Abitibi-Consolidated. Not long after that Resolute abruptly shut the mill down, considering it surplus to need, thereby putting Liverpool's biggest employer and only industry out of business, a transaction done for the shareholders with scant concern for the people thus unemployed or the town thus devastated. A familiar story. Shareholder capitalism doing its best for the shareholders, whoever and wherever they are, at ruinous local cost.

In any case, before Resolute became less so, it would hold occasional open houses, and invite the locals out to the woodlands to see how things were done. We went on one of those excursions. The site was a hillside, but not very steep, perhaps a twenty-degree slope. To the right of the access road, a section had been cleared a few years earlier, and was now growing up in alder and red oak, the first species to recolonize a clearcut. The real action was to the left, where a machine called a feller-buncher was to be put through its paces. This was not your ordinary harvester. It was the size of a three-story row house, and cut a track six metres wide through the forest. The machine simply grabbed a tree, or a bunch of trees if they were growing close together, hugged it or them to its steel bosom, and deployed its metre-wide disk saw to cut them off at the knees. That was the felling part. The bunching part was to lay the cut trees on the ground, where a crew would limb them and buck them into four-metre lengths, where another machine, called a skidder, would find them and drag them out to the road, where they would await loading onto the eighteen-wheelers soon to arrive. A skilled operator on a good-quality feller-buncher could clear twenty hectares in a day, whole forests in a week or so, depending on size. The mill used to have a harvester, a machine that did it all in one pass, the felling and the bunching and the bucking, but it had broken and was somewhere being repaired. Still, this was impressive enough. The only thing left behind was called slash: limbs and twigs and needles. It was useless and left to rot, though it remained a fire hazard for several years.

As we were turning to leave, a small convoy of vehicles pulled onto the access road. Half a dozen men got out. They strapped spray tanks to their backs, and set off into the fields that had been logged several years before. Red maples, the first to venture onto cleared land, had grown to about a metre to a metre and a half. They were no use. Red maples aren't useful to a pulp-and-paper company, so they needed to go. I don't know whether the herbicide was Roundup or one of its clones. I do know that all the saplings sprayed died. That was the point.

* * *

There are many ways of managing forests. The simplest is to do nothing, neither cut, nor thin, nor clear, nor groom, but just leave the forest to manage itself. Such forests will be a fire hazard, but then, as suggested earlier, fires have historically been a way for new trees and new species to establish themselves, and are not harmful per se. Natural forest regeneration after trauma, whether fires, pests, storms, or human harvesting, is called "second growth," and it stays second growth until enough time has passed so the trauma is no longer evident, a period that could take anywhere from a century to several millennia. (The time scale is generally 150 to five hundred years for deciduous forests, 120 to 140 years for the conifers of British Columbia's interior forests, and more than 250 years, and up to a thousand, for the coastal rainforests.) Do-nothing management is the way most pre-industrial societies dealt with woodlands. Sometimes their inaction was overlaid with spiritual values (reverence for the forest itself and for the life it maintained, as the Druids insisted), but often just because the hunting that forests offered outweighed the necessarily arduous task a small population faced in clearing them. This hands-off practice had the not inconsiderable virtue of maintaining a complex ecosystem of mammals, birds, and plants, not to mention fungi and lichens.

On the other end of the management scale is the practice of clear-cutting the forest entirely and planting monoculture stands of commercially viable timber, in neat (that is, accessible by harvesting machines) rows.

Somewhere in the middle range are the best practices most often employed by logging companies, at least in countries with viable legal codes: clear-cutting in patches to allow natural regeneration, leaving behind enough trees for the forest to reseed itself, and selective cutting, which entails cutting only some of the trees in a forest, leaving other species or a different age cohort of trees for subsequent cuts. Sometimes loggers cut and replant at once with nursery-grown seedlings, which is labour-intensive but time-efficient. This enlightened view is not really new. The chief forester at the court of Versailles, one "Monsieur Le Roy," always insisted on the great benefit to be found "if one cares . . . for the preservation of the soil in which the trees have their roots. Excessive rejuvenation alters growth and exhausts the earth. Since every terrain has a certain depth, beyond which the roots cannot reach, excessive cutting will only hasten the moment when trees begin to decay."[169]

Clear-cutting is the practice most abhorred by environmentalists, for mostly good reasons, although often through disingenuous messaging. A favourite technique is to contrast the bare ground of a newly cut stand with photographs of lush temperate rainforests, often a couple of time zones away. Still, the good reasons remain good. Clear-cutting is ruinous for biodiversity, and equally ruinous to the habitat of multiple species. It is bad for carbon retention: since the soil is one of earth's great terrestrial carbon sinks, clear-cutting liberates the carbon and sends much of it into the atmosphere, where it does maximum harm. Nutrients are leached from the soil and carted away, not to be replenished. Clear cutting also reduces water-retention, thereby making downstream flooding worse. One of the defences of radical cutting is, or used to be, that new trees consume more carbon dioxide, and give off more oxygen, than mature ones do, and that "forest rejuvenation" (a nice euphemism) was therefore justified. This agreeable theory has been thoroughly debunked. A study that looked at hundreds of thousands of trees on every continent found a then-surprising result: the older the tree, the more quickly it grows. Trees with trunks a metre in diameter generated three times as much biomass as trees that were only half as wide. Peter Wohlleben: "If we want to use forests as a weapon in the fight against climate change, then we must allow them to grow old, which is exactly what large conservation groups are asking us to do."[170]

In fact, most logging companies don't like clear-cutting natural forests either, except in forests that are naturally single-species. Cutting everything forces them to spend time and money on trees for which they have no use. The British Columbia Forests Practices Code, a set of rules widely accepted and adopted by the major logging companies, itself criticizes past clear-cutting practices, and now limits cutblock size, requires extensive riparian strips to preserve streams and wetlands, mandates irregular boundaries to mimic natural patterns, and restricts harvesting on unstable soils and steep slopes. Cutblocks must also be smaller and more dispersed. Longer "green-up" periods have been introduced before adjacent stands can be logged, and sufficient trees must be left standing to provide wildlife with a refuge and a home. And carefully done, selective cutting does have advantages. Deer and some songbirds like the open spaces thus provided, while the sun exposure thus gained helps seedlings thrive.

No one thinks an industrial economy can maintain itself without major interventions, which in this case means large-scale forest harvesting and large-scale plantings. Jim Drescher and his cohorts can't begin to supply the demand for wood for papermaking, or for construction, even less now that designers are turning their attention away from concrete and toward wood for high-rise buildings. Nor would they want to, or want to forbid the practice altogether. They are, however, asking for a little more sensitivity toward the larger ecological impacts of what loggers are doing. And asking for a little more sustainability. And, certainly, demanding that the mass application of pesticides to kill selected species should be banned, immediately and outright. Hardly anyone can now be found to disagree. At least not in public, or where they can be overheard.

You can also manage forests by growing new ones. Not just trees. Whole forests. They may not be lovely, but they might help save a few old forests along the way. On the other hand, they may replace natural forests instead. Depends.

Most "planted forests" are essentially monoculture plantations, manufactured woodlands, industrial forests with their focus on product, not on ecosystem services. There are two kinds of such forests. The first is what the Food and Agriculture Organization (FAO) oddly calls "roundwood forests," by which they mean trees planted for timber and pulpwood (for biofuels and paper, among other uses). The second are forests planted for their by-products, often oil, but also fruit. Examples of such planted forests are the endless linden groves of China, the pulpwood spruce plantations of New Brunswick, coffee and tea plantations in Colombia, Kenya, and India, and, most controversially, the palm oil plantations of Indonesia and Malaysia. These planted forests are often excoriated by environmentalists and their allies, sometimes for good reasons and sometimes for spurious ones. They are also defended, not just by corporate spokespeople but also by sober-minded organizations like the FAO. The defenders, too, have their good reasons and their bad.

As global "natural" forest cover fluctuated over the last thirty-five years (up, then sharply down, then up again, though not so sharply, an overall increase of not quite a million square kilometres, mostly in temperate regions) planted forests increased steadily, from 167.5 million hectares to 277.9, though a more recent figure has the latter number at 299 million. The increase in plantations was greatest in the temperate zone, not the tropics.

A good estimate for 2020 is that natural forests still account for 93 per cent of the world's forested area, with planted forests coming in at the remaining 7 per cent. This number will increase. To meet the added demand caused by population growth and expanding industry, the WWF, in its Living Forests Model, calculates that 250 million new hectares of planted forest "for all end uses" will become necessary by 2050. Europe alone will need an additional eleven million hectares.[171] A multi-authored piece in the journal *Forest Ecology and Management* headlined "Changes in planted forests and future global implications" suggests that plantings are not keeping up with demand: the rate of increase to supply new demand should have been 2.4 per cent annually, while the actual increase was only 1.2 per cent. Population pressure on land use and increasingly variant weather and climate were the prime reasons for the shortfall, and these factors were not likely to diminish anytime soon. This new forest will not necessarily replace natural forest, though it may (there are assertions on both sides of this issue). Europe's eleven million new hectares, for example, will create entirely new forests, not replace old ones. Only about a fifth of the planted forests are species introduced to new areas; overwhelmingly, plantations consist of native species.

All of these points most people can agree on.

Opponents of planted forests hate them for many reasons. Most superficially, they hate them because their typically rigid geometry seems so antithetical to nature: they hate boring forests because they *are* boring, lacking diversity, spontaneity, complexity, *beauty*. In plantations, the biodiversity of natural forests is entirely absent: they are groomed and trimmed and weeded, so nothing but the desired trees are left, more like gardening than forestry. There is little refuge for wild creatures; habitat is lost. At the same time, as per the discussion above, many plantations replace older forests, rather than pioneering new ones. Palm oil plantations are a particularly egregious example. The United National Environmental Program (UNEP), which is the world body's angrier counterpart to the FAO, maintains that palm oil plantations are the leading cause of rainforest destruction in tropical areas. A UNEP publication title conveys the angst directly: *The Last Stand of the Orangutan—State of Emergency: Illegal Logging, Fire and Palm Oil in Indonesia's National Parks*. The report, says, inter alia, this: "A scenario released by UNEP in 2002 suggested that most natural rainforest in Indonesia would be degraded by 2032. Given the rate of deforestation in the past five years, and recent widespread investment in oil palm plantations and biodiesel refineries, this may have been optimistic. New estimates suggest that 98 per cent of the forest may be destroyed by 2022, the lowland forest much sooner."[172]

The NGO Rainforest Rescue (which, you will be unsurprised to learn, is against rainforest deforestation) makes two main points: if rainforest is cleared, or if the plantation was on a former peatbog, up to six thousand tons of carbon dioxide is released into the atmosphere for every hectare cut. Indonesian and Malaysian rainforests and peatlands are among the most species-rich environments on the planet, and are home to iconic endangered animals such as orangutans, Sumatran tigers, and Bornean rhinos. As an aside, Rainforest Rescue quotes the Center for Orangutan Protection as registering 1,500 orangutans being clubbed to death after they wandered out of neighbouring forests into palm oil groves.

Another factor is that manufactured forests are often manufacturing the wrong wood for the wrong zones. An example, from the Canadian provinces of Nova Scotia and New Brunswick, is the replacement of Acadian mixed forests with plantations of spruces, a species better suited to a more northerly climatic zone. This has been called the "borealization" of deciduous hardwoods. A more northerly drift of deciduous forests would better suit the changing climate, so these plantations have it backwards.

Proponents, for their part, make a number of simple points. The main one is that well-managed planted forests (a nice hedge) reduce the pressure on natural forests and can provide other environmental benefits. Importantly, planted forests are essential in any transition to a green economy: natural forests cannot take up the added burden. Moreover, in many places, particularly in Europe, planted forests are not replacing natural forests but supplementing them. Planted forests can be more productive since they grow faster than natural forests. They can provide new habitat and shelter for wildlife, and they can contribute to rural development. What's more, planted forests can prevent soil degradation and erosion.

Is this last point true? Can such forests actually prevent soil degradation? Plantation owners say yes, environmentalists say no, vigorously and vociferously and often. The truth, as so often happens, is somewhere in the middle (if shading toward the no). Any removal of biomass from any patch of forest degrades soil in the long term by a gradual removal of what otherwise would be returned as nourishment. This means that monoculture plantations do degrade the soil. So does the careful logging of natural forests. Plantations only degrade it faster because they grow more efficiently and are harvested more often.

Even the hated palm oil has its defenders. Palm oil has a high melting point, making it easy to work with. Indeed, it is used in thousands of products: you can find it in foods ranging from frozen pizza to chocolate bars, in laundry detergents and cleaning agents, in cosmetics, even in diesel fuel tanks. It is also cheap to produce, as long as you don't factor in the negatives. Among palm oil's defenders, interestingly, is the organic food industry, which uses palm oil in literally hundreds of products. As the Rainforest Rescue people note, snarkily, "[while] organic farming prohibits the use of pesticides, chemical fertilizers, and genetic engineering, organic labels do not establish standards against rainforest destruction and land grabbing. Furthermore, vast industrial monocultures, including those that fulfill organic production standards, can hardly be deemed environmentally sound."

Some planted forests are hard to criticize, even by zealots. A lovely example was recounted by Eric Asimov, the *New York Times* wine writer, in a piece about Andy Brennan, a New York artist, and his wife, Polly Giragosian, who decamped into upstate New York's hardscrabble Sullivan County to make apple cider. Writes Asimov: "[there] he planted an orchard, but it failed. Modern orchards, with their reliance on dwarf trees, [limited] varietal selections, clonal rootstocks and chemically supported monocultures, are weak and practically require industrial crutches. He wanted to farm organically. Desperate for apples, [he] discovered that Sullivan County was a trove of old apple trees, both wild and in preindustrial orchards long abandoned, buried behind brambles or hidden in dense forest growths. He set about foraging these apples and, as the proprietor of Aaron Burr Cidery, began to produce wonderful examples of what he calls 'locational ciders,' meant to convey the nuances of the different places from which the apples were gathered. What he loves most, it turns out, is not the apple and not the cider but the tree, which he sees ideally as a reflection of a place. Inspired by the wild trees he has discovered, he spreads their assorted seeds on a hillside by his home, creating a forest of apple trees, a 'forchard.'" Brennan's book, *Uncultivated*, "is more than anything a meditation on the industrialization of agriculture and all that's been lost as a result."

The future of trees

I T WAS ONCE SAID that "a squirrel could get from New York to Chicago [sometimes expressed as "from Maine to Georgia"] without ever touching ground", simply by hopping from chestnut tree to chestnut tree. Indeed, it is hard to overestimate the place of the chestnut in rural America, its ubiquity and utility. In the Appalachians, a quarter of all hardwoods were chestnuts, and not for nothing was it known as the cradle-to-grave tree. Farmers and town folk alike used its wood for rot-resistant chestnut houses, were warmed by chestnut fires, housed their hogs in chestnut-beam barns, fed their flocks and hogs and themselves on the chestnut's many bushels of nuts, were rocked in chestnut cradles, were entertained by chestnut fiddles, and buried in chestnut coffins. Split-rail fences, railroad ties, flag poles, and supportive pilings were all chestnut. The trees were also once known as the redwoods of the east, sixty metres tall, commonly, and perhaps three metres in diameter: in the fall, there would be a carpet of chestnuts on the ground four inches thick, a deposit that sustained wild turkeys and black bears, wild and tame hogs, raccoons, chipmunks and, yes, squirrels, who squirrelled them away for winter, as squirrels do.

Then a fungus came to America, *Cryphonectria parasitica*, a stowaway on imported Japanese seedlings of a pretty little ornamental Asian chestnut, and more than three billion trees died, maybe four billion, with startlingly speed. By the 1940s, they were gone.

Now, it is possible that through genetic engineering chestnuts will cautiously and slowly be able to repopulate their historic lands. A decade ago, three spindly trees were planted in the gardens of the New York Botanical Society, the only genetically modified plants allowed in its 250 acres, also the only chestnuts in America older than ten years. They were born in a lab in Syracuse, New York, and replanted in New York with caution and trepidation, with an underlay of optimism. Triumph of science, or sheerest folly?

That forests and trees need help is hardly a secret. As recorded in *Forests in Danger*, the U.S. Department of Agriculture, in 2019 suggested that insects and diseases could destroy a quarter of all trees in somewhere around 7 per cent of American forests. A quarter of 7 per cent doesn't sound like a lot, but it's still a lot of two-by-fours. Warming forests and increasing international travel have made it easier for invasive pests and diseases to take hold. I reported earlier on initiatives to help forests migrate to new climatic zones, as well as other sustaining efforts. All good initiatives, all comfortably within the Earth Day approval envelope, although not without complications.

Few scientific endeavours are as rife with emotions, some of them bitterly antagonistic, as the genetic modification of living things, particularly the insertion of genetic material from one species into another. True, most of the antagonism has been reserved for genetically modified foods, but transgenic trees have not been spared the opprobrium.

It is also true that the issue has recently been somewhat muted (not so many genetic modification labs picketed or burned down). The softening has come about partly because transgenic crops have shown some obvious advantages as research continues. Genetically modified food crops already allow greater yields with less water, less energy use, and fewer chemicals, which even skeptics acknowledge, if somewhat grudgingly, as a good thing. Similarly, genetically modified crops are almost certainly less harmful than the noxious chemicals routinely sprayed by crop-dusters on non–genetically modified crops. Even the Great Satan, Monsanto, has moved some minds. Researchers at Monsanto have found a way to mitigate the effect of drought on corn, and in field trials their new variety maintained yields under harsh test conditions.

There have been successes in trees, too. In one example, Ray Ming of the Hawaii Agricultural Research Center reported in 2008 on a successful fight against the Papaya Ringspot Virus that had been devastating the island's crop by making it difficult for trees to photosynthesize. The solution was to plant a transgenic variety of papaya whose genetic makeup included a mild mutant of the virus, which conferred resistance through a technique called post-transcriptional gene silencing. Reassuringly, a *post facto* study found that the inserted genetic material occurred in only three places in the papaya genome, and that no nuclear genes were disrupted. Ming's report included photographs of the vigorous new trees next to rows of the blighted older ones.[173] "Without biotechnology, there's no papaya industry. Simple as that," said Dennis Gonsalves, one of the mutant's developers.[174] Similarly beneficial research is under way to provide a genetically modified organism fix for the phylloxera blight that almost destroyed the European wine industry a century and a half ago.

What has all this got to do with chestnuts?

Two separate efforts are under way to resurrect the American chestnut. One is the traditional method of hybridization, by successive waves of cross-breeding between surviving American chestnut saplings (which currently always die once they reach nut-bearing age) with a more fungus-tolerant Chinese variety. This is painstaking work, since trees grow much more slowly than most food crops, and multiple generations of careful cross-breeding are necessary to make any changes. "The challenge has been to select seedlings with enough Chinese blood in them to ward off the disease and yet still look like the American chestnut. At maturity, the American tree is tall and spreading with a thick, straight trunk. The Chinese species is shorter and more branching."[175] By 2020, 60,000 seedlings had been planted at Meadowview Research Farms in Virginia, and four thousand had made the first cut. The final cut would be six hundred trees planted in selected areas of Appalachian forest.

The second effort involves true genetic modification techniques. Plant geneticist William Powell of the State University of New York in Syracuse has over the past forty years targeted the acid that the chestnut blight secretes, an acid that efficiently kills plant cells. To do so, he and his team have inserted a gene from wheat that enables the trees to detoxify the acid; the trees that have resulted are reliably blight-resistant—they can protect themselves, even when blasted with huge doses of the blight. Defending himself against vigorous attacks from environmental groups, Powell says the bacterium he used to carry the wheat gene into the chestnut chromosome is already found, naturally, in the DNA of some tree species, including the walnut. "Walnut is a natural GMO," he said.[176]

Even so, transgenic chestnuts face formidable bureaucratic obstacles. By 2020, neither the U.S Environmental Protection Agency or the U.S. Food and Drug Administration had allowed the release of such trees into the wild.

Commercial limitations have further hampered trials. Plant geneticist Steven Strauss of Oregon State University in Corvallis, who used to collaborate with commercial forest companies, is now facing objections from them. Few companies will allow him to plant his trees on their land because doing so could lose them their certification by such organizations as the Sustainable Forestry Initiative. Many key consumers, such as home-improvement stores, will not buy wood without such certification, which is intended to demonstrate that the wood was harvested responsibly.[177]

Nevertheless, a report from the U.S. National Academies of Sciences, Engineering, and Medicine, which highlighted "regulatory and research challenges" before such trees can be released into the wild, also noted that "genetic engineering's potential to boost forest health is promising enough to warrant further research." As Heidi Ledford wrote in *Nature*, "the academies' report highlights several challenges that are unique to forests. Unlike food crops, which are typically harvested after a few months, engineered trees would persist in the environment for decades, and they could migrate undetected across national borders. The report authors say that some modified trees could even escape regulation altogether, like some engineered [food] crops already do, because of gaps in the rules." And a release into nature would be "a massive and irreversible experiment," as Rachel Smolker of the NGO StopGEtrees put it in a report called *Biotechnology for Forest Health? The Test Case of the Genetically Engineered American Chestnut*.[178] Her report rather ambiguously quotes a 1936 rhyming verse by Robert Frost . . .

> *Will the blight end the chestnut?*
> *The farmers rather guess not.*
> *It keeps smouldering at the roots*
> *And sending up new shoots*
> *Till another parasite*
> *Shall come and end the blight . . .*

Smolker points out, accurately, that while the blight was a horror, many chestnut forests succumbed as much to loggers as to disease. She also notes, acidly, that Powell's group at SUNY is "deeply connected" to timber, energy, and biotechnology interests, and is partly funded through companies such as Monsanto (now Bayer), Duke Energy, and ArborGen, a venerable guilt-by-association smear.

There are also technical difficulties in genetic modification. Dario Grattapaglia of Embrapa, a state-owned research corporation in Brasília, says that "disease resistance is often controlled by small contributions from hundreds or even thousands of genes, too many to tackle using genetic engineering." Initial optimism often turns to disappointment. In 2015, regulators in Brazil approved a modified eucalyptus tree that grew much faster than trees in the wild, but, as Grattapaglia points out, the results didn't hold up in tests conducted in other locations around the country, and the project fizzled. Powell still maintains that the efforts are worthwhile, pointing to "growing concerns about tree diseases, including sudden oak death. The American chestnut is not the only tree that could benefit from genetic engineering . . . There is probably going to be a wave of trees behind it . . . There are so many problems out there."

As in Brazil, tree geneticists are not only focused on solving problems, they also want to make what they are pleased to call "improvements." Some labs are working to modify the genome of natural trees, aiming to increase their tensile strength, make it easier for trees to survive drought and freezing, and to change fertility patterns. They want, in short, to make new and improved natural trees. These changes are being done, according to the propagandists for the labs, "to enhance biomass production in a sustainable and environmentally responsible manner."

Sustainable? Environmentally responsible? To environmentalists, calling trees "biomass" and their growth "production" is redolent of the problem.

A certain skepticism is in order. Toward both sides.

Engineered wood

ALL THREE OF THE iconic buildings mentioned above—
Kizhi's Church of the Transfiguration, Notre Dame's roof
"forest," and the Sakyamuni pagoda—used post-and-beam
timber construction, as did almost all large pre-modern buildings; what
dimensional lumber (two-by-fours, etc.) existed was used only in detail
work and furnishings. Humbler buildings used a construction method
called "coulisse," or "pièce coulissante," which mostly involved erecting
vertical posts with deep grooves cut into them, down which thick planks
could be dropped and pegged, thus serving as solid walls and giving the
whole rigidity without the need for metal fastenings.

Across many cultures, posts and beams were squared off with adzes
and carefully fitted, the joints, again, secured by wedged hardwood
pegs. Elizabethan-era half-timbering was a version of this style, the most
famous examples being in Germany and Alsace, though Rouen in France
has many splendid specimens. Half-timbering refers to a frame of load-
bearing timber, creating panels (*Fächer* in German) between the beams
that are then filled with a non-structural material, such as plaster and lathe
(or wattle and plaster), often in an intricate pattern. The post and beam
frame itself is usually left exposed on the exterior of the building, giving
it the desired architectural feel.

The post and beam method of building was imported into the American colonies. Eighteenth- and nineteenth-century American houses and barns were constructed in this way. We once owned a nineteenth-century barn near Bancroft, in the deciduous forest belt of Ontario, that was twelve meters high and maybe twenty meters on its long axis, not a metal fastening in the whole place, except for the roofing shingles. It was crude—this was no Kizhi—but it was strong and spacious enough for its purpose, which was housing for cattle and their winter feed.

As America developed and spread westwards, building methods changed. Some communities still used heavy timber construction techniques, the Amish among them, but from the 1840s onward, as the expansion accelerated, most new buildings began to use a system invented in Chicago called balloon-frame building, with wooden cladding. This involved a frame made of much smaller pieces of wood, typically two-by-four or two-by-six inches, regularly spaced at small intervals and nailed into a rectangular frame, connected at corners to other similar frames, essentially the same system used in tract housing today. The only significant change since then came after World War Two, when the balloon frame was modified to a platform frame, each story resting on a solid wood floor. This made multi-story buildings easier to erect and, by eliminating a clear air channel from basement to eaves, mitigated the fire hazard.

There were downsides to frame building. For one, small lumber rots easily unless meticulously protected from damp and mould. For another, its sound insulation properties are poor compared to either block or larger wood dimensions. But three main factors eased the transition to frame buildings, the first two being the development of large-scale sawmills that used industrial techniques to produce dimensional lumber in predictable sizes, and the sheer abundance of softwood forests—there seemed to be trees everywhere, and the supply seemed inexhaustible. The third factor was the invention and subsequent large-scale rollout of the first "engineered wood," plywood.

Plywood is made by gluing together thin sheets of veneers, with the grain of each sheet running in an alternate direction. This made it possible to manufacture sheets much wider than boards from the widest trees, while giving the whole sheet dimensional strength not possible with planks butted together. It was not a new technique—examples of multiple veneers have been found dating back to the Egyptian Old Kingdom, somewhere around 2,500 BCE—but it was never widely adopted because the tools available for veneer work were crude and the cutting was painstaking and the wood prone to split. European and early American furniture makers also used multiple veneers in some pieces, but even by the early 1800s, plywood making was still difficult and frustrating.

In the 1830s, a Swedish engineer and inventor, Immanuel Nobel (father of Alfred of dynamite and prize fame) invented a rotary cutter that made possible veneering on a larger scale. The family moved from Sweden to Russia to sell Immanuel's inventions (which included improved underwater exploding mines for naval defense) and lived on grants from the Tsar for twenty years. A few decades later, Nobel's invention was introduced into the United States; the first patent for modern plywood was granted in 1865. Still, the new material wasn't widely marketed for use as a building material until 1910, and the first standard-sized sheets (eight-by-four feet) were sold in 1928. Since then, the number and range of engineered wood products have (to use a favourite Nobel family term) exploded.

As defined on its Wikipedia page, engineered wood (also called mass timber, composite wood, or manufactured board) is "a range of derivative products which are manufactured by binding or fixing the strands, particles, fibres, veneers, or boards of wood together with adhesives or other methods of fixation to form composite material . . . The panels vary in size but can range upwards of 64-by-8 feet (19.5-by-2.4 metres) and . . . can be of any thickness from a few inches to 16 inches or more."

So far, so banal. But some of this "range of derivative products" are ingenious at attempting to improve on what nature has wrought. Take, as an example, "densified wood," or "chemically densified wood." This is lumber treated with steam, heat, or ammonia, impregnated with resin and subjected to high pressure to increase density and strength, generally reducing its volume by 40 per cent and increasing density similarly. More recent developments have been able to double the compression to about 20 per cent of the original, by first boiling the wood in a brew of caustic soda mixed with sodium sulphite, a preservative, and then squashing it flat under high pressure, plus removing most of the hemicellulose and lignin. The cellulose is left intact, but compressed to nanofibers, which greatly enhances its strength. How strong? About the same as steel. Engineers at the University of Maryland, who developed the technique, put its strength to the test by firing a bullet at it. The new stuff stopped the bullet half way through, while it went right through normal wood.[179]

There are many other derivative products. Glulam is an engineered stress-rated beam composed of wood laminations bonded with adhesives. Fiberboard, obviously enough, is made from wood fibres compressed and glued; medium density fiberboard (MDF) has become a darling of woodworkers because of its weight and stability, a fine substrate for veneers. Particleboard has the advantage of being cheap (it is made basically from sawdust pressed with resin). Oriented strand board (OSB) is similar to particleboard but made with strands instead of sawdust; it is stronger than plywood in shear tests.

Laminated veneer lumber is like plywood, except that the plies are thick planks and not thin veneers, a very high-strength product. Trusses are devices for transferring loads from where you don't want them to where you do; a roof truss takes the weight of the roof and whatever snow load is on it and transfers it to load-bearing walls. There are many different kinds of trusses: Warren trusses, Pratt trusses, K trusses, Fink trusses, Gambrel trusses, and Howe trusses among them.

Laminated strand board cuts softwoods like aspen and poplar into foot-long strands and then pressure-bonds them in a waterproof adhesive; they are useful because long beams can be made in this way from small trees.

Fibre cement siding is self-explanatory—it is made from cellulose fibres bound in cement. Builders like it because it is resistant to rot and termites; aesthetes hate it because it is ugly, apparently meant to resemble wood but only poorly.

Finally, a product highly anticipated by architects but not yet (early 2022) out of the laboratory is a transparent wood composite that combines transparency and stiffness via a chemical process that replaces light-absorbing compounds, such as lignin, with a transparent polymer. Lab samples let 90 per cent of the light through but are stronger (with "higher mechanical properties" in the jargon) than wood. There it is: see-through wood.

* * *

In 2018, over some objections and despite some reservations, the International Building Code was amended to allow wooden buildings of up to eighty-two meters, ground to roofline, or about eighteen stories, a substantial change from the previous limit of twenty-five meters. Even so, the authors of the code were, in a way, playing catch-up: in the spring of the same year, an office and residential tower was completed in Brumunddal, Norway, a satellite town an hour's drive north of Oslo, designed by Voll Arkiteker. It was called Mjostarnet (Mjøstårnet in its Norwegian orthography). On its roof was an open wooden structure, a simplified pergola with a rakish tilted roof. The building was eighty meters tall, including the pergola. That made it the tallest mass-timber building in the world so far. It is constructed of glulam, LVL (laminated veneer lumber) and CLT (cross laminated lumber, also known as "plywood on steroids"), with a few concrete elements and metal brackets here and there.

A push for massive timber buildings began in the 1990s, mostly in Europe, fuelled by a watchful Green movement and a belated recognition of the environmental cost of cement manufacture, the increasing availability of engineered wood (and an understanding of its properties), the relative benignity of construction sites without steel and concrete, and the notion, largely justified, that wooden buildings are aesthetically and environmentally superior.

Most of the early forays into high-rise wooden towers were relatively modest, eight or ten stories. In the US, a seven-story building was erected in Minneapolis, and an eight-story residential tower in Portland, Oregon. Canadian building codes generally restricted wooden buildings to six stories, although Vancouver architect Russell Acton was given a "special exemption" to build an eighteen-story student residence at the University of British Columbia, the world's tallest when it opened in 2017. In 2020, Acton was building a ten-story building on the campus of George Brown College in Toronto. On the drawing boards were a twelve-story condo building in Victoria, BC, and thirty-story wood towers for Toronto, part of the proposal by Google's Sidewalk Labs to redevelop a neglected part of downtown Toronto. (In the middle of 2020, Sidewalk Labs abruptly cancelled its Toronto project. Community opposition, popular fears of intrusive technology, and diminishing commercial prospects in the Covid-19 aftermath were the stated reasons.)

The Sidewalk Labs proposal was one of many from the pencil of Vancouver architect Michael Green, who is still pushing for much higher buildings. He has conceived a thirty-five-story tower for a project at Porte Maillot in Paris. Already built is the whimsically named HoHO Vienna, the same height as Norway's Mjostarnet, although with six more stories, twenty-four in all. In the words of its developer, translated from the German, it is "reminiscent of huge wooden blocks with a tree bark facade; the naturalness and, above all, the visibility of the wooden surfaces in the interior, are part of the core idea for the additional noticeable improvements and new tangible experience of the element of wood, in the world's tallest wood structure high-rise."

But far taller buildings are contemplated. The Japanese timber company Sumitomo Forestry has already proposed an 1,100-foot tower for Tokyo that would be Japan's tallest building of any material. Several US architects have modeled wood skyscrapers between forty and eighty stories. Long buildings, too: the new Swatch watch headquarters northwest of Bern is a honeycomb of timber 240 meters long. Microsoft is building a new campus, almost all of it from wood. Britain is a contrarian voice here. Spooked by the deadly fire in the (non-wood) Grenfell Tower in 2017, Britain's building code in 2020 reduced the approved height for wooden buildings from six stories to four.

The eighteen stories of the Norwegian Mjostarnet project are shared between offices, thirty-two apartments, seventy-two hotel rooms, a cafeteria, a restaurant, a conference room and a rooftop terrace. Brumunddal, where it is located, is a small town in wooded countryside, not prepossessing, although it does have a pleasant view to Norway's largest lake, Mjosa. Why there? The building was a pet project of Arthur

Buchardt, an investor who favors hotel properties, and who was born in Brumunddal. To Green applause, he decided he wanted to build the world's tallest wood structure, using only local resources, local suppliers, local tradespeople, and using only sustainable wood. The glulam structural members were built at a factory only fifteen kilometers away. The factory is owned by Moelven, a major industrial building supply company, but it *is* local, or at least this one of its factories is.

The building was erected with only minor hitches. One of the massive glulam members was mis-measured and had to be replaced (the others fitted perfectly, with a millimeter tolerance). Some adjustments had to be made for the rooftop pergola, a last-minute fancy of the client's: a full kilometer of glulam beams had to be shipped off to get their corners rounded to minimize wind resistance, the work done at a flagpole factory in the south of the country. When the building was topped off, the maximum deviation from the theoretical vertical at the eighteenth level was nineteen millimeters.

Were prospective tenants worried about fire, wind, strength, rot? About living and working in what amounted to a Podunk town? The building sold out before it was finished.

Among the environmental arguments in favour of wood high-rises is that wooden buildings sequester carbon. A study in *Nature* found that a five-storey residential building constructed of wood can store up to 180 kilograms of carbon per square meter—three times more than a high-density forest with the same footprint.[180] The same study suggested that if 50 per cent of buildings were of wood, they could store up to 700 million tons of carbon a year, and cut emissions from steel and cement manufacturing in half.

Not everyone is enthusiastic. Absent a global commitment to sustainable forestry practices, the effects on the world's forests could be severe, if not catastrophic. And what happens when the buildings are demolished, as they inevitably will be? No building lasts forever. If the wood decays, the benefits will be lost.

Other critics ask whether enough data has been accumulated to prove such buildings safe and strong enough. Do we trust the engineers? How fireproof are they, really? Tests by the US forest service indicate that they meet all relevant code standards. Is that surety enough? How do they deal with the stresses of high winds? Hurricanes? Earthquakes? Computer models suggest their combination of flexibility and rigidity would make them stable, but absent real buildings of the relevant height, are models enough? Accelerometers were installed throughout the Norwegian project to allow constant real-time monitoring. Is *that* enough? Would excessive moisture be a problem? Excessive desiccation? Do they *age* well? No one yet knows.[181] Is this a good use of wood, or a misuse? We will find out, in due time. Meanwhile, use it we will.

Afterword

THE LONGBOW, THE SCHOONER, AND THE VIOLIN are hardly the only uses humans have found for wood, as this book has made obvious. Wood has been everywhere in our lives, and still is, and so are the trees from which it comes, and the forests that are those trees agglomerated. But these three remain iconic, and not in the trivial sense of "the music of Justin Bieber is iconic" (a real example, alas, from a web search for the definition of iconic), but in the sense that they represent something more than just themselves: caught, as I said in the introduction, at the absolute pinnacle of their craft, they are linked in history, root and branch, through wood and human ingenuity.

Sure, the longbow eventually yielded to the musket, and the musket to the carbine and the carbine to a long series in the ever-expanding arsenal of death-dealing. A lone gunman in a tower can fire six hundred rounds a minute, somewhat faster than the bowmen at Crécy.

The schooner yielded to the steamer, and the coal burner to diesel and then came aircraft and then we headed out to space, always faster, higher, stronger, the wood diminished to accents and fancies, like mahogany steering wheels and thuya dashboards. Sailing vessels are now made of fibreglass and aluminum, even dinghies are pressed from a mould, smelling of formaldehyde and glue.

Of the three icons, only the violin is still used for the purpose for which it was conceived. Yes, there are electronic violins and rock guitars made of queer composites and amplifications, but carbon fibre has not replaced maple, not yet and maybe not ever. A difficult piece on a mellow violin, the vibration of the violin string on spruce and maple, still represents the best artistic balance between head and heart, and audiences are still moved, and likely always will be.

So just one survives of the three, except in sport and in story.

Even so, wood is still with us. Indeed, "the hottest commodity on the planet [right now] is lumber," an economist wrote in 2021, during the pandemic.[182] Even shipping is not quite out of the wood yet: the schooner not quite dead. A small company in Costa Rica, Sail Cargo, is reviving the idea of cargo vessels made from wood and propelled by sail, albeit high-tech sail, and assisted by a series of electric motors whose energy is produced by the sun and by what the car industry calls "regenerative braking," in this case propellers under water that generate power as the vessel is moving under sail. In looks, the ship is based on a trading schooner built in Finland in 1906, albeit with containers on deck.

Prodigious wood, indeed. Sumitomo, the Japanese forestry company eyeing the hundred-story high-rise described above, has even loftier goals for its manufactured wood: space. Along with scientists from Kyoto University, they are planning a series of low-orbiting earth satellites. As *The Economist* put it, a little cheekily, they "are pondering the idea of building satellites out of an advanced, high-performance composite made from cellulose and lignin, a pair of complex polymers which are strong in tension and compression respectively. This material is both cheap and abundant. It is self-assembling and requires only simple chemical inputs. Manufacture can be entirely automated, requiring no human oversight."[183]

Self-assembling, yes: those would be trees.

Bibliography

The Longbow

Ascham, Roger, *Toxophilus: The First Book of the School of Shooting*, 1545, https://www.archerylibrary.com/books/toxophilus/dedication.html.

de Villiers, Marq and Sheila Hirtle, *Into Africa: Journeys Through the Ancient Empires*, Toronto, Key Porter, 1997.

Euripides, *Heracles*, R. Potter translation, https://uh.edu/~cldue/texts/herakles.html.

Froissart, Jean, *Chronicles* (The *Chroniques de Jean Froissart par Jean Froissart*), Createspace.com.

Gest of Robyn Hode, Knight, Stephen and Ohlgren, Thomas H. (eds.) https://d.lib.rochester.edu/teams/text/gest-of-robyn-hode.

Hardy, Robert, *Longbow: A Social and Military History*, New York, Lyons and Burford, 1992.

Herodotus, *The Histories of Herodotus of Halicarnassus*, London, Penguin Classics, 2014.

Hurley, Vic, *Arrows Against Steel: The History of the Bow*, New York, Mason Charter, 1975.

Langland, William, *The Vision and Creed of Piers Ploughman*, Volumes 1 and 2, Project Gutenberg, http://www.gutenberg.org/files/43660/43660-h/43660-h.htm.

Miller, Madeline, *Circe*, New York, Little, Brown and Company, 2018.

Oman, Charles, *The Great Revolt of 1381*, Kitchener, Batoche Books, 2001.

Riche, Barnabe, *Riche his Farewell to Militarie Profession Conteining Verie Pleasaunt*

Discourses Fit for a Peaceable Tyme, edited with introduction and notes by Donald Beecher, Ottawa, Dovehouse Editions/Binghamton, New York, Medieval & Renaissance Texts & Studies, 1992.

Stockel, Henrietta H., *The Lightning Stick: Arrows, Wounds, and Indian Legends*, Reno, University of Nevada Press, 1995.

The Schooner

Backman, Brian and Phil, *Bluenose*, Toronto, McClelland and Stewart, 1977.

Dana, Richard Henry, *Two Years Before the Mast*, New York, Modern Library, 2001.

Darrach, C K (Captain Claude), *Race to Fame: The Inside Story of the Bluenose*, Hantsport, Lancelot Press, 1989.

—— *From a Coastal Schooner's Log*, Halifax, Nova Scotia Museum, 1979.

De Villiers, Marq, *Witch in the Wind*, Toronto, Thomas Allen, 2007.

Garland, Joseph E., *Down to the Sea: The Fishing Schooners of Gloucester*, Boston, David R. Godine, 1983.

Hayden, Sterling, *Wanderer*, New York, W.W. Norton, 1977.

Howe, Octavius Thorndike and Frederick C. Matthews, *American Clipper Ships, 1833-1858*, Mineola, Dover Publications, 2012.

Lyon, Jane D, Clipper Ships and Captains, New York, American Heritage Publishing, 1962.

Wallace, Frederick William, *Wooden Ships & Iron Men*, London, Hodder and Stoughton, 1924.

The Violin

Hill, W. Henry, Arthur F., Alfred E., *Antonio Stradivari, His Life and Work*, Mineola, Dover Publications, 2014.

Nelson, Sheila, *The Violin and Viola: History, Structure, Techniques*, Mineola, Dover Publications, 2003.

Pierce, John Robinson, *The Science of Musical Sound*, New York, W.H. Freeman and Co., 1992.

Rault, Christian, L' Organistrum ou l'Instrument des premières polyphonies écrites occidentales: étude organologique, iconographie, Paris, Editions Klincksieck, 1985.

—— "How, where and when did the specific technological matters of the violin family appeared," Musikalische Aufführungspraxis in nationalen Dialogen des 16. Jahrunderts, Augsburg, 2007, pp. 123-152.

The Essays

Anon. *Gilgamesh*, tr. by Stephen Mitchell, New York, Atria Books, 2010.

Bechmann, Roland, *Trees and Man: Forests in the Middle Ages*, New York, Paragon House, 1990.

Birmingham, David *Trade and Conflict in Angola: The Mbundu and Their Neighbours Under the Influence of the Portuguese 1483-1790*, Oxford, Clarendon Press, 1966.

Burroughs, Edgar Rice, *Tarzan of the Apes*, Amazon Classics, undated

Ciottone, Dr. Gregory, *Disaster Medicine*, Toronto, Elsevier, 2015.

Conrad, Joseph, *Heart of Darkness*, Project Gutenberg, 1995.

Constantine, Albert, *Know Your Woods*, New York, Charles Scribner's Sons, 1975.

Cooper, James Fenimore, *The Pathfinder*, Penguin, London, 1989

—— *The Last of the Mohicans*, Penguin, London, 1986

Crichton, Michael, *Congo*, London, Arrow, 2003.

Doyle, Arthur Conan, *The White Company*, Project Gutenberg, 1997.

Grew, Nehemiah, *The Anatomy of Plants Begun*, London, W. Rawlins, 1682.

Haggard, Rider, *She*, Project Gutenberg, 2001.

Harrison, Robert Pogue, *Forests: The Shadow of Civilization*, Chicago, University of Chicago Press, 1992.

Hawthorne, Nathaniel, *The Scarlet Letter*, Boston, James R. Osgood & Co., 1878.

Holthouse, Hector, *Cannibal Cargoes*, Toronto, Seal Books, 1970.

Jemisin, N.K, *The Broken Kingdoms*, Orbit, London, 2010, part 2 of *The Inheritance Trilogy*

Kingsley, Mary, *Travels in West Africa* (1897), Washington, National Geographic, 2002.

Kipling, Rudyard, *The Jungle Book*, Suzeteo Enterprises, replica 1894 edition

LeGuin, Ursula, *The Word for World is Forest*, New York, Berkley, 1976.

Longfellow, Henry Wadsworth, *Evangeline*, https://poets.org/poem/evangeline-tale-acadie.

Lovelock, James, *The Revenge of Gaia*, New York, Basic Books, 2007.

Marris, Emma, *The Rambunctious Garden*, New York, Bloomsbury, 2013.

Mercader, Julio (Editor) *Under the Canopy: The Archaeology of Tropical Rainforests*, New Brunswick, Rutgers University Press, 2002.

Schama, Simon, *Landscape and Memory*, Toronto, Vintage Canada, 1996.

Sheldrake, Marlin, *Entangled Life*, London, Random House, 2020.

Thoreau, Henry David, *Walden*, Project Gutenberg, 1995.

Tolkien, J.R.R., *The Lord of the Rings*, New York, HarperCollins, 1991.

Tompkins, Peter and Christopher Bird, *The Secret Life of Plants,* New York, Harper, 2018.

Trotsky, Leon, *History of the Russian Revolution*, London, Victor Gollancz, 1932-33.

Trouet, Valerie, *Tree Story: The History of the World Written in Rings,* Baltimore, Johns Hopkins University Press, 2020.

Tudge, Colin, *The Tree*, New York, Three Rivers Press, 2005.

von Humbolt, Alexander, *Personal Narrative of Travels to the Equinoctial Regions of the New Continent during the years 1799–1804,* New York, Penguin Classics, 1996.

Walker, Aidan, ed., *The Encyclopedia of Wood,* New York, Facts on File, 1989.

Wohlleben, Peter, *The Hidden Life of Trees*, Vancouver, Greystone, 2016.

Notes

1 Some of this from Robert Pogue Harrison, *Forests*.
2 A good survey of these penitents can be found in Roland Bechmann's *Trees and Man*.
3 A Forest Hymn was published in 1834.
4 See https://agroforestry.org/the-overstory/74-overstory-195-trees-forests-and-sacred-groves.
5 Many of these from Sarah Laird.
6 In the survey of shooting he called *Toxophilus: The first book of the school of shooting*.
7 A newton, named obviously enough after the physicist Isaac Newton, is a unit of force that will accelerate one kilogram of mass one meter per second squared.
8 Interview with the *The Guardian* February 24, 2020.
9 See the excellent Wikipedia summary.
10 The team's findings were published in the journal *Antiquity* 84:635–648.
11 Some of the Pygmy material in this book was used in another form in my book *Into Africa*, co-written by Sheila Hirtle.
12 *Wikipedia* article on archery.
13 Herodotus (VII.61–80).
14 This from Livy XLII. 35.
15 Translated by Philip Vellacott for Penguin, 1973
16 This from Madeline Miller's engaging retelling of the *Odyssey in her goddess's-eye-view book, Circe*.
17 This last from Hector Holthouse's book *Cannibal Cargoes*, p.141. Others from personal observation or from a survey in sciencedirect.com ("Chemical and Biological Warfare in Antiquity"). Adrienne Mayor, in History of Toxicology and Environmental Health, 2015 2.3.
18 Arthur Conan Doyle, *The White Company*.
19 Wikipedia, *The Design of Longbows*.
20 Some of this material on yews from a delightful essay by Paul Kendal on the website https://treesforlife.org.uk/into-the-forest/trees-plants-animals/trees/yew/.

21 *Myths of the Sacred Tree* by Moyra Caldecott, on http://www.thegoddesstree.com/trees/Yew.htm.

22 Siobhan Roberts, *The New York Times*, April 9, 2020.

23 http://warbowwales.com/the-welsh-longbow/4557703062,

24 This story has been told many times, not least by Bradmore himself in his memoir he called *Philomena*. A good recounting can be found at https://www.medievalists.net/2013/05/prince-hals-head-wound-cause-and-effect/. Michael Livingston, novelist and scholar, described the operation at the 48th International Congress of Medieval Studies.

25 https://www.navyhistory.org.au/englands-first-naval-victory-the-battle-of-sluys-ad-1340/3/.

26 These anecdotes are recounted in an engaging piece by J. Ruben Valdes Miyares, pubished by the *National Geographic*, February 5, 2019.

27 A good summary of this in https://wwnorton.com/college/english/nael/middleages/topic_1/uprise.htm.

28 Also from Miyares, see note 26.

29 www.newscientist.com/article/dn11701-mystery-prehistoric-fossil-verified-as-giant-fungus/#ixzz6P9mi3eYq.

30 https://www.scientificamerican.com/article/plants-created-earth-landscapel/.

31 http://www.devoniantimes.org/opportunity/massExtinction.html.

32 https://www.nature.com/collections/fycvsrqngn.

33 https://www.adonline.id.au/plantevol/tour/mega-clubmoss-flora/.

34 From devoniantimes.com.

35 https://www.jehsmith.com/1/2020/01/do-trees-exist.html.

36 Quoted by the BBC, January 23, 2021.

37 See Edward Gilman, *Dispelling Misperceptions About Trees*. University of Florida Institute of Food and Agricultural Sciences Extension, August 2011.

38 Among other sources, see Mary Jo Dilonardo, How to identify a tree by its bark https://www.mnn.com/earth-matters/wilderness-resources/blogs/how-identify-tree-its-bark.

39 https://www.forbes.com/sites/trevornace/2018/10/18/the-worlds-largest-organism-pando-is-dying/#12fb7715554c. See also *The Glorious, Golden, and Gigantic Quaking Aspen* by Michael Grant and Jeffry Mitton, of the Department of Ecology and Evolutionary Biology, University of Colorado at Boulder, in *Nature Education*.

40 Edward Newbigin, of the University of Melbourne, who described the clone in the journal PlosOne https://journals.plos.org/plosone/article?id=10.1371/journal.pone.0008346.

41 https://www.oldest.org/nature/trees/.

42 In a 2002 essay in *Ageing Research Reviews*.

43 Sarah Zhang in *The Atlantic*, February 5, 2020

44 *The Hidden Life of Trees* (pp. 79–80).

45 http://sciencenetlinks.com/blog/snl-educator/weird-wonderful-creatures-dragon-blood-tree/.

46 https://rare.us/rare-news/science-and-nature/sandbox-tree-hura-crepitans/.

47 https://www.rainforest-alliance.org/species/kapok-tree.

48 See Erin Alvarez and Bart Schutzman, University of Florida environmental horticulture department, http://hort.ufl.edu/.

49 Adam Morton, *The Guardian, January 15, 2020.*

50 Wikipedia article on Campbell Island.

51 https://fivethirtyeight.com/features/the-bugs-of-the-world-could-squish-us-all/.

52 For an interesting exposition of this process, see https://www.waldwissen.net/wald/tiere/insekten_wirbellose/wsl_insekten_oekosystem_wald/index_.

53 https://apps.fs.usda.gov/r6_decaid/views/fungi.html.

54 https://mmbr.asm.org/content/81/2/e00063-16.

55 https://www.fs.fed.us/wildflowers/beauty/lichens/about.shtml.

56 Robert Macfarlane in *The Guardian*, November 2, 2019.

57 This from a 2019 *Paris Review online essay written by Cody Delistraty.*

58 https://www.nationalgeographic.com/science/2020/07/tree-crown-shyness-forest-canopy/

59 https://www.quantamagazine.org/soils-microbial-market-shows-the-ruthless-side-of-forests-20190827/

60 See for example a piece in Nautilus by Mike Newland, http://nautil.us/issue/90/something-green/when-plants-go-to-war-rp.

61 http://www.bbc.com/earth/story/20141111-plants-have-a-hidden-internet.

62 Gabriel Popkin in *Quanta.*

63 *Paris Review* online 2019.

64 *The Hidden Life of Trees*, p 83

65 *Plant Signaling and Behavior*, December 2009; 4(12): 1121–1127. Baluška et al.

66 Quoted by the BBC.

67 https://www.sydney.edu.au/news-opinion/news/2019/11/20/multispecies-justice-a-new-approach-to-a-growing-environmental-threat.html.

68 Quoted by Robert Macfarlane in *The Guardian*, November 2, 2019.

69 From Hayden's introduction to Joe Garland *Down to the Sea: The fishing schooners of Gloucester.*

70 This from https://www.smithsonianmag.com/history/the-great-tea-race-of-1866-8209465/.

71 See Jean Vaucher, Université de Montreal, http://www.iro.umontreal.ca/~vaucher/History/Prehistoric_Craft/.

72 https://teara.govt.nz/en/pacific-migrations/page-2.

73 Story recounted in *Le Roi d'Afrique et la reine mer, by Jean-Yves Loude.*

74 From my *Witch in the Wind*

75 Karl Heinz Marquardt, *The Origin of Schooners* for the Australian Association for Maritime History.

76 This also from *Witch in the Wind;* so too the construction details that follow.

77 Quote from Brian and Phil Backman, *Bluenose*, McClelland and Stewart, Toronto, 1977.

78 http://www.bbc.co.uk/ahistoryoftheworld/objects/Gqboa2VnQSSl4KNoG8fJRA.

79 Some of this from an engaging website operated by the USS Constitution Museum, at https://ussconstitutionmuseum.org/2016/07/19/canvasing-the-navy/.

80 https://www.explainthatstuff.com/pulleys.html.

81 This, too, is from *Witch in the Wind.*

82 See Lyon, Jane D, Clipper Ships and Captains, p. 138.

83 Recounted in *American Clipper Ships, 1833-1858,* by Octavius Thorndike Howe, Frederick C. Matthews.

84 Details of the Great Tea Race from a piece in *Smithsonian* magazine, by Mike Dash, published online, December 15, 2011.

85 See www.newworldencyclopedia.org/foreststypes.

86 http://mosquitia.tripod.com/index.html.

87 See for example http://www.borealforest.org/index.php?category=world_boreal_forest.

88 http://northword.ca/features/the-ancient-forest-a-walk-through-bcs-hidden-treasure.

89 Good piece on Tongass in *The Guardian*, February 16, 2020, by Mike MacEacheran.

90 Published in *NYT Style magazine, May 17, 2018.*

91 Some of this adapted from my own *Down the Volga in a Time of Troubles.*

92 https://www.nature.com/scitable/knowledge/library/restoration-of-deciduous-forests-96642239/.

93 https://www.nature.com/scitable/knowledge/library/restoration-of-deciduous-forests-96642239/.

94 https://ocean.si.edu/ocean-life/plants-algae/mangroves.

95 https://www.weforum.org/agenda/2019/02/5-reasons-to-protect-mangrove-forests-for-the-future/.

96 Numbers variously from World Bank 2002; World Bank 2004; World Bank 2008; World Bank 2009; the Rainforest Foundation; the World Rainforest Movement 2005.

97 http://www.fao.org/3/w7732e/w7732e04.htm.

98 Julio Mercader (ed.), *Under the Canopy: The Archaeology of Tropical Rainforests*, Rutgers University Press, 2002.

99 Froment.

100 Some of this conversation was first published in another form in my earlier book called *Into Africa.*

101 Grew's book *The Anatomy of Plants Begun was published in 1682. He was quoted in Albert Constantine's Know Your Woods.*

102 https://www.wood-database.com/wood-articles/janka-hardness/ and https://www.engineeringtoolbox.com/wood-density-d_40.html.

103 Some of this from https://www.americanforests.org/magazine/article/edible-trees-foraging-food-forests/.

104 https://www.quora.com/What-happens-if-someone-eats-wood.

105 https://www.iforgeiron.com/topic/12808-whats-the-best-wood-for-charcol/.

106 B. Anglicus, *The Great Owner of all Things Very Useful and Profitable for Keeping the Human Body Healthy, Jean Longis publisher, 1556.*

107 https://www.washingtonpost.com/opinions/2020/05/19/if-trump-likes-hydroxychloroquine-hell-love-camel-urine/.

108 wooddatabase.com.

109 http://www.visual-arts-cork.com/history-of-art/altarpiece.htm.

110 Albert Constantine's *Know Your Woods*, p. 62.

111 https://www.bbc.com/news/world-africa-48964785.

112 This from Steinhardt, Nancy Shatzman, *Liao: An Architectural Tradition in the Making, Artibus Asiae* (volume 54, number 1/2, 1994): 5–39.

113 http://www.horti-expo2019.org/2017-09/14/content_41587165.htm.

114 These were excavated by a team of British and American archeologists, headed by Leonard Woolley. For trivia buffs, Agatha Christie's *Murder in Mesopotamia was inspired by these royal tombs; Christie herself later married Woolley's assistant.*

115 http://sumerianshakespeare.com/117701/117801.html.

116 http://www.christianrault.com/fr/publications/how-when-and-where-the-specific-technological-features-of-the-violin-family-appeared.

117 http://www.madehow.com/Volume-2/Violin.html.

118 Sheila Nelson, *The Violin and Viola: History, Structure, Techniques* p. 14.

119 Heidi Werber, from Daily Art.

120 Sheila Nelson, op. cit.

121 http://www.historyofinformation.com/detail.php?id=2368.

122 Jim Collins in *Chicago* magazine. [date?]

123 https://www.sciencemag.org/news/2017/05/million-dollar-strads-fall-modern-violins-blind-sound-check#.

124 www.pnas.org/cgi/doi/10.1073/pnas.1619443114.

125 This last from *Wikipedia.*

126 https://tarisio.com/cozio-archive/property/?ID=40111.

127 Good articles on the Messiah controversy at https://www.catgutacoustical.org/journal/nov02.htm https://www.forbes.com/2001/01/10/0110connguide.html#6c6b9ba83269.

128 Sheila Nelson, op.cit, p. 51

129 https://www.theguardian.com/music/2020/oct/09/mozart-violion-bring-instrument-back-to-life-christoph-koncz.

130 See the writings of musicologist Elisabeth Le Guin, whose own website described her thus: "Elisabeth Le Guin is a performer and musicologist whose dual allegiances manifest as a series of dialogues, in tones and words, between theory and practice."

131 Terry Borman in *The Strad*, May 2018. www.thestrad.com.

132 Norman Lebrecht / October 22, 2008, http://www.scena.org/columns/lebrecht/081022-NL-violin.html.

133 The descriptions of the violin-making process in the following passages is derived from multiple sources, and from watching luthiers work, but the clearest and most useful working outline is from http://www.madehow.com/Volume-2/Violin.html#ixzz6MFfMSW6W.

134 https://www.runthemusic.com/parts-of-a-violin/.

135 http://www.christianrault.com/fr/publications/how-when-and-where-the-specific-technological-features-of-the-violin-family-appeared.

136 Richard Cownie on Quora, https://www.quora.com/Why-does-the-violin-have-4-strings.

137 https://www.forbes.com/sites/quora/2018/09/26/what-is-catgut-really-made-from/#4dacfeed7fce.

138 https://www.violinist.com/wiki/violin-strings/.

139 These details from many sources, including Yamaha's guide to musical instruments, which itself is sourced from Takatomo Kurosawa, *World Dictionary of Musical Instruments*, 1984; Yuzankaku, Tomoyasu Fujinuma, *The Story of Music Through Instruments*, 1973; Radio Gijustsusha, and others.

140 *The Economist*, May 23, 2020.

141 Sheila Nelson, op. cit. p. 141.

142 A version of the Yulin passages was published in my *Water*, revised edition, 2003.

143 Quoted by Daimen Hardie, co-founder of Community Forests International, in *Rural Delivery* magazine, July–August 2020.

144 Helen Briggs, BBC, January 26, 2021.

145 Some of this from a study in Nature's Scientific Reports by lead author Neil Roberts, see https://www.sciencedaily.com/releases/2018/01/180116111121.htm, and some from a piece by Rhett A. Butler, https://psmag.com/environment/the-planet-now-has-more-trees-than-it-did-35-years-ago.

146 The biggest gains in tree cover occurred in temperate continental forest (+726,000 square kilometres), boreal coniferous forest (+463,000 square kilometres), subtropical humid forest (+280,000 square kilometres). Russia (+790,000 square kilometres), China (+324,000 square kilometres), and the United States (+301,000 square kilometres) experienced the largest increase in tree cover among countries during the period.

147 https://www.sciencemag.org/news/2015/09/earth-home-3-trillion-trees-half-many-when-human-civilization-arose.

148 Rhett A. Butler op. cit.

149 Reported by Reuters, May 28, 2020.

150 U.S. Department of Agriculture, 2019.

151 *The Guardian*, August 2019.

152 https://www.airclim.org/acidnews/2009/AN4-09/boreal-forest-dieback-may-cause-runaway-warming.

153 https://www.nrcan.gc.ca/climate-change/impacts-adaptations/climate-change-impacts-forests/adaptation/assisted-migration/13121.

154 https://www.resilience.org/stories/2017-03-07/helping-forests-migrate/.

155 https://www.theguardian.com/environment/2020/sep/17/shoots-and-leaves-the-shotgun-scientist-who-hunts-moving-trees-aoe.

156 Quoted in *The Washington Post by Brady Dennis, April 29, 2020.*

157 https://www.theguardian.com/world/2020/sep/02/amazon-fires-brazil-rainforest-bolsonaro-destruction.

158 This from a gleeful piece in *Forbes magazine:* https://www.forbes.com/sites/michaelshellenberger/2019/08/26/why-everything-they-say-about-the-amazon-including-that-its-the-lungs-of-the-world-.

159 Quoted in the *Forbes* piece.

160 https://www.theatlantic.com/science/archive/2019/08/amazon-fire-earth-has-plenty-oxygen/596923/.

161 Matt McGrath, BBC environment correspondent, July 2021. The research was published in *Nature.*

162 https://www.ncbi.nlm.nih.gov/pmc/articles/PMC5414690/.

163 https://untamedscience.com/blog/the-environmental-impact-of-forest-fires/.

164 Bailey material from a review by Andrea Donsky on https://www.treehugger.com/natural-sciences/research-suggests-frequent-fires-could-help-forest-ecosystems.html.

165 This from Valerie Trouet, professor of dendrochronology at the University of Arizona, writing in *The Guardian*, September 2020.

166 https://www.nytimes.com/2020/09/22/us/forest-fires-fighting-history.html?referringSource=articleShare.

167 https://www.fs.usda.gov/pnw/pnw-research-highlights/wildfire-can-be-good-fish.

168 https://www.worldwildlife.org/stories/forest-fires-the-good-and-the-bad.

169 From Robert Pogue Harrison.

170 Peter Wohlleben, *The Hidden Life of Trees*, p. 97.

171 WWF, Living Forest Report 2012, chapter 4.

172 https://www.rainforest-rescue.org/topics/palm-oil/questions-and-answers#start.

173 *Nature*, April 24, 2008.

174 https://foodinsight.org/how-gmo-technology-saved-the-papaya/.

175 Adrian Higgins, *The Washington Post, December 18, 2019.*

176 Adrian Higgins.

177 Heidi Ledford, *Nature*, January 2019.

178 https://stopgetrees.org/wp-content/uploads/2019/04/biotechnology-for-forest-health-test-case-american-chestnut-report-WEB-1.pdf.

179 https://www.thechemicalengineer.com/news/new-densified-wood-is-as-strong-as-steel/

180 www.nature.com/articles/s41893-019-0262-4

181 Some of this from "Wooden Towers," Stephen Wallis, *New York Times*, November 20, 2019, and Emily Chung, CBC news, February 6, 2010.

182 Dustin Jalbert, an economist at the market-research firm Fastmarkets, quoted by Robinson Meyer, *The Atlantic*, April 27, 2021.

183 January 16, 2021.